I0793166

IMAGES
of America

FORGOTTEN FOSTER PARK

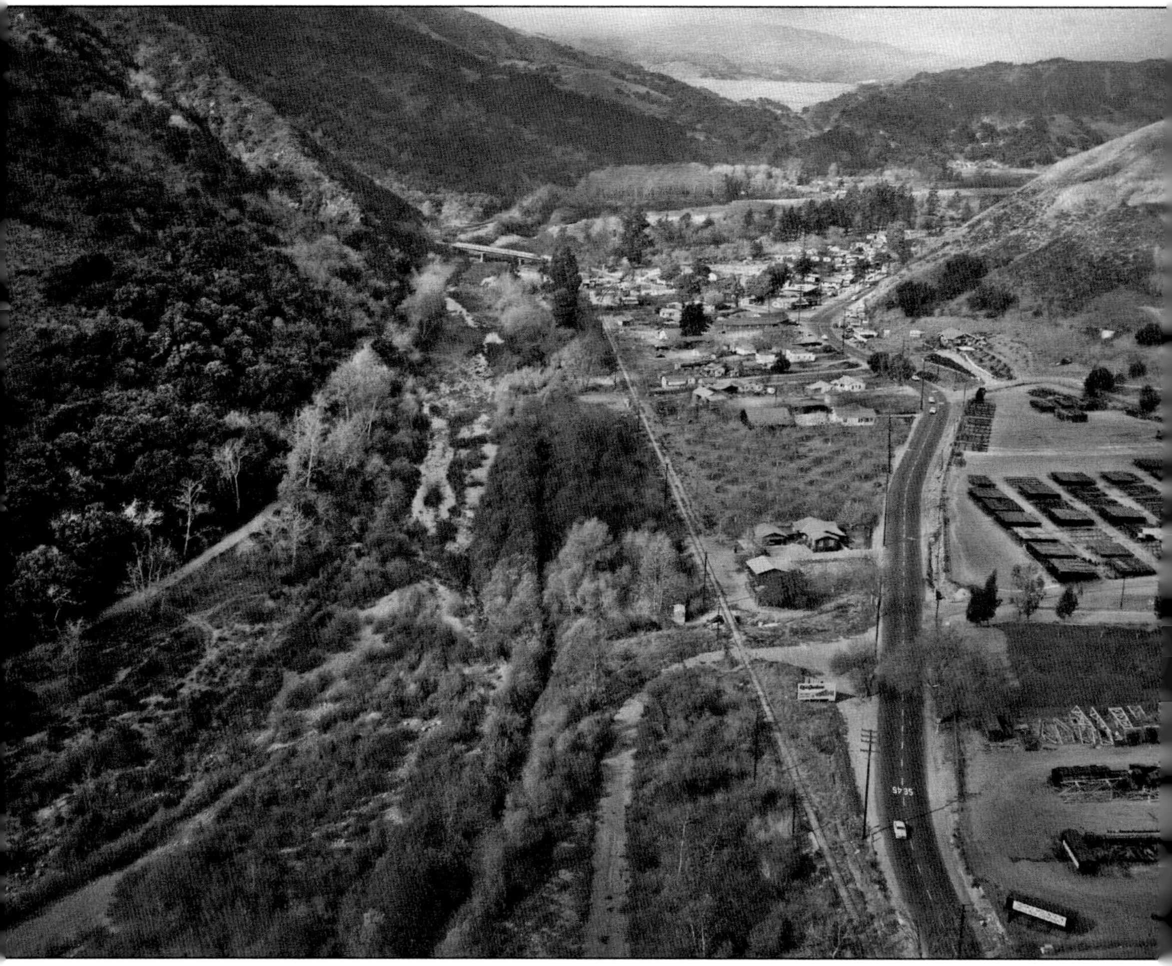

This captivating aerial facing north shows Foster Park as it appeared in 1963. The approach into town is North Ventura Avenue, better known as Highway 33. In the lower right corner is a partial view of the Rocky Mountain Drilling Company pipe yard. The train whistled and clanked as it traveled along the Southern Pacific Railroad track (center) on its daily run into Ojai. To the left is the Ventura River flowing along Red Mountain with the Foster Park Bridge in the distance. At the top sits the crowning glory of this image—the newly developed Lake Casitas. (Photograph by Walt Dibblee©, courtesy of Steve Dibblee.)

On the Cover: This 1960 photograph of the Foster Park Market depicts a charm and quaintness of an era long past. Located at the intersection of North Ventura Avenue and Casitas Pass Road, the market was the hub of town for its denizens and offered a variety of wares and services. (Photograph by Joseph P. Pluim, author's collection.)

IMAGES
of America

FORGOTTEN FOSTER PARK

Gwen Alferes

ARCADIA
PUBLISHING

ISBN 978-1-4671-3277-0

Published by Arcadia Publishing
Charleston, South Carolina

Printed in the United States of America

Library of Congress Control Number: 2014944609

For all general information, please contact Arcadia Publishing:
Telephone 843-853-2070
Fax 843-853-0044
E-mail sales@arcadiapublishing.com
For customer service and orders:
Toll-Free 1-888-313-2665

Visit us on the Internet at www.arcadiapublishing.com

Dedicated to the one who has always been there to guide, strengthen, and encourage me—Jesus Christ, my lord, my savior, my friend

Contents

ACKNOWLEDGMENTS

Writing *Forgotten Foster Park* was quite an undertaking. It started with a box of family slides and a dream. Thanks to so many wonderful people from coast to coast and Arcadia Publishing, that dream came true. Outside of my personal knowledge, the information I acquired was largely sourced from oral history through recorded interviews and memoirs. There were so many contributors. A most appreciated thanks to Steve Dibblee of Ventura Views Photography for the historical aerials taken by his late father, Walt Dibblee; C. Robert Lee, esteemed photojournalist and author, for his Canet Ranch and family photographs; Casitas Municipal Water District and Cinnamon McIntosh, water conservation specialist, for her hard work scanning the historical Casitas Dam images; and Jackie Springer for sharing his knowledge and history of the dam. Much gratitude to KCBS-TV for the usage of DVD outtake images from *Ralph Story's Los Angeles*; Charles Johnson, research library director at the Museum of Ventura County for the finishing touch; San Buenaventura Mission's Fr. Tom Elewaut and Barbara Duran for historical information and images of Rev. Daniel Hurley; Brook's Institute of Ventura for the Mill School historical information; Laurie Dunning at E.P. Foster County Library for her research; and Stephanie and Carlos at Ventura Photograpix and Greg at Dexter's Camera for their expertise. For images, interviews, and memoirs, a most grateful and unending thanks to Phil Foster Ranger, Ed Brown, Steve Riley, Ileana and JiJi Lee, Ernie Sawyer, Jo Ann Moore, Gary Moore, Barbara Randall, George Turner, Jim Hall, Jean Davis, Linda Oliver, Rick Mungo, Kit Mungo, Jim Capito, Pete and Frank Duran, Gracie Varela, John and Erma Lorenzana, Mike, John, Edward, and Alex Pulido, Ethel Mullikin, Joan Robles, Ted Robinson, Ray "Windmill" White, Jennifer Kennedy, Vicky Beria-Jefferson, Bud Allison, Blaine Cook, Les McDowell, Rob Garvin, Jeff Maulhardt, Jim Maxwell, Charlie Eskew, Becky Enlow, Edgar Henke, John Colla, Kathy Hartman, Ruth Rosemann, Brian Aikens, Armand Keeter, Drace Barnes, Drew and Neil Mashburn, Jim and Rick Bach, Wanda Nelson, and Jim, Bob, and Bud Miles. To my family, thank you for your love, support, and of course, the images.

Introduction

Foster Park was a tiny community that sprang up like a blade of wild grass in the way of progress. In the early years of Ventura's development, the northern Ventura Avenue area was sparsely populated with farms, ranches, and small cabins along the Ventura River until of one of the deepest oil pools in the world at that time was discovered in the Ventura River valley. As oil companies began to develop the oilfield in the early 1920s, folks came from all over the country looking for steady work and a place to settle in. About five miles north of Ventura, where the valley narrows, a small "oil patch" community began to develop along Foster Memorial Park, from which it got its name.

During World War II, while bivouacked servicemen rested at Foster Memorial Park, the young ladies of town put on their lipstick and youngsters loaded their Radio Flyer wagons with bags of home-made popped corn and candy and lined their pockets with cash selling snacks to the weary soldiers.

Located outside the Ventura City limits, Foster Park offered more affordable housing, especially for large families such as Harold and Mona Miles, who came to Ventura from Olympia, Washington, in 1947 with their six sons, Larry, Tom, Bill, Jim, Bob, and Bud. They lived in a tent on the Rincon for three weeks until Harold found employment in Port Hueneme. However, he found the wooded beauty of Foster Park worth the long drive to work and settled his family at the Foster Park Auto Courts, which he also managed. To accommodate the family, they took up three of 10 cabins. Two daughters, Susan and Christy, were later additions to the family.

Before the completion of the Matilija Dam in 1948, the Ventura River provided a healthy spawning ground for steelhead trout and a cultural heritage for county anglers. Foster Park had a favored fishing spot around the bridge. The tiny town bustled with action as folks gathered at open season to catch their legal limits. Despite efforts to create upstream passage to spawning grounds, the steelhead have virtually disappeared.

Another local disappearance was the Santa Gertrudez Chapel, built in the early 1800s by Franciscan padres. For many years its existence was known, but pinpointing its location awaited discovery. Historical accounts put it about one half-mile south of Foster Park in the vicinity of the Canet Ranch along Ventura Avenue. With the help of ranch foreman Mike Pulido, an archeological team unearthed its foundation and artifacts in the ranch bean field in 1966. A monumental plaque was erected in 1970 on the old highway about 500 feet from the original site of the chapel, now under the Ojai Freeway.

Ventura Avenue, which led to Ojai, was the contemporaneous route of the historical El Camino Real, which branched westward at the center of what became Foster Park, winding over the Casitas Pass and rejoining the coastal route at Rincon point. The pass was used when the coastal route was impassible due to high tide. It was considered the main artery of travel between Ventura and Santa Barbara until the early 1900s, when the popularity of the automobile led to the modernization of roads. Presently, it ends at the site of the Casitas Dam and is part of the lake bed; it is now known as Casitas Vista Road. Beyond the lake, the road continues west at Highway 150.

On the northwest side of the Ventura Avenue and Casitas Pass intersection sat the Foster Park Market, which became known for its "real Western jerky" during the 1950s and 1960s and was the hub of town. On the south corner was the competing Elwell's Market, also known as Spadt's Grocery during the 1930s, which had two Shell gasoline pumps to offer travelers. On the east side of the highway was Foster Park Café, a full service gas station, and an auto repair garage. The café had several owners over the years and at one time was known for its mouth-watering, train-stopping pies, for it was not uncommon for Southern Pacific railroad engineers to stop the train and enjoy a slice after making their daily run from Ojai.

During the 1930s and early 1940s before World War II, big band sounds filled the humble community's ballroom located next door to Spadt's Grocery. It was part of the Loyal Order of

Moose and known as the Moose Hall. After the war, the ballroom became host to the country western and hillbilly music circuit, booking some of the biggest acts of that era, which included Maddox Brothers and Rose, Tex Ritter, Jim Reeves, Lefty Frizzel (whose family were once Foster Park residents), the Everly Brothers, and Johnny Cash (Cash later moved his family to Casitas Springs in 1961). But the biggest act to ever appear at the Moose Hall was "Texas Tiny" Guy Cherry, who, as announced in a 1948 *Star-Free-Press* ad, was "640 Pounds of Fun." Cherry, a comedian and cowboy personality, appeared regularly on the popular music television program *Town Hall Party* during the 1950s and was billed as the "World's Biggest Cowboy."

In the late 1950s, the Moose Hall changed ownership and its name to "Okie's" and continued to book popular crowd-pleasers, including Buck Owens, Freddie Hart, and Jerry Lee Lewis. A boxing gym was added to Okie's in the 1960s, forging state championship light-heavy-weight boxer Ray "Windmill" White.

Next door to Okie's was the Shanty Tavern. It had originally been an Army surplus building pulled into Foster Park in the mid-1940s by an entrepreneurial resident known as "Doc Voight." Voight erected the portable building at the entrance of his small cattle ranch on Highway 33, transforming it into a restaurant, and served barbecued beef from cattle he slaughtered on his ranch just yards from the back door.

In the early 1960s, the Shanty operated under the ownership of the Lavender Hill Corporation. The corporation got its name from the 1951 British comedy *The Lavender Hill Mob*, starring Alec Guiness, in which two "honest men" (a bank clerk and an artist) form a gang and hijack a gold bullion delivery van. The Lavender Hill Corporation consisted of nine men and one woman who owned three other bars in Ventura County that they ran during evening hours while they robbed banks and business in Los Angeles during the daytime. After the hold-up ring was smashed, they were dubbed the "Lavender Hill Mob." Among gang members were two Korean War heroes, both recommend for the Army's Silver Star (which one veteran received), two former police officers, a local athletic star, and a psychology graduate. The case lasted over a year and brought scandal to the small community. The Shanty later became Brown's Trading Post.

In 1966, the 40-year-old wild-grass community was mowed over to make room for the extension of the Ojai Freeway, but its roots still remain in the memories of those who once called it home.

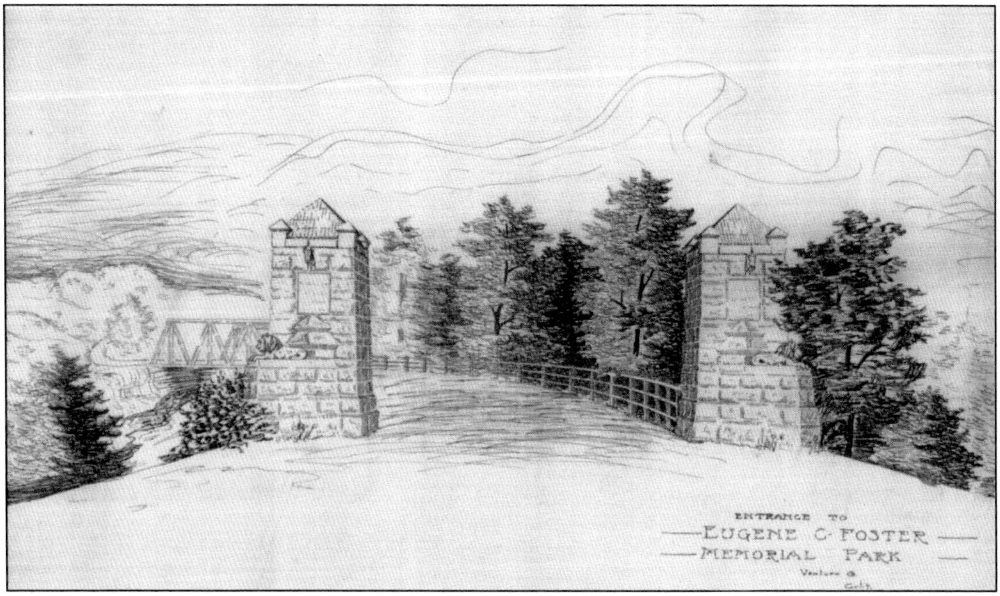

Lion statues sit and guard the gateway to the Casitas Pass at the entrance of Eugene C. Foster Memorial Park in this sketch that was presented to Ventura County supervisors by architect Charles C. Rittenhouse in 1908. (Courtesy of the Museum of Ventura County.)

One

Agriculture, Oil, and a New Town

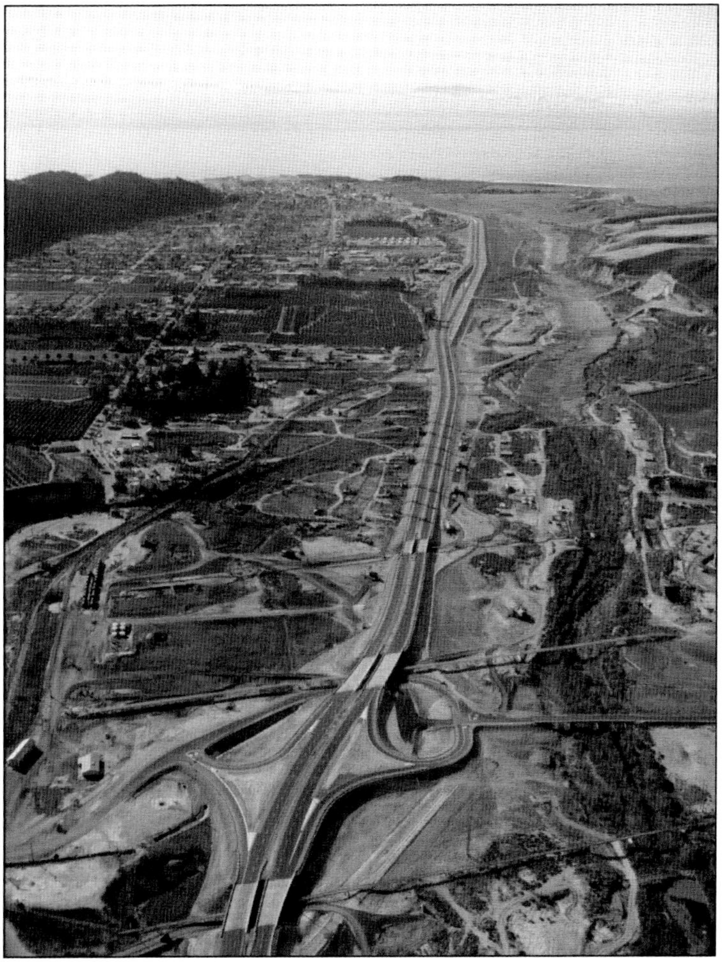

Anacapa Island peaks up through the offshore marine layer in this southward view of the Ventura River Valley. Nearly 40 years after the Ventura oil boom of the 1920s, farmlands and the oil industry appear to be thriving in harmony. Striped with the shadows of oil derricks, the newly completed section of the Ojai Freeway made access to the Avenue Oilfield much easier, with the loopy Shell Road exits shown in the foreground. (Photograph by Walt Dibblee©, courtesy of Steve Dibblee.)

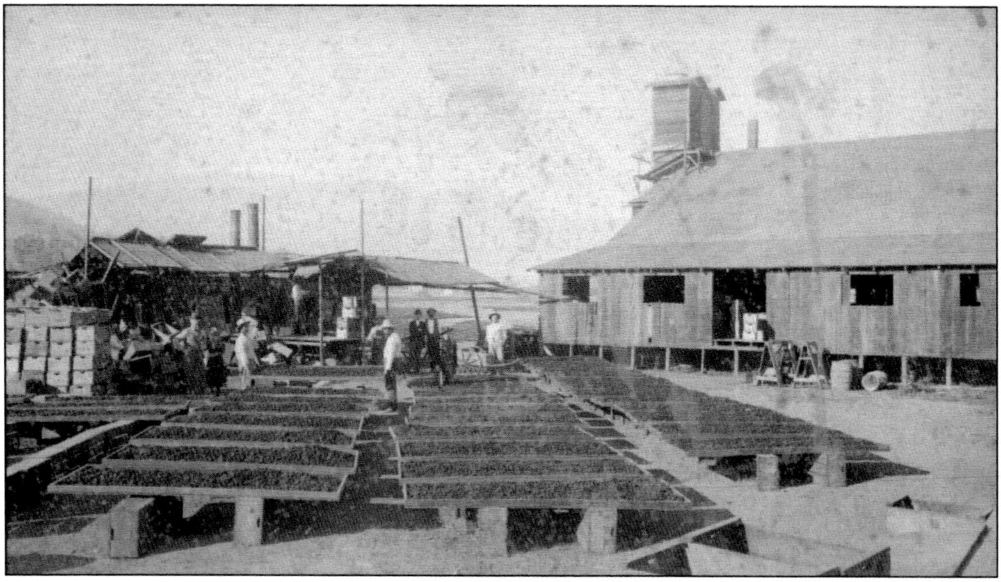

Before towering oil derricks dominated the Ventura River Valley landscape, this was a typical scene along Ventura Avenue during apricot season, pictured here in the late 1800s. County growers originally used artificial methods to dry fruit. After much expense, they finally discovered the sun supplied ample heat to cure the fruit and produced a much better product. (Photograph by Brewster, courtesy of Edgar Brown.)

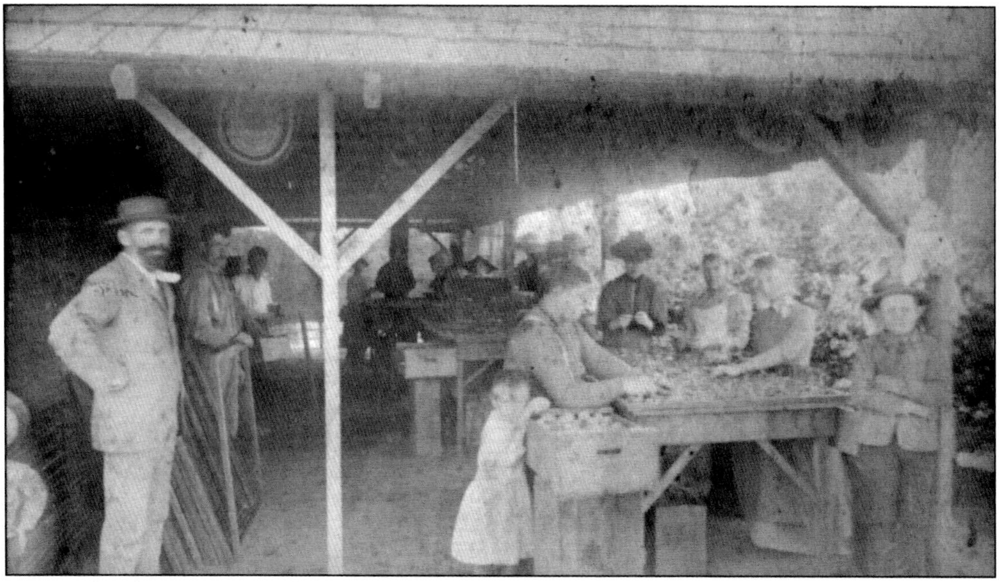

Women busily pit apricots while the men and the boy on the right appear to be taking a break. A notation on the back of this photograph reads, "The pitting room matter indistinct. Allen could hardly keep from laughing and nearly upset the rest," dated 1891. The identity of this ranch is possibly that of William Ware "W.W." Sparks; however, like the "pitting room matter," it remains a mystery. (Photograph by Brewster, courtesy of Edgar Brown.)

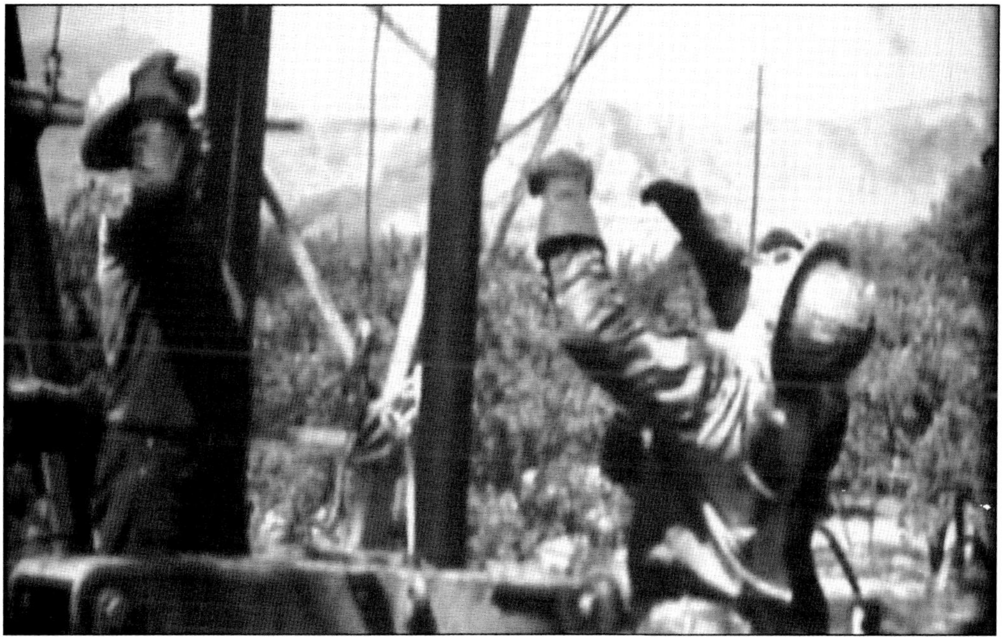

In this 1949 photograph, a crew from Costal Drilling Company drills for oil on a lease in the middle of an apricot orchard using the second-largest drilling rig in the world. This apricot ranch, owned by Lee and Pauline Barnes, was located on North Ventura Avenue. The Barneses purchased the property from Henry Sparks, son of W.W. Sparks. After the change of ownership, Sparks maintained a shared interest in the oil rights. The lease was found to have the deepest oil well in the Avenue Oilfield. Below, Pauline Barnes bears a joyful smile as a gusher of fortune spews a fountain of black gold from the Barnes-Sparks No. 1 of three wells that were drilled on the ranch. The Barneses also developed a mobile home park on their property, known today as the Magnolia Mobile Home Park. (Both, courtesy of Drace Barnes.)

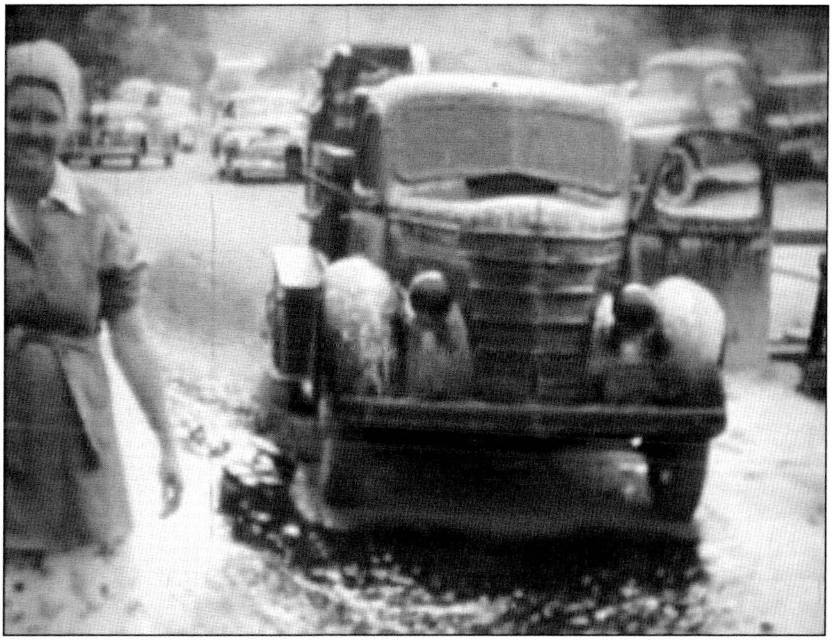

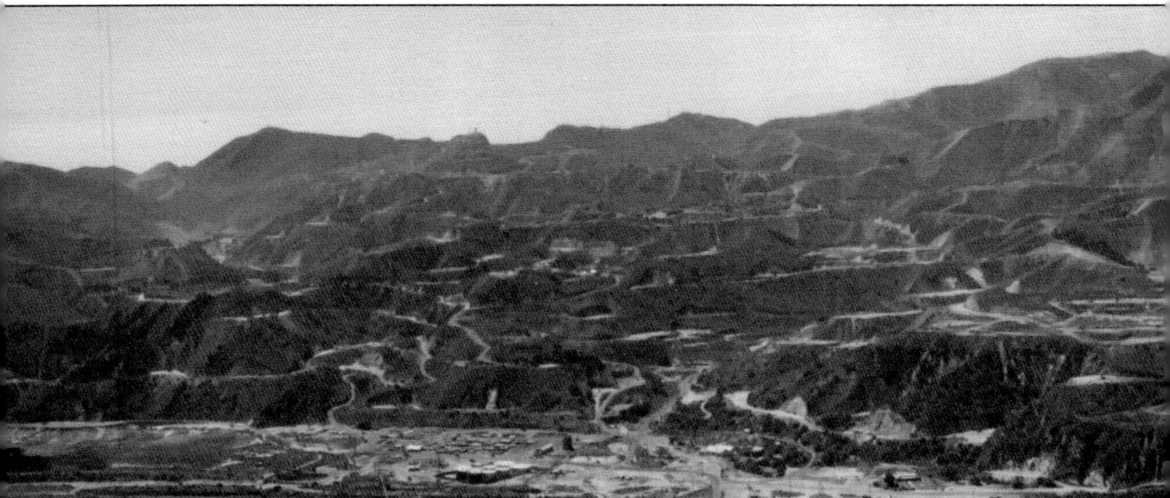

In the lower-left corner of this westerly view is a Shell Oil Company natural gasoline refinery sitting next to an orchard on the hillside above Ventura Avenue. Although the Ventura River valley, once checkered and striped with lush, fertile farmlands, has been scarred by years of oil production, the oil industry brought prosperity and growth to the county. In his 1926 publication *The History of Ventura County*, Sol N. Sheridan had this to say about the development of the Ventura Avenue Oilfield: "That development has made the old Mission town of San Buenaventura a city trebling its population in five years; and starting it on a career of growth that will make it an industrial center . . . For San Buenaventura has a beautiful location, a climate unsurpassed, a magnificent beach and the backing of the richest agricultural and horticultural section on the Pacific coast." (Photograph by Walt Dibblee©, courtesy of Steve Dibblee.)

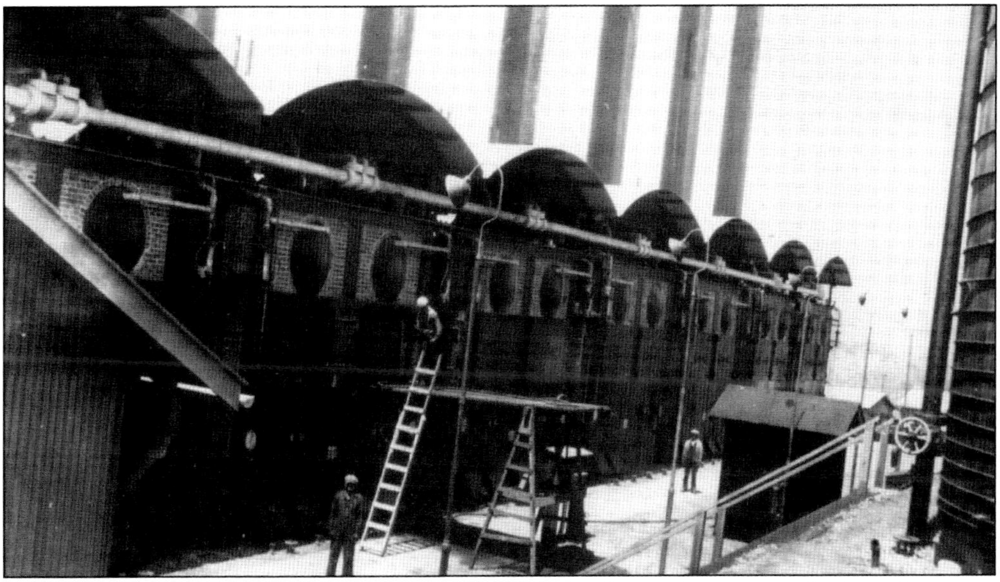

The discovery of black gold indeed brought folks from all over the country looking for steady work, such as these men pictured at this thermal cracking boiler at a Shell Oil gasoline refinery plant in the Avenue Oilfield in the early 1930s. The exact location is unknown. Boilers are still used today, creating heat needed to aid in the refining process. (Courtesy of the Leslie Ray Moore family.)

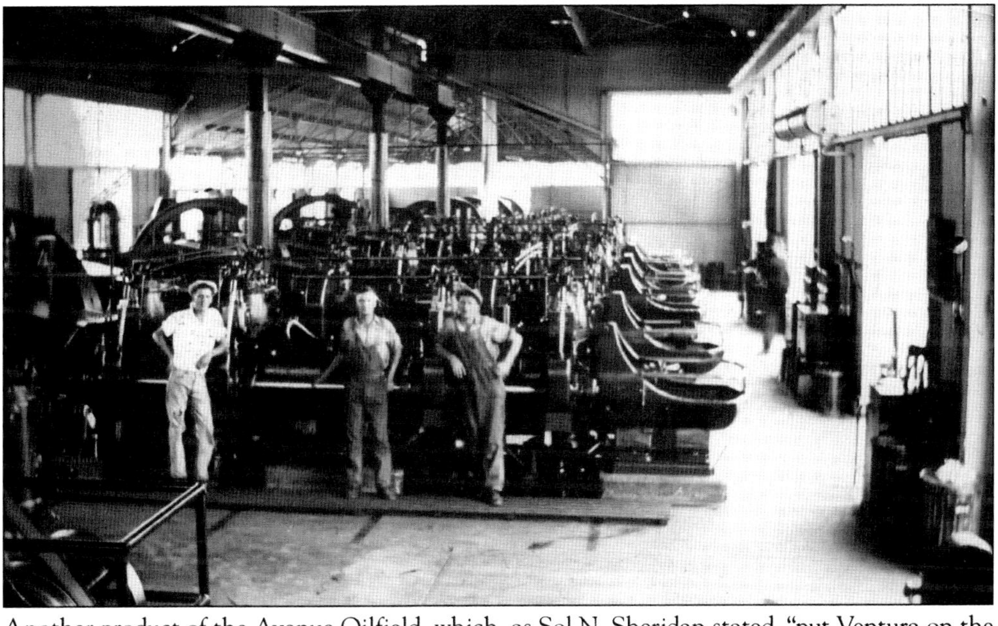

Another product of the Avenue Oilfield, which, as Sol N. Sheridan stated, "put Ventura on the map," was natural gas. By 1926, the peak of production was 100 million cubic feet per day. Pipelines were built to Santa Barbara and Los Angeles Counties. Picture here in the 1930s, workers take a break at this natural gas compressor plant that was located on the east side of Ventura Avenue just north of Shell Road. (Author's collection.)

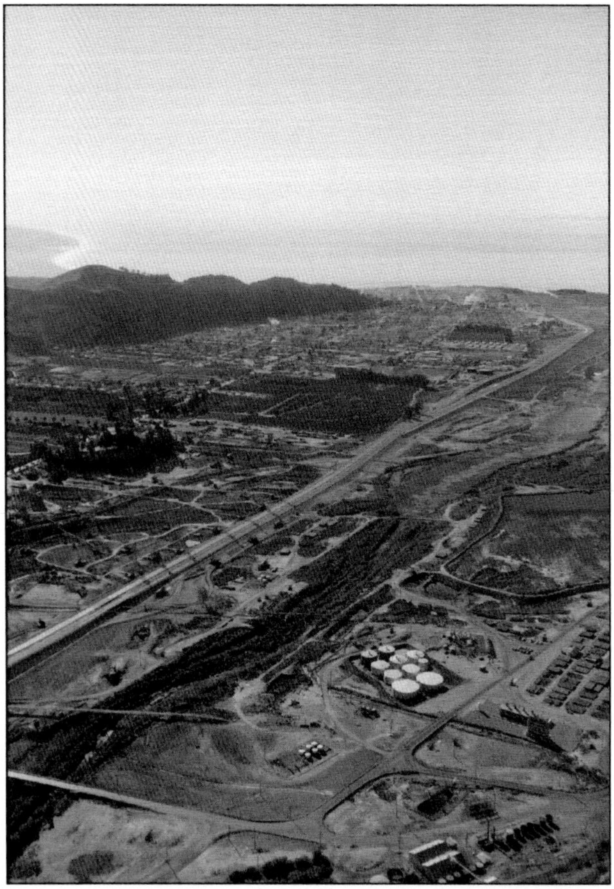

Between the Ojai Freeway and the oil storage tanks in the foreground, the Ventura River makes its way to the sea. In the upper left corner, the Pacific Ocean appears calm as waves roll upon the shoreline beyond the eastern slope. This southeasterly view of the Avenue Oilfield, now known as the Avenue, is certainly an image of Sol N. Sheridan's 1926 prediction regarding its development. While oil production fervently continued, farmlands of the Avenue receded, giving way to dense residential construction. As Ventura's population steadily multiplied, its tentacles spread beyond the city limits, reaching northward and creating small oil patch communities along the unincorporated area of Ventura Avenue. One such community was Foster Park (below), located about five miles inland. Facing west is an image of the tiny community as it appeared in 1962. (Both photographs by Walt Dibblee©, courtesy of Steve Dibblee.)

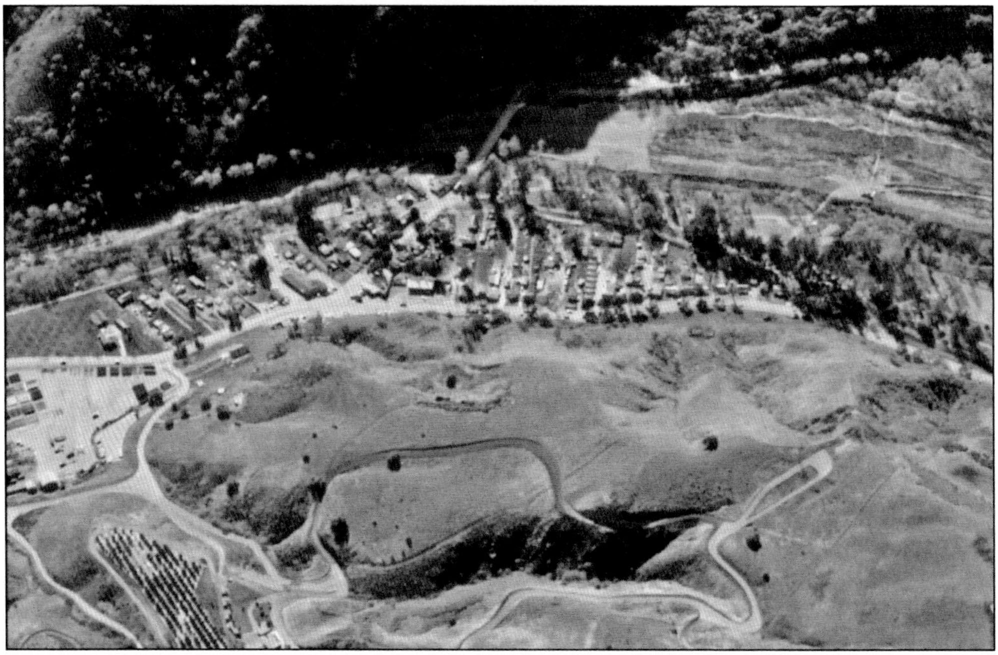

Two

The Town and Its Folks

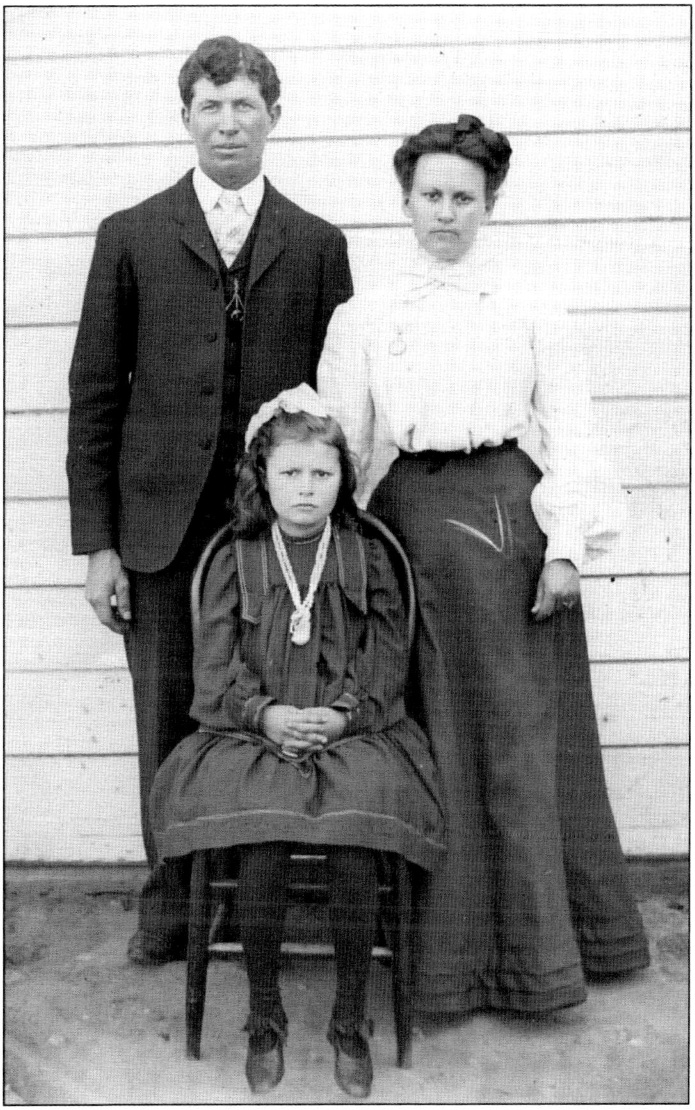

Before the oil boom years and Foster Park began to develop, small cabins were scattered along the Ventura River, mostly for anglers and hunters. The area was primarily farmland, and one such farm was Trains Dairy, located at the southeastern end of Foster Park. The Trains also grew apricots and walnut trees. In this 1908 photograph, owner Charles Train poses with his wife, Addie, and daughter Relda. (Courtesy of the Leslie Ray Moore family.)

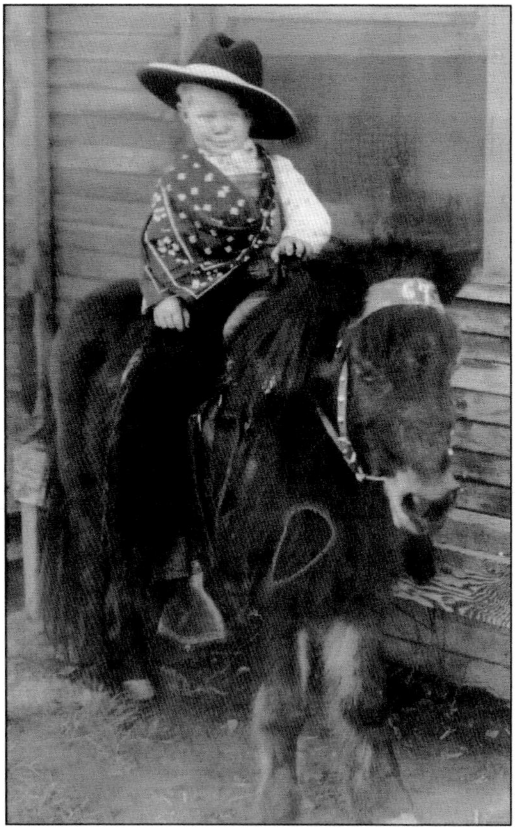

This 1930 photograph reveals more than a young cowboy on a pony. The weathered house in the background was located on the south side of Casitas Pass Road and may very well be one of the aforementioned sportsman cabins. Atop the miniature steed is three-year-old Archie H. "Poke" Allison, who was born in this house in 1927. (Courtesy of Bud Allison.)

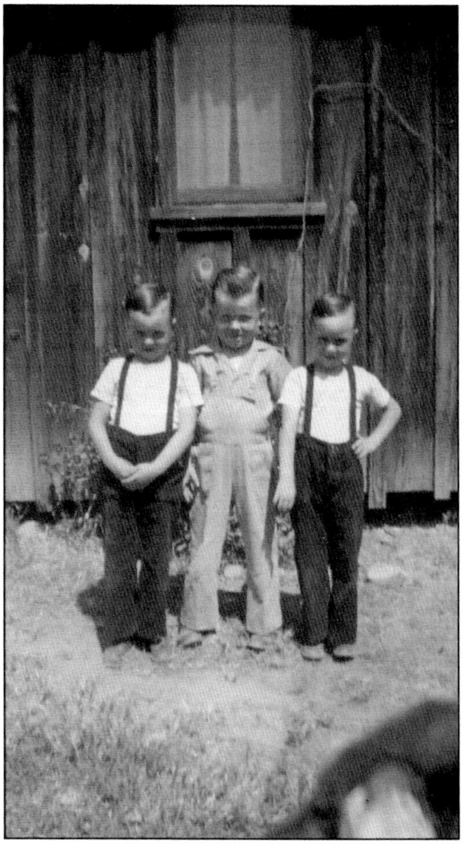

This house was in the same vicinity as the home pictured above and was possibly another cabin built before the town's development. Neighbor Gary Moore stands between bookend-looking twins Donald (left) and Ronald Godsy (right) as they pose for this 1946 photograph. The Godsy twins were grandsons of this home's owners, Kirk and Myrtle Keeter. (Courtesy of the Leslie Ray Moore family.)

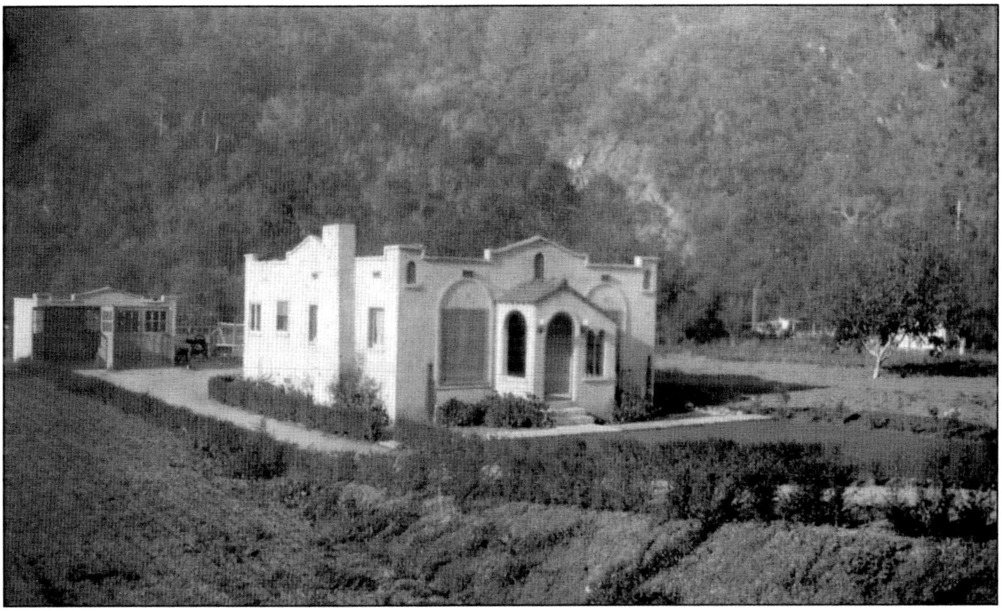

Spanish architecture became very popular in Ventura County during the 1920s; however, only a few examples made their way into the landscape of Foster Park. With the precipice of Red Mountain as a backdrop, this lovely Spanish fort-like home and matching two-car garage were the property of Shell Oil employee Chet Griffith. (Courtesy of the Leslie Ray Moore family.)

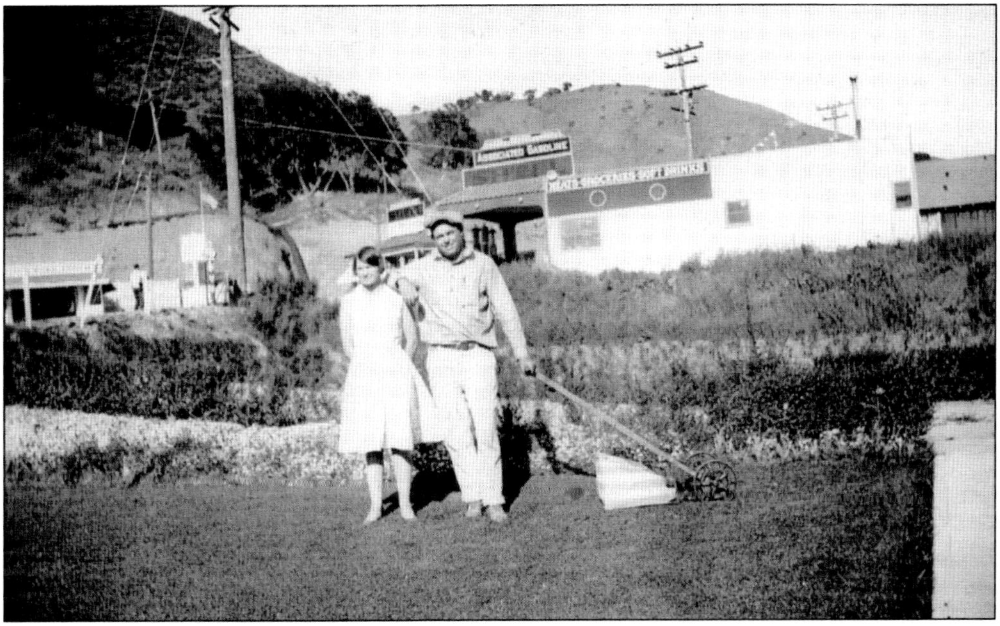

Chet Griffith poses with wife, Blanche, in this 1930 photograph. Behind the couple is a mini-market equipped with two Shell gas pumps. To the right is the Foster Park Café. Blanche was the second and youngest child of Charles and Addie Train. Relda had been the Trains' only child for 12 years, and she married Charles Hood. The Hoods were Foster Park residents also. (Courtesy of the Leslie Ray Moore family.)

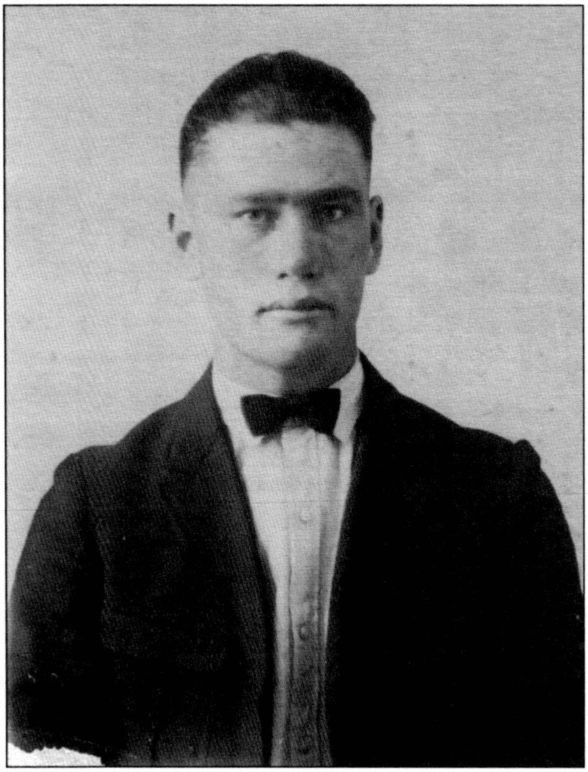

Determined not to end up a Missouri farmer, Leslie "Ray" Moore came to California in 1925 seeking better opportunities. Moore took a vacation back to Missouri to visit family, and while there he met Neva Pitts, a switchboard operator who could also drive a car. Impressed with her driving ability, he decided, "Any gal who had enough spunk to drive a car is the gal for me." (Courtesy of the Leslie Ray Moore family.)

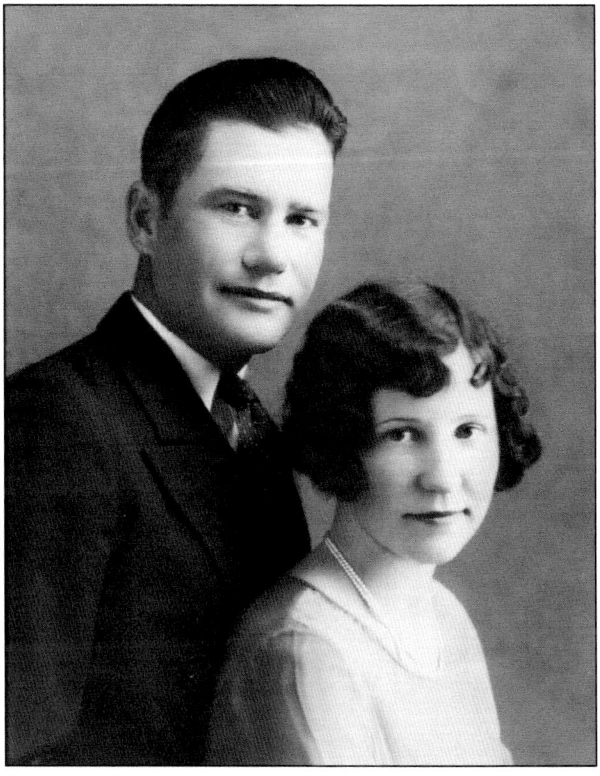

"I went to old Missouri looking for a bride. Soon Miss Neva Pitts was seated by my side." This was the first verse as Ray and Neva Moore recalled their early years in a song. Their honeymoon was driving a friend's newly purchased automobile back to California. "Stopped at a motel and went to bed. If this is married life I think I will cover up my head." Neva's verse during the couple's 60th anniversary celebration further details that road trip. (Courtesy of the Leslie Ray Moore family.)

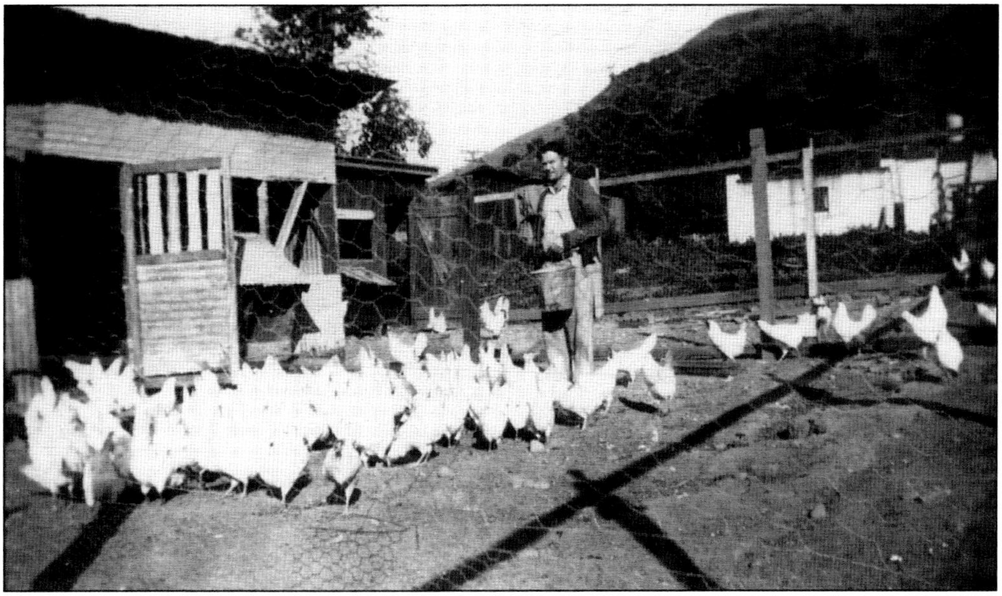

For some folks who pulled up stakes in the Midwest, Foster Park offered the best of both worlds. Ray Moore (above), who left his family's farm in Missouri, found permanent employment with Shell Oil Company and eventually planted stakes in Foster Park. With a mild climate and a sizable piece of land, Moore resumed farming as a hobby. (Courtesy of the Leslie Ray Moore family.)

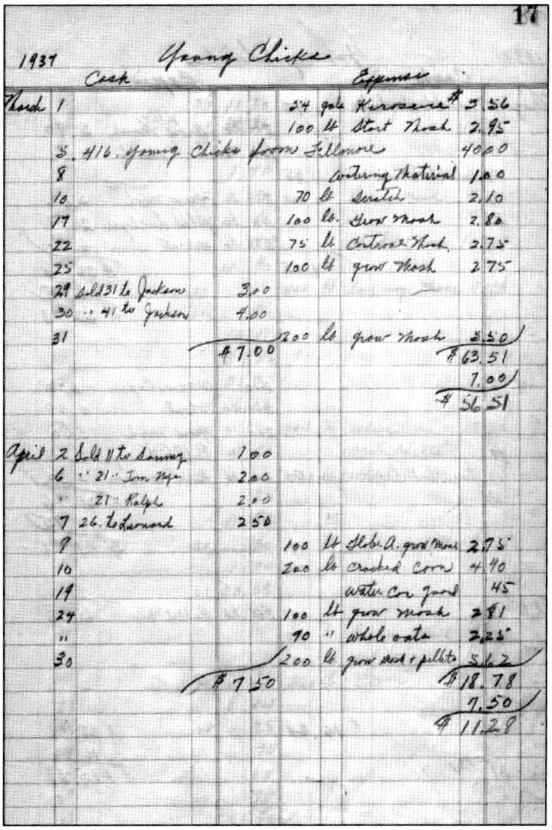

17

1937 Young Chicks

Date	Cash		Expenses	
March 1			24 gals Kerosene	$3.56
			100 lb Start Mash	2.95
3	416 young chicks from Fillmore			40.00
8			Wiring Material	1.00
10			70 lb Scratch	2.10
17			100 lb Grow Mash	2.80
22			75 lb [illegible] Mash	2.75
25			100 lb grow Mash	2.75
29	sold 31 to Jackson	3.00		
30	" 41 to Jackson	4.00		
31			200 lb grow mash	5.50
		$7.00		$63.51
				7.00
				$56.51
April 2	Sold 11 to Sammy	1.00		
6	" 21 " Jim Nye	2.00		
"	21 Ralph	2.00		
7	26 to Leonard	2.50		
9			100 lb Globe A. grow mash	2.75
10			200 lb cracked corn	4.40
19			water con [illegible]	45
24			100 lb grow mash	2.81
"			90 " whole oats	2.25
30			200 lb grow mash + pellets	5.12
		$7.50		$18.78
				7.50
				$11.28

Whether it was household expenses—utility bills to a pair of socks for one of his two sons—or his chicken-farming venture, Ray Moore kept a tidy ledger. He recorded every cent that came in and went out, to whom, and when, as displayed on this page of his personal ledger, dated 1937. (Courtesy of the Leslie Ray Moore family.)

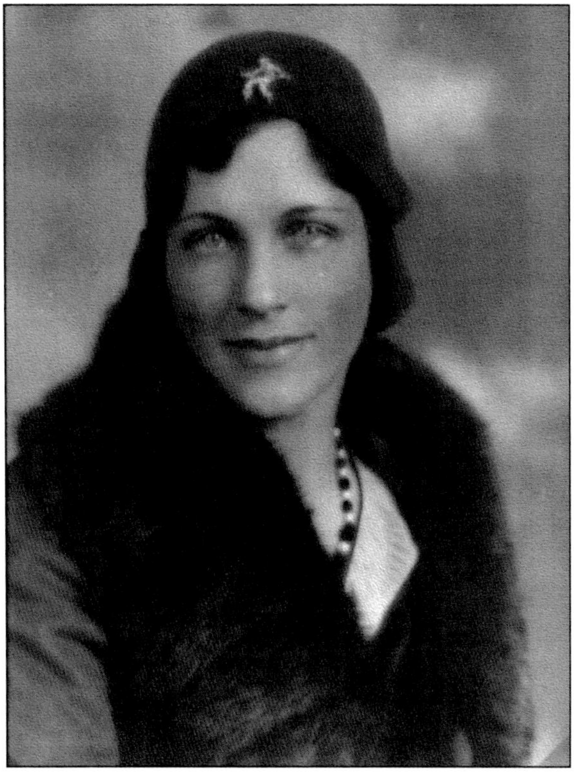

India Homa Petty was born in Hugo, Oklahoma, on November 16, 1907. As she entered the world, fireworks burst across the Oklahoma sky in celebration of the Indian and Oklahoma Territories merging to become the 46th state to enter the Union. Petty, named for her birthplace and Cherokee heritage, came to California in 1925 and found employment on the Austin Denny Barnard Ranch on Ventura Avenue as a live-in housekeeper and driver. (Courtesy of Naomi Guinn.)

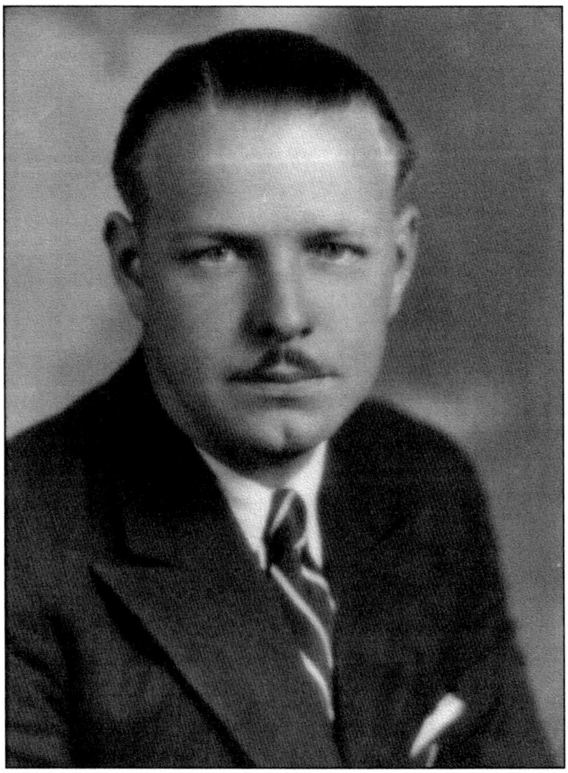

Joseph "Joe" Peter Pluim, the son of Dutch immigrants, was born in Sioux City, Iowa, in 1902. His family came to Los Angeles when he was a teenager. Pluim's performance on a temporary job gained him permanent employment with Southern California Gas Company, and he later became president of the Pacific Gas Workers Union. Pluim married India Petty on Valentine's Day in 1929. (Courtesy of Naomi Guinn.)

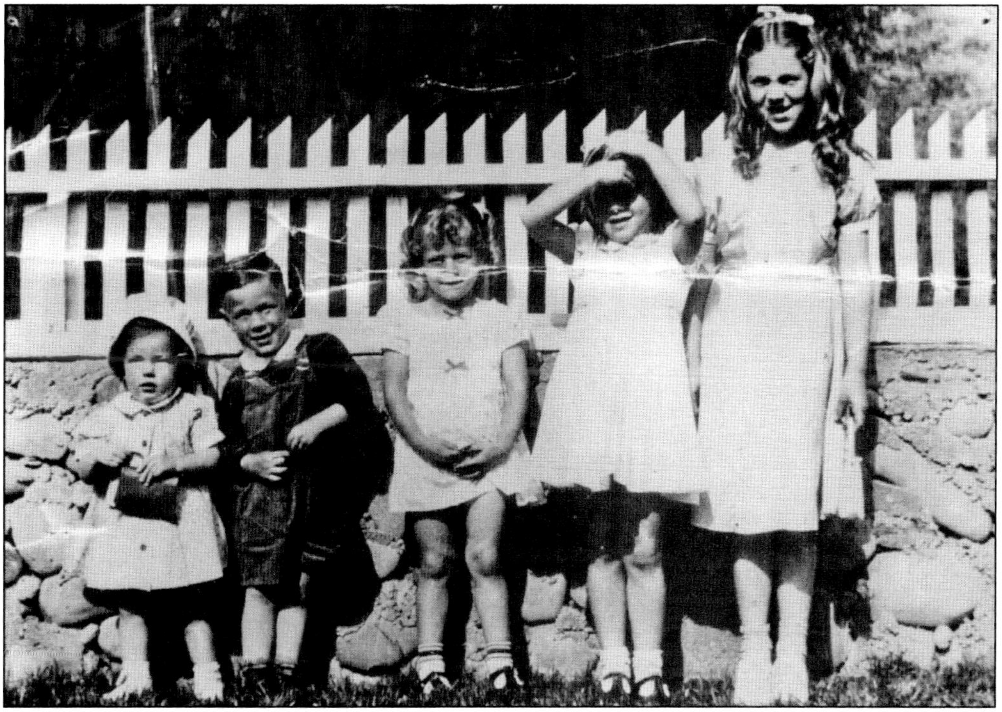

Joe and India Pluim lived on McFarland Lane before moving their family to Foster Park in 1939. The Pluims bought a two-bedroom house along North Ventura Avenue. When they needed more space, Joe Pluim had the house raised and put in a basement for a game room. From left to right, the Pluim children are Naomi, Jan, Mary Ann, Virginia "Jeannie," and Joan. (Courtesy of Mary Ann Aguilar.)

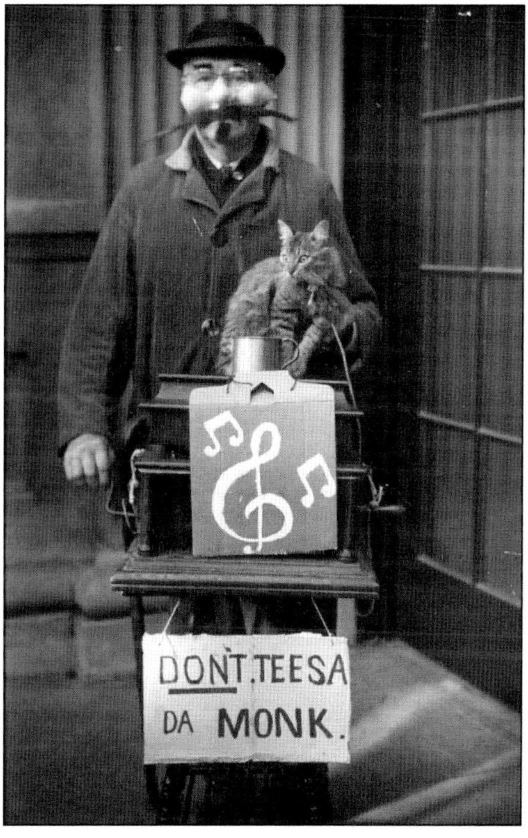

When Joe Pluim's father, Jan Wilhelm Pluim, came to Foster Park from Los Angeles to visit his grandchildren, it was always a treat. The elder Pluim was a practical joker and loved to perform gags. In this photograph, Pluim does his best improvisation as an organ grinder. (Courtesy of Teresa Ross.)

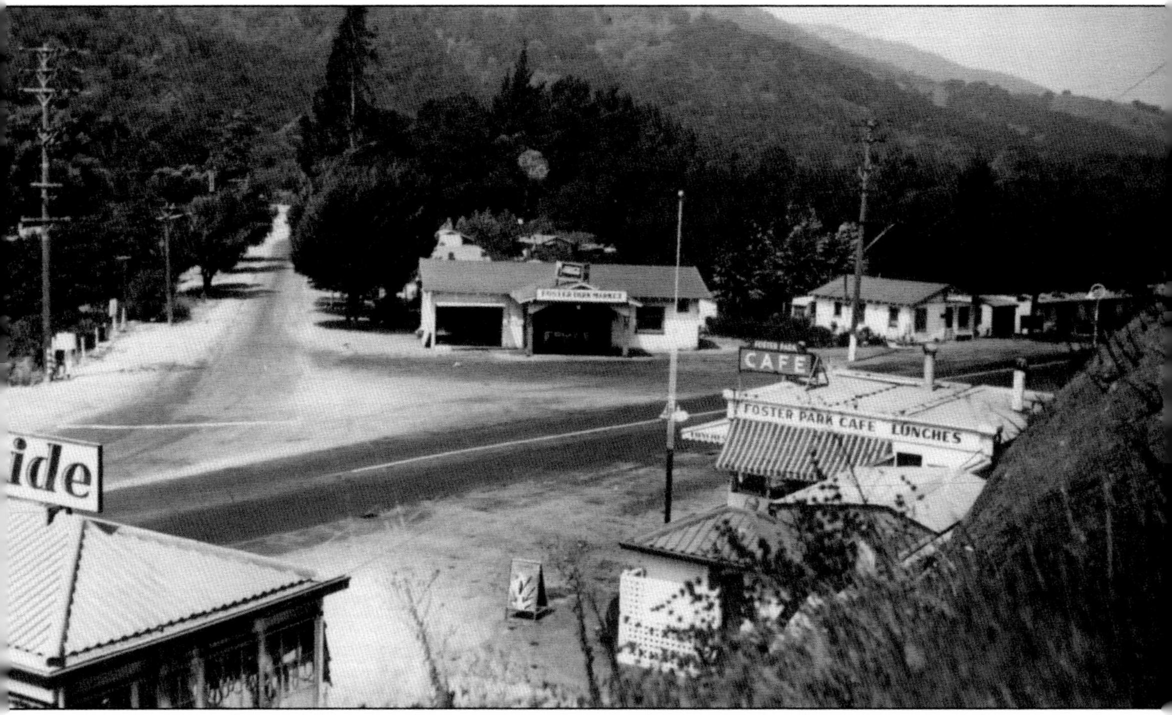

This westerly view facing Red Mountain is a partial image of the downtown area of Foster Park as it appeared in 1939. The Foster Park Market sits quietly at the intersection of Highway 399 (later known as Highway 33) and Casitas Pass Road. A single advertisement for Coca-Cola rests atop the open-air entrance. Not so visible through the trees behind the market are homes, which made up part of the residential area. The building to the right of the market is a barbershop owned by local barber Jack Young. Across the highway, in the left corner, fan belts hang in the window at the Foster Park Seaside Service Station. To the right, striped awnings give a quaint invitation to lunch at the Foster Park Café. The market may have been established before the town's development, supplying goods for sportsmen and travelers. As the town's population grew, the market became the hub of the town. (Courtesy of the Museum of Ventura County.)

The Foster Park Service Station, located on the east side of North Ventura Avenue, had different owners over the years. It was originally a Shell service station until the mid-1930s, when it switched to Seaside Oil Company. Sporting a bow tie and a white uniform, owner Orly Shullanberger, posing with his mother, looks dressed to play the role of a service station attendant in a period film about 1935. (Courtesy of the Leslie Ray Moore family.)

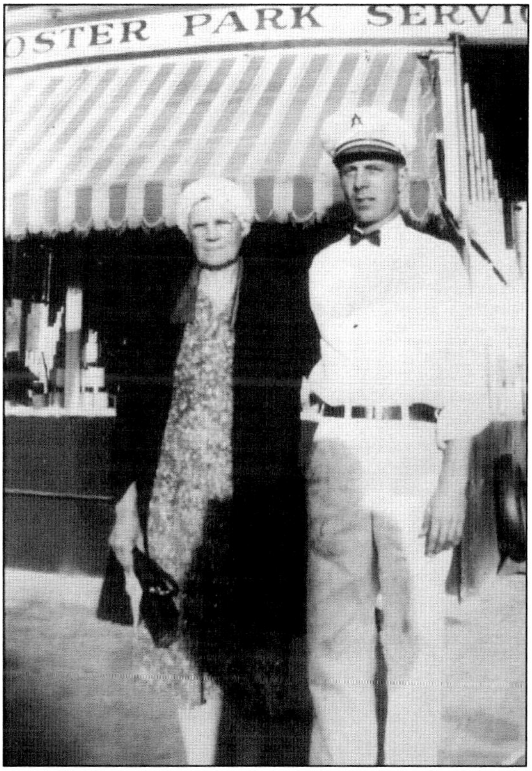

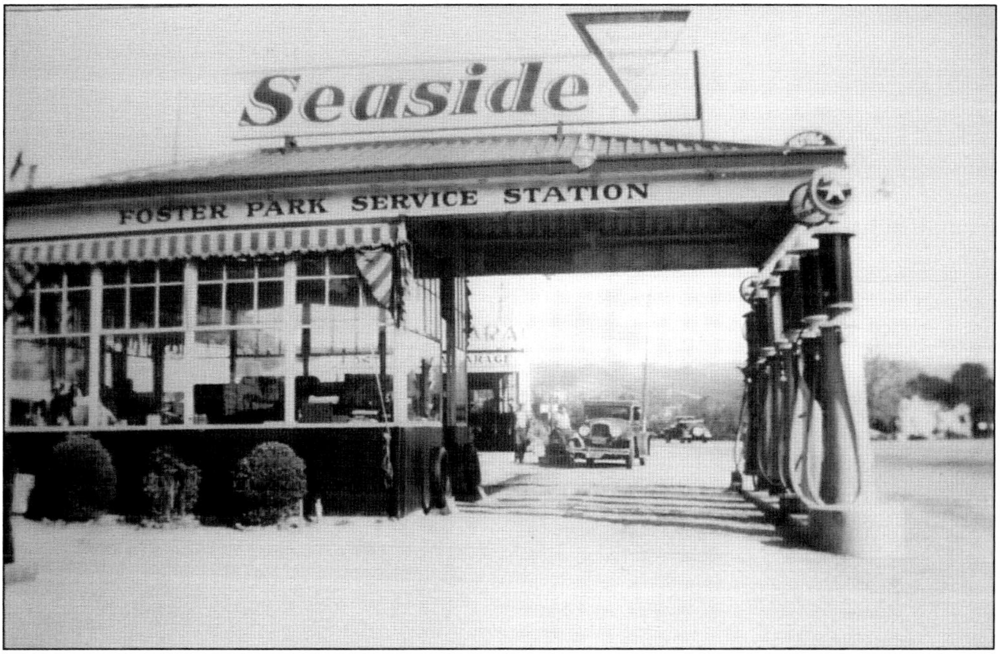

In this view facing south, the building directly behind the service station is the Foster Park Garage, later owned by Jess Hamby from the late 1930s to the mid-1960s. The white building on the west side of the highway is the Foster Park Ballroom. It was also known as the Moose Hall until the late 1950s, when it became Okie's Tavern. (Courtesy of the Leslie Ray Moore family.)

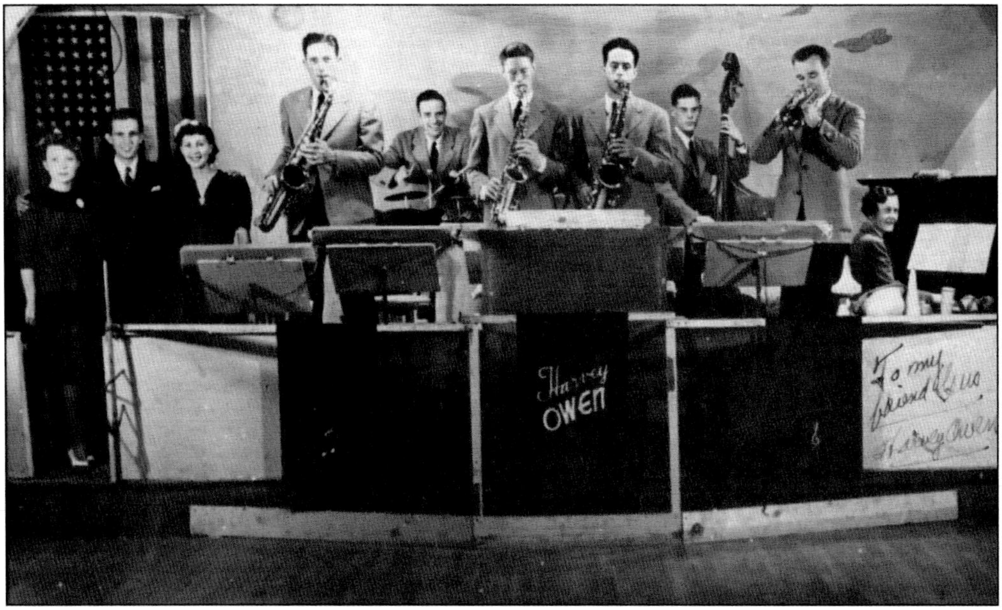

During the 1930s and early 1940s, big band music blared as folks got their swing on at the Foster Park Ballroom. Harvey Owen and his orchestra played there regularly before World War II. Owen (far right), a Ventura resident, played in a naval band under John Phillip Sousa during World War I. After the invasion at Pearl Harbor, Owen rejoined the Navy and its band. The ballroom was of the Royal Order of Moose. (Courtesy of Steve Riley.)

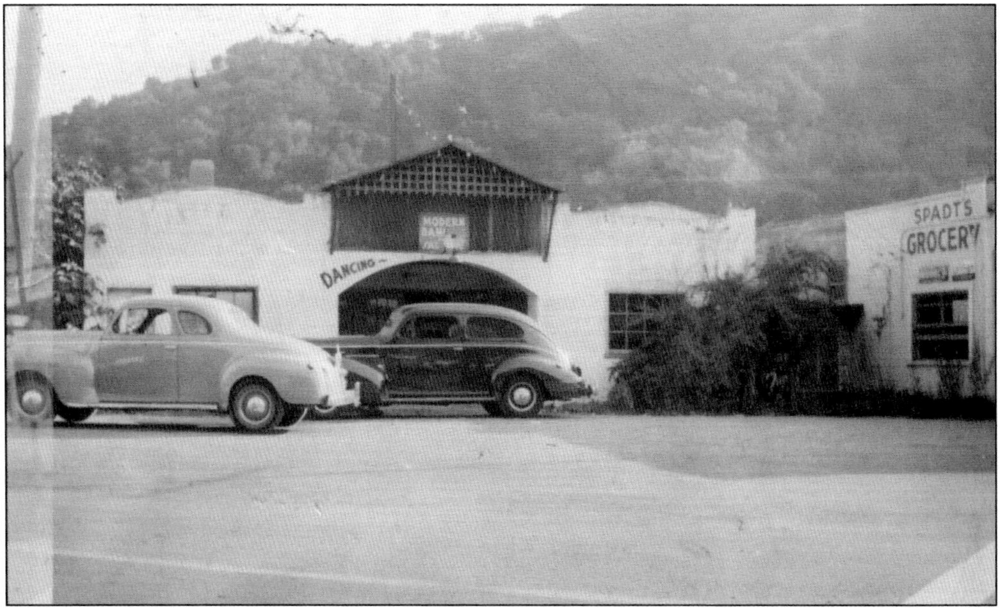

"Ye Old Stomping Ground, September 1944," was the notation on the back of this photograph taken by Harvey Owen as he stopped to reminisce about his big band days at the Moose Hall. "MOOSE BOOK OPRY' STAR" was another notation made by the *Ventura Star-Free-Press* when announcing that newcomer Johnny Cash would be appearing at the hall in December 1956. Other booked stars included the Everly Brothers, Lefty Frizzel, and Jim Reeves. (Courtesy of Steve Riley.)

Members of the Kenney family stand on the Foster Park Bridge for this 1941 photograph. Foster Park resident Carter Bryan Kenney worked as a roughneck in the Avenue Oilfield. In the foreground is the youngest Kenney family member, Carter "Ray," family dog Cricket, wife Minnie Marie, and daughter Lucille. Their daughter Ethel Marie is not pictured. (Courtesy Ethel Marie Mullikin.)

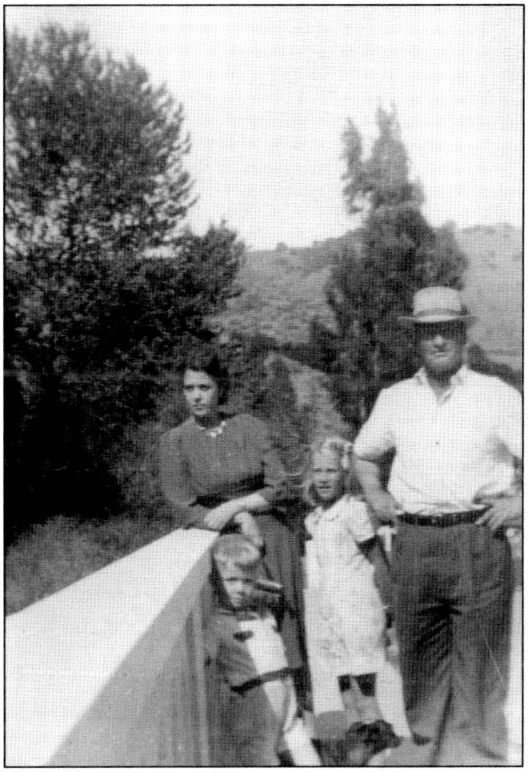

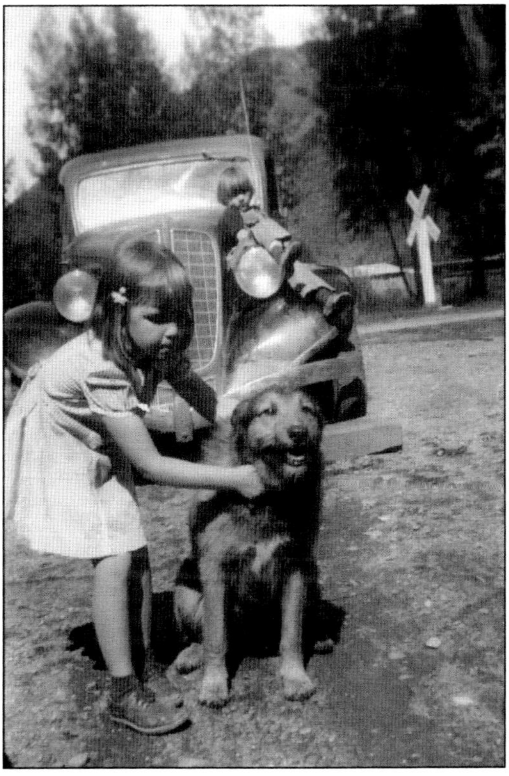

The youngest Kenney daughter, Ethel Marie, plays with the neighbor's dog while playmate Jeanine England reclines on the fender of the car in the background. The Kenneys lived below the bridge in the first house east of the railroad tracks on Casitas Pass Road. Note the railroad crossing sign to the right. (Courtesy of Ethel Marie Mullikin.)

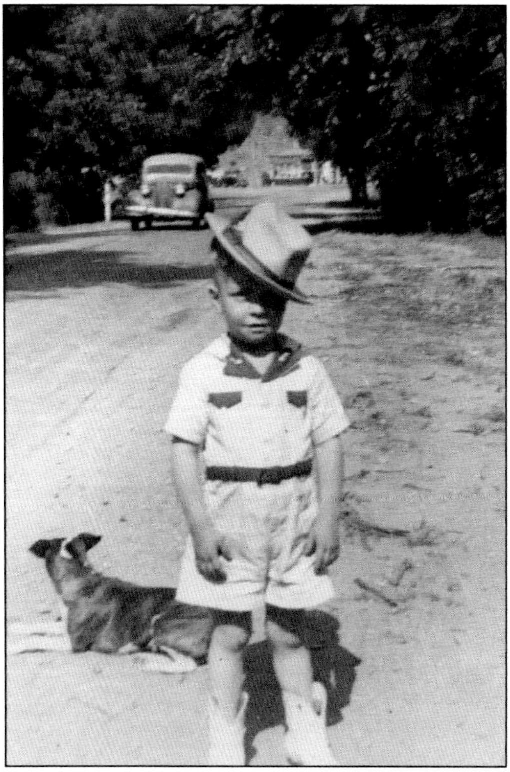

Picturesque Foster Park was inviting to Hollywood filmmakers. As the camera was rolling during the filming of a scene on the bridge, a voice echoed from below. "Mom, Mom!" "Cut!" the director yelled. "Whose kid is that?" When the crowed looked down to see who it was, Minnie Kenney saw her little Ray. Overcome with embarrassment, she did not say a word. Young Kenney, wearing his father's hat tilted atop his head, shows off his new cowboy boots while Cricket watches the oncoming car. At the end of the arbor tunnel is the service station and café. Below is a 1965 image facing the intersection of Casitas Pass Road and Highway 33. It is a view of the same area shown and described on the previous three pages. (Left, courtesy of Ethel Marie Mullikin; below, courtesy of KCBS-TV©.)

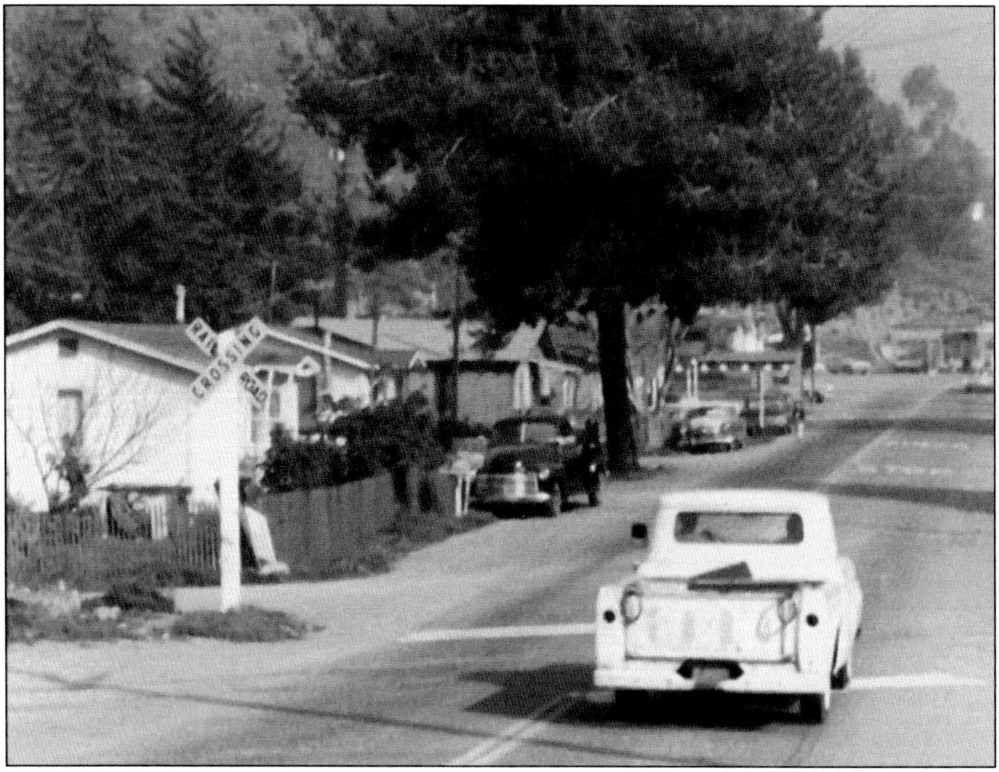

Milton and Mildred Maxwell share a happy moment with their only child, James "Jimmy" Milton, in this 1946 photograph. The Maxwells, originally from the California Central Valley area, lived in Casitas Springs before moving to Foster Park in 1941. Maxwell worked at the Foster Park Service Station from 1937 to 1940, when he was hired by a construction company. On this smiled-filled occasion, the Maxwells celebrate Jimmy's fifth birthday. (Courtesy of Jim Maxwell.)

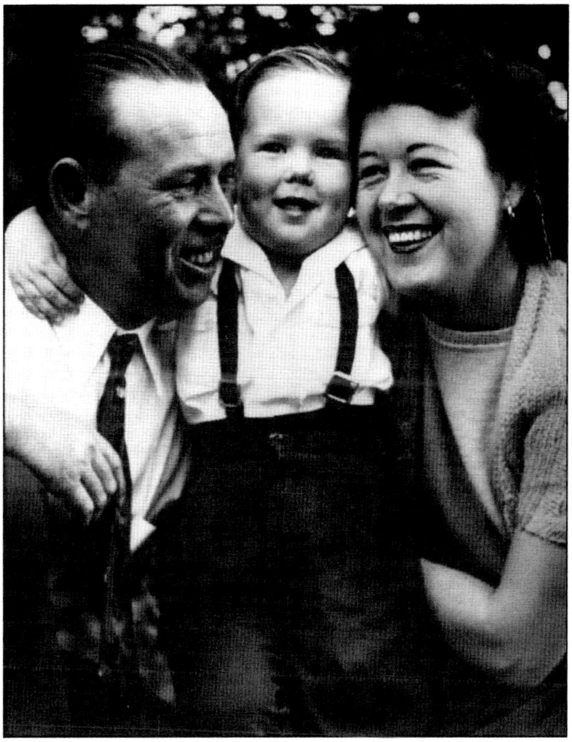

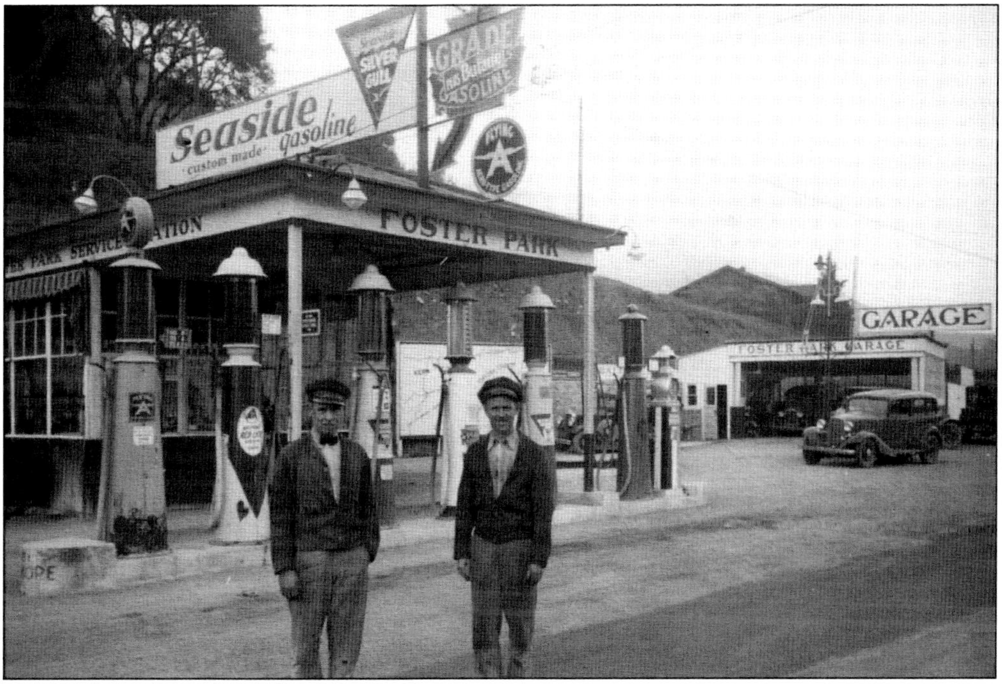

Milton Maxwell (left) and his brother Lloyd Maxwell, from Casitas Springs, take a break from their duties as service station attendants for this photograph around 1937. The station and garage were owned by Jess Hamby at this time. Hamby hired help to run the station while he spent his time and mechanical expertise at the garage. (Courtesy of Jim Maxwell.)

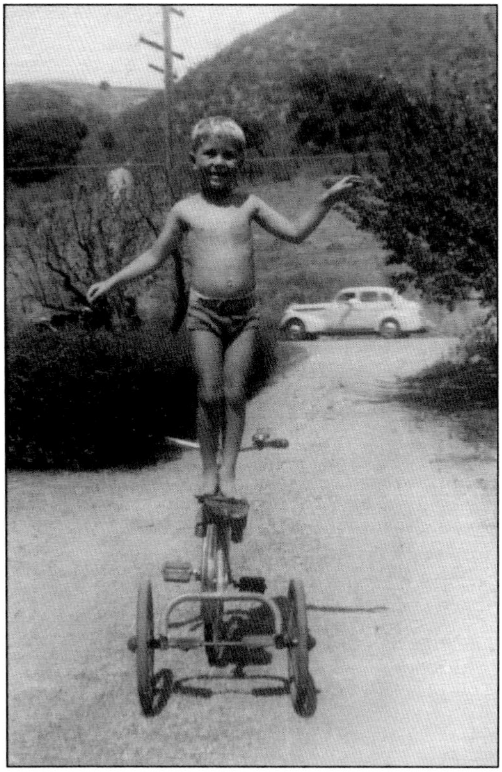

Donald "Don" Moore was born on Christmas Day, 1931. He was 18 months old when his parents, Ray and Neva Moore, moved to Foster Park. In the background, a car passes on Highway 33 as seven-year-old Moore does a balancing act—something he became very good at. After his marriage to Joann Russell, an E.P. Foster Elementary School teacher (below), in 1956, Moore continued his studies at Fresno State University and earned a bachelor's degree in mathematics. When the computer age was on the ground floor, Moore's mathematical skills took him on a diverse career journey, including civil employment with the US Navy at Point Mugu writing computer programs for testing missile trajectories. His Christian faith later led him to positions as assistant pastor at Ojai Valley Community Church in Ojai and Live Oak Fellowship in Oak View. (Both, courtesy of the Leslie Ray Moore family.)

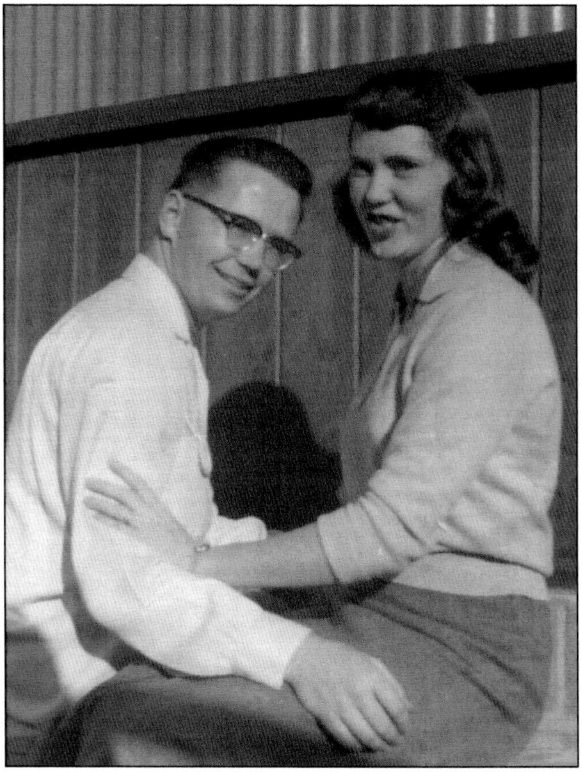

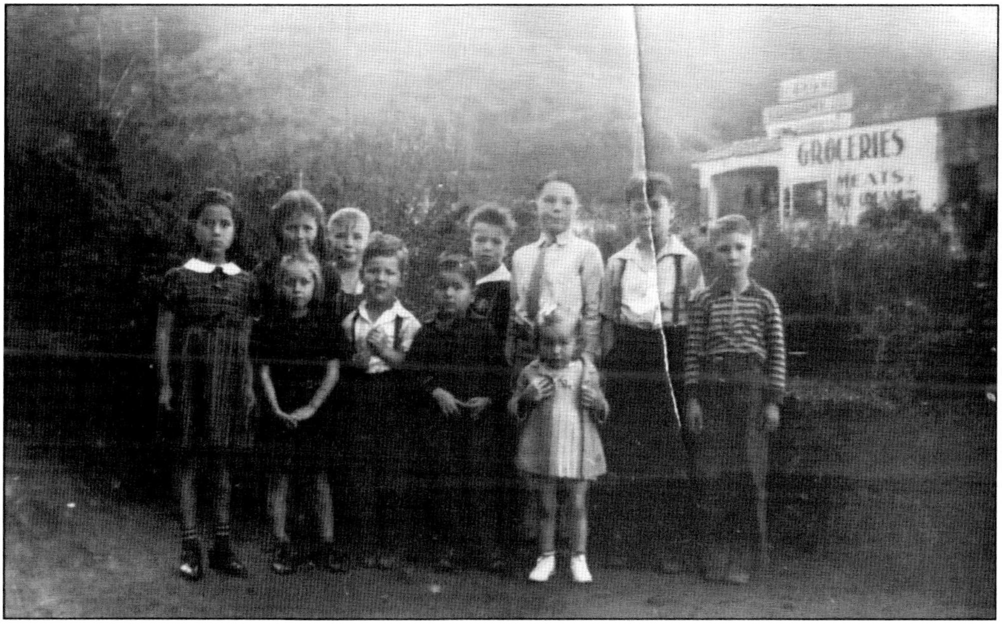

This was a special day for eight-year-old Don Moore (back row, third to the right). Being that he was born on Christmas Day, he never had a party on his birthday. Neighbor Blanche Griffith had no children and was very fond of young Moore. On this Christmas in 1939, as a gift, she gave him a party. Moore and Griffith remained lifelong friends. In the background is Spadt's Grocery. (Courtesy of the Leslie Ray Moore family.)

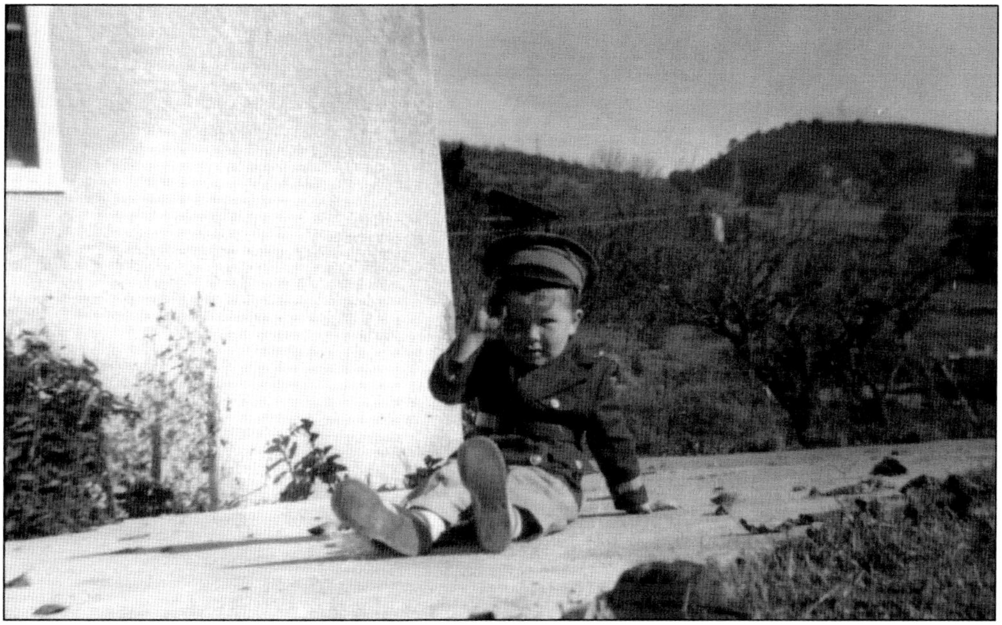

This uniformed young man saluting for the camera is Gary Moore. The miniature uniform caught the eye of frugal Ray Moore as he walked with his three-year-old son through a department store in downtown Ventura during World War II. He had no intention on buying it; nonetheless, he showed it to little Gary. With open arms and a jubilant, "Oh thank you Daddy!", Moore made an unexpected but rewarding purchase that day. (Courtesy of the Leslie Ray Moore family.)

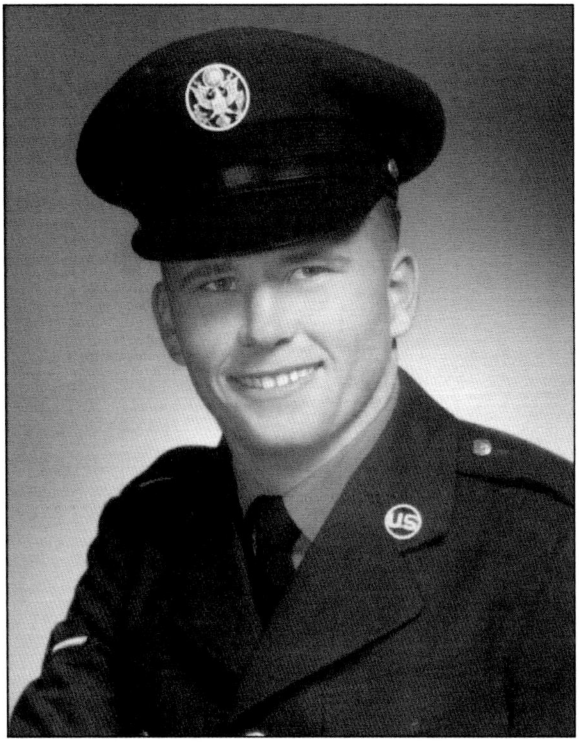

In this photograph, a mature Gary Moore wears a US Air Force uniform. He served as an airman, first class, at Ellsworth, South Dakota, in the Intercontinental Ballistic Missile unit (ICBM) from 1958 to 1966. After his military service, Moore earned a bachelor's degree in criminology from Fresno State University. (Courtesy of the Leslie Ray Moore family.)

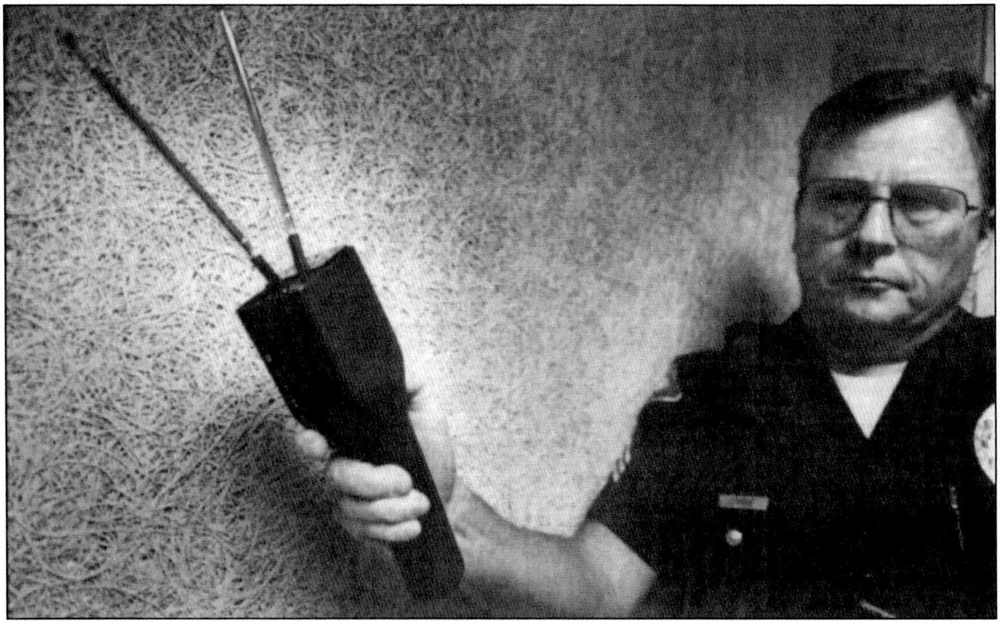

Now wearing a police uniform in this 1990 photograph, Ventura Police sergeant Gary Moore displays the latest alternative to lethal force weaponry—the Taser gun. Through a pair of rabbit ear–like antenna, 50,000 volts of electricity could be delivered into the body of a combatant suspect up to 14 feet away. Moore was the first officer in the department to deliver its debilitating effect. "It worked," Moore recalls, "he dropped like a sack of potatoes!" (Photograph from *Ventura Star-Free-Press*; courtesy of the Leslie Ray Moore family.)

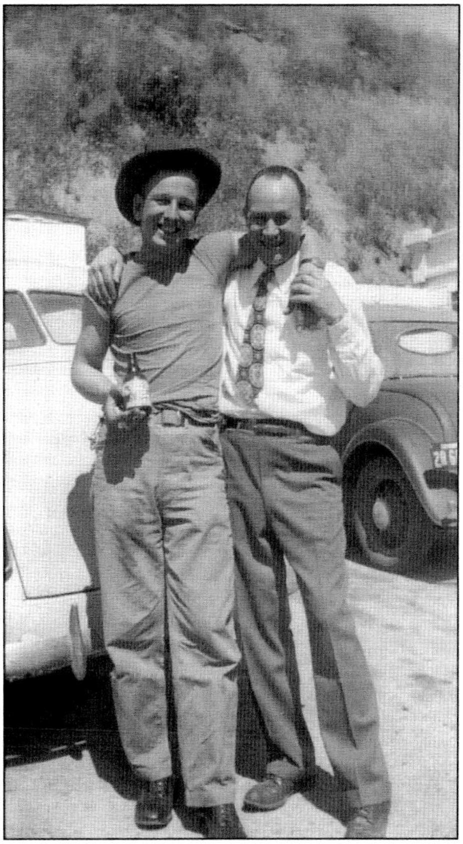

Here, Ray Roberson (right in the image at right) poses with friend Dutch Valine in the parking lot between the Foster Park Service Station and the Foster Park Café. Roberson and his wife, Inez, owned the Foster Park Market from 1941 to 1946. Among items sold there, the most memorable were the mouth-watering dill pickles. However, a piece of bubble gum rarely sold, since he often gave them away. Roberson was generous and easygoing, and he always had a joke and a winning smile to offer those around him. He was nicknamed "Mayor of Foster Park." Pictured below is Roberson with hunting buddies who stopped by to show off their trophy. From left to right are, Roberson, Monte Vanegas, Dan Sheff, and Camilo Escarena. (Right, courtesy of Becky Enlow; below, courtesy of Linda Oliver.)

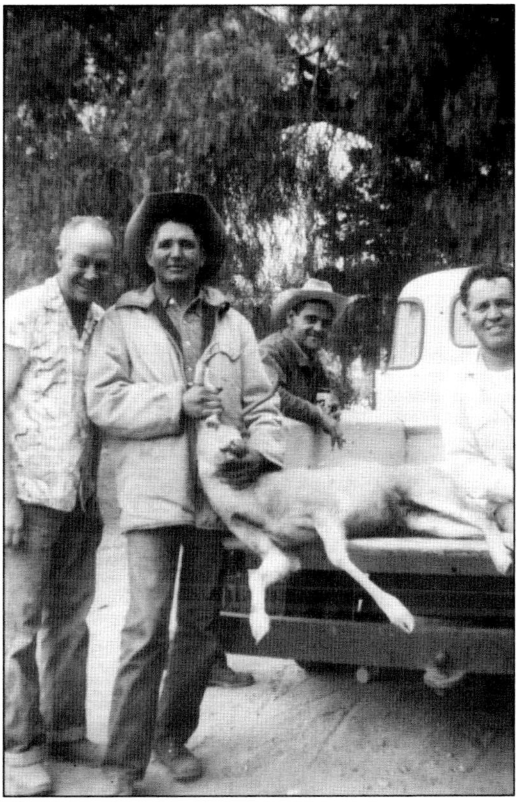

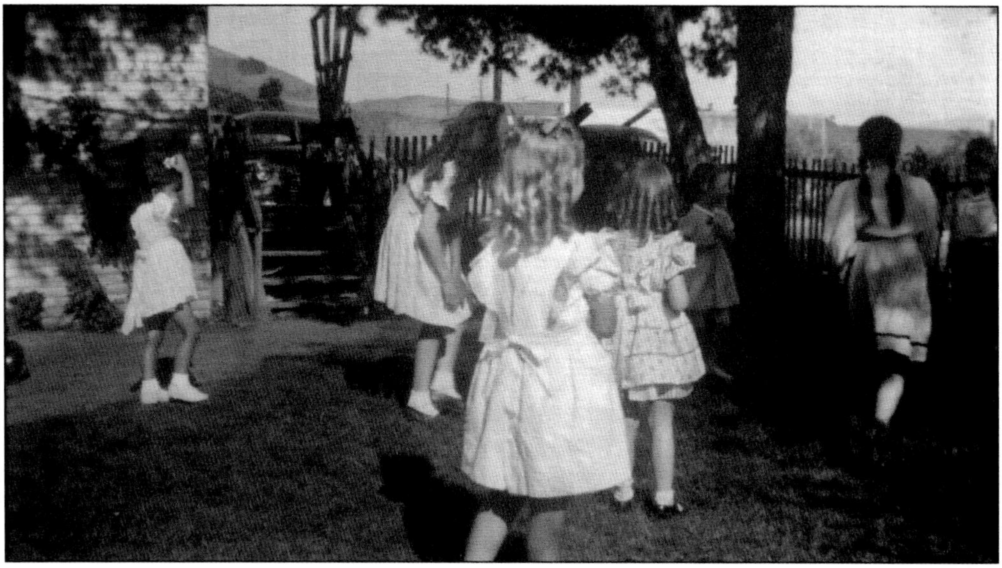

Children and parents alike adored Ray Roberson, especially when the little ones had a loose tooth. It all started with one child who would not let his parents touch his loose tooth. Roberson, with his calming tone and warm smile, offered to lend a hand. Using a gentle tug, he pulled out the tooth. The child was then rewarded with a soda pop. After the story got around, parents were bringing their loose-toothed children to Roberson. In these 1946 photographs, children gather behind the market in the Roberson front yard for daughter Linda's birthday party. Party guests pictured below are, from left to right, (first row) Judy Bartholomew, Meggy Nye, Linda Roberson, and Norma Lee Cline; (second row) Linda Smith, Tommy Nye, Ray Roberson Jr., and Pat Kingston; (third row) Betty Bartholomew and Joan Roberson. (Both, courtesy of Linda Oliver.)

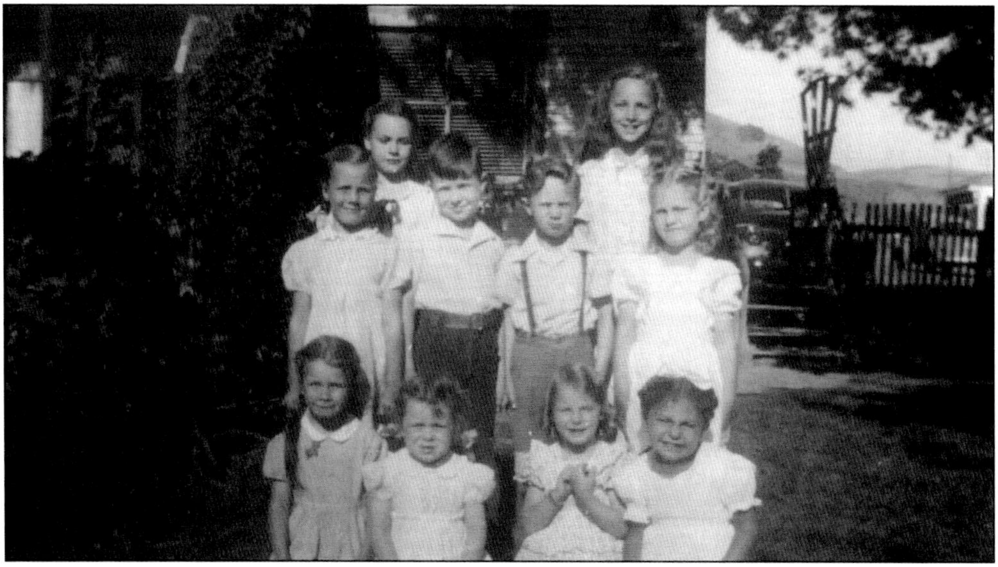

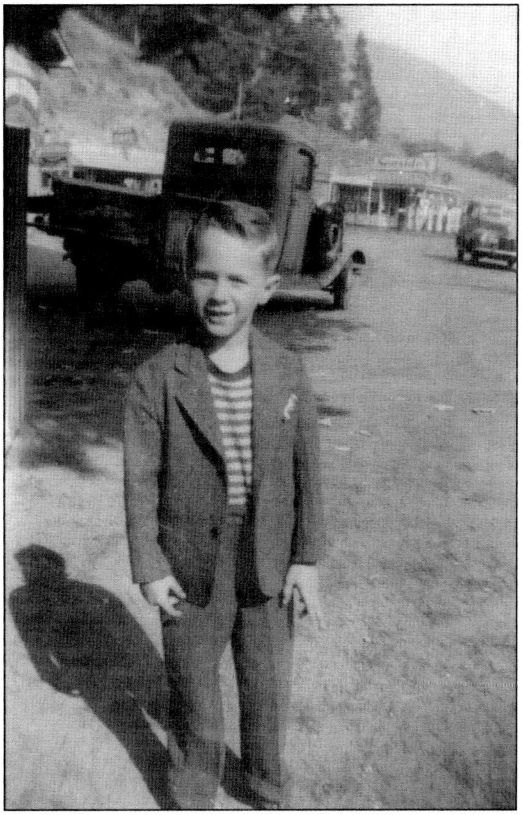

Ray and Inez Roberson had six children within a 23-year span—Patsy, Jean, Joan, Linda, Susan, and Ray Jr. The Robersons lived behind the market on Casitas Vista Road, where Ray Jr. stands for this early-1940s photograph. In the background is a partially obscured view of the service station (right) and the café. The bathing beauty below is 17-year-old Jean Roberson, who made sure she had on her lipstick when soldiers bivouacked in the park during World War II. Doing her best to boost military moral, Jean sent such lovely photographs of herself with letters of encouragement to servicemen she had met. However, it was former serviceman Larry Davis who walked into the family's market and stole her heart. The couple married in 1945 and rented their first home in Foster Park. (Right, courtesy of Becky Enlow; below, courtesy of Linda Oliver.)

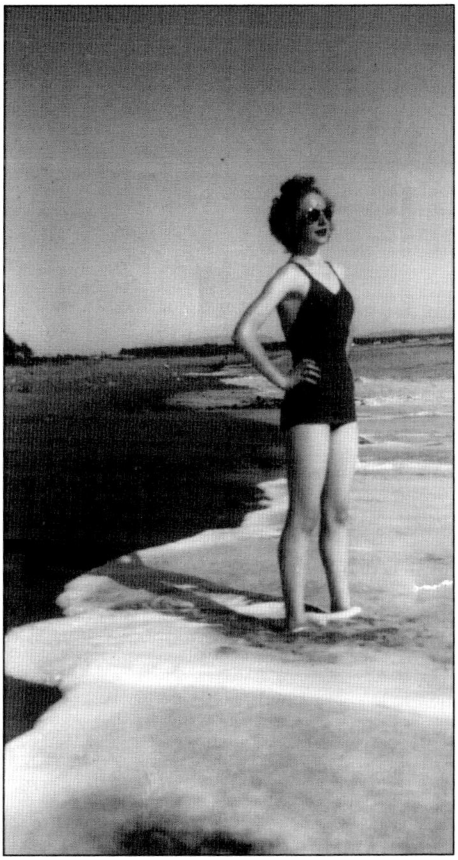

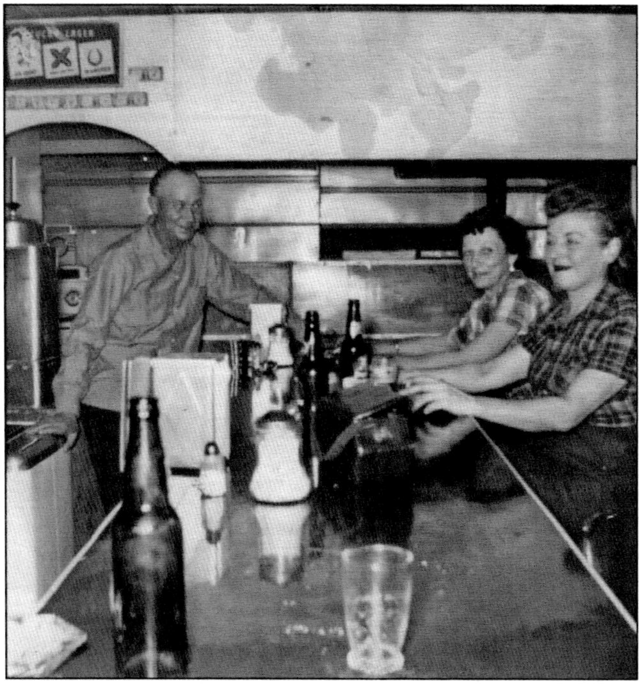

During their years in Foster Park in the mid-1940s, the Robersons owned the café for a short time. Inez, who was highly skilled in the kitchen, ran the restaurant. When she made short ribs, it was standing room only. Her fresh-baked pies were also a draw to the café. Ray Roberson stands behind the counter while Inez (back) takes a break and pops the top off a cold brew with a patron. Pictured below, Ray Jr. escapes the adult chatter to test his skills with a game of Tucson pinball. The pinball machine was tucked away in a corner behind the booths. In the upper-right corner is a window sign advertising Lucky Lager beer. (Both, courtesy of Linda Oliver.)

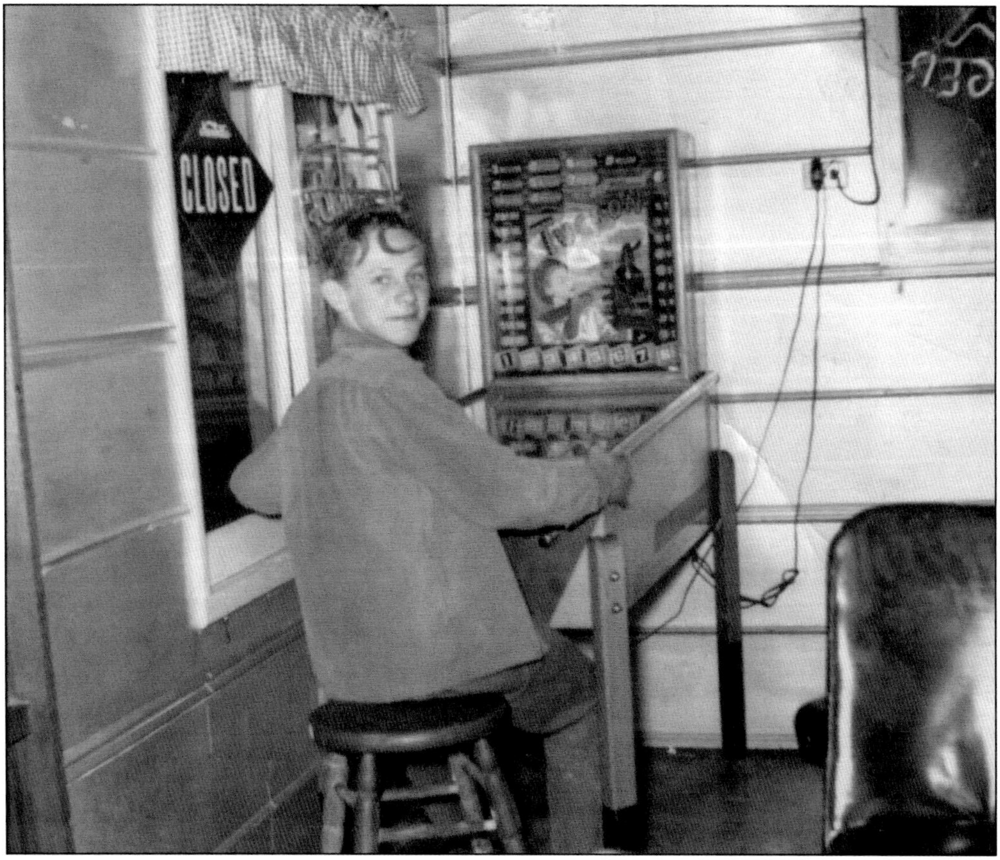

The handsome fellow on this park bench is George Turner, who served as Foster Memorial Park's residential caretaker from 1944 to 1966. Turner was born in New York City in 1908, and his adventurous nature and athletic ability took him on a variety of career paths. In the early 1920s, Turner was the youngest Harley Davidson salesman on the East Coast, and he performed motorcycle stunts as well. Turner came West and worked as a carpenter at Scotties Castle in Death Valley and as a Hollywood stuntman, doubling once for Errol Flynn. In 1927, he found a steady career working for the US Forestry Service before employment with County of Ventura Parks Department. Below, Turner stops to chat with local youth Gene Hale during a drive through the designated camping area of the park in this 1965 photograph. (Right, courtesy of Barbara Turner Randall; below, courtesy of Annie Cody.)

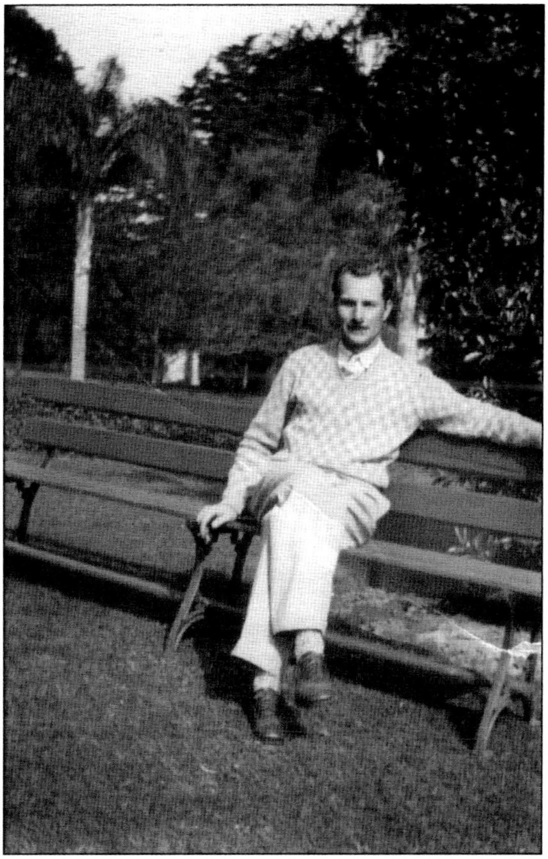

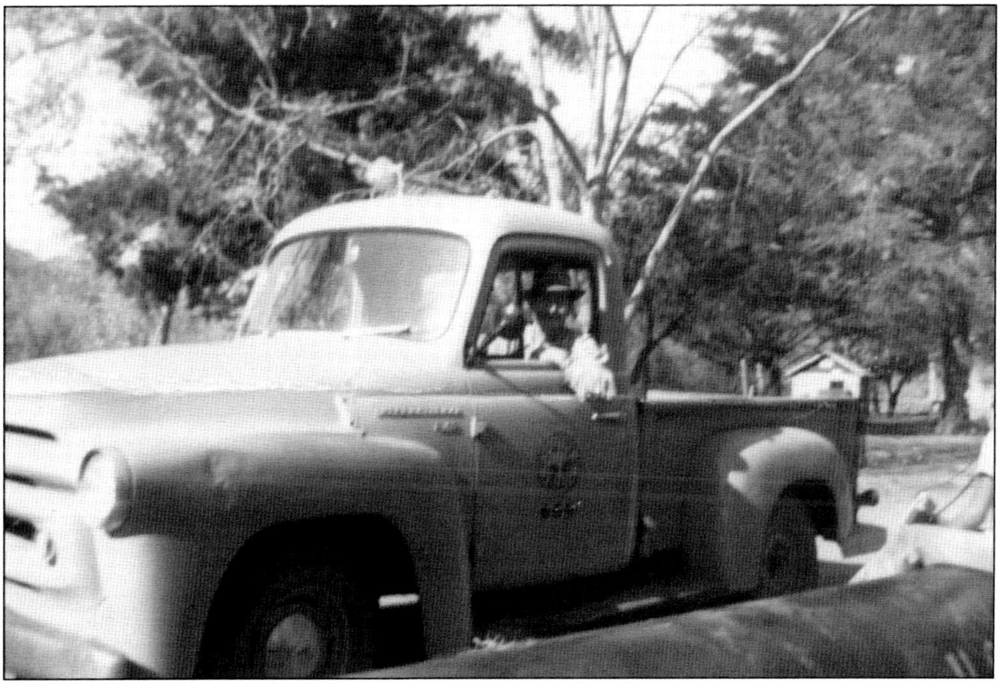

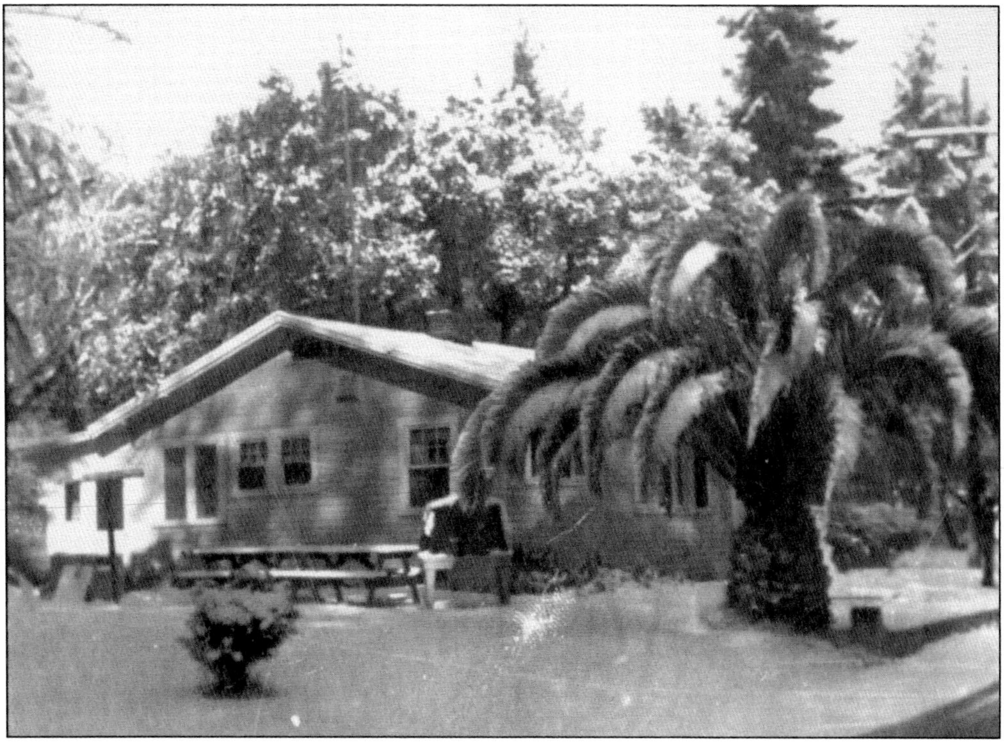

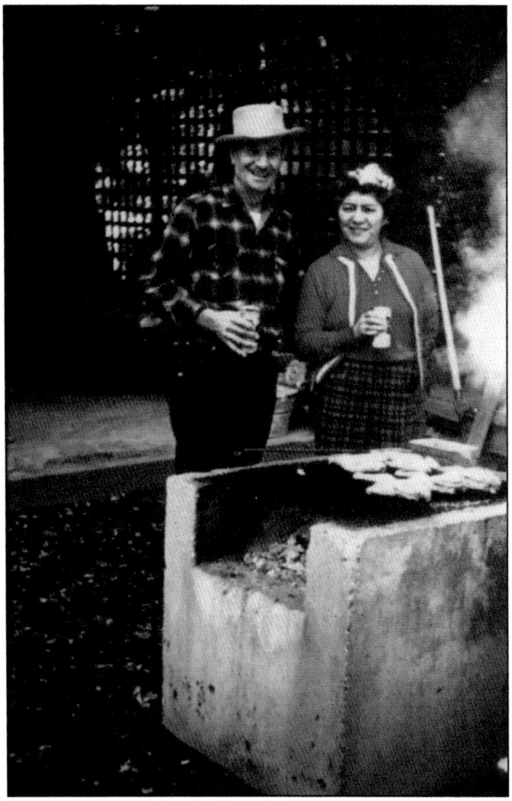

As the resident park caretaker, George Turner moved his family into this house, which is still located on Casitas Vista Road; however, the palm tree has since been removed. In this photograph, the caretaker's residence is dusted white with snow after a flurry hit the area in 1962. (Courtesy of George Turner Jr.)

George Turner and his wife, Olivia "Ollie," enjoy a brew and barbecue chicken at their home in the park. They met in the mid-1920s, when Turner was working as a stunt man. Ollie was visiting an aunt whose ranch was often used as a movie set. Handsome Turner drove up in a fancy car, and that was all it took. The couple were married in 1927 and had three children, George Jr., Patricia, and Barbara. (Courtesy of John Hall.)

Barbara Turner affectionately poses with horse Silvia "Sil" in this 1952 photograph. Her father, George Turner, bought Sil from the Hoffmans, who owned Rancho Casitas, located about a mile north of the caretaker's house. Turner built this corral for Sil in the area between Coyote Creek and the east side of the road across from the house. A maintenance building, which is still there, was used as a tack room. (Courtesy of Barbara Turner Randall.)

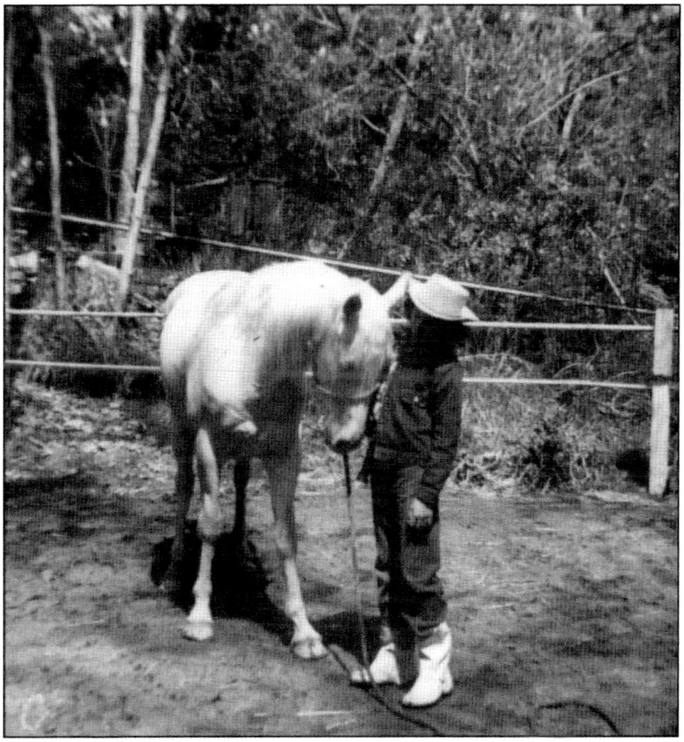

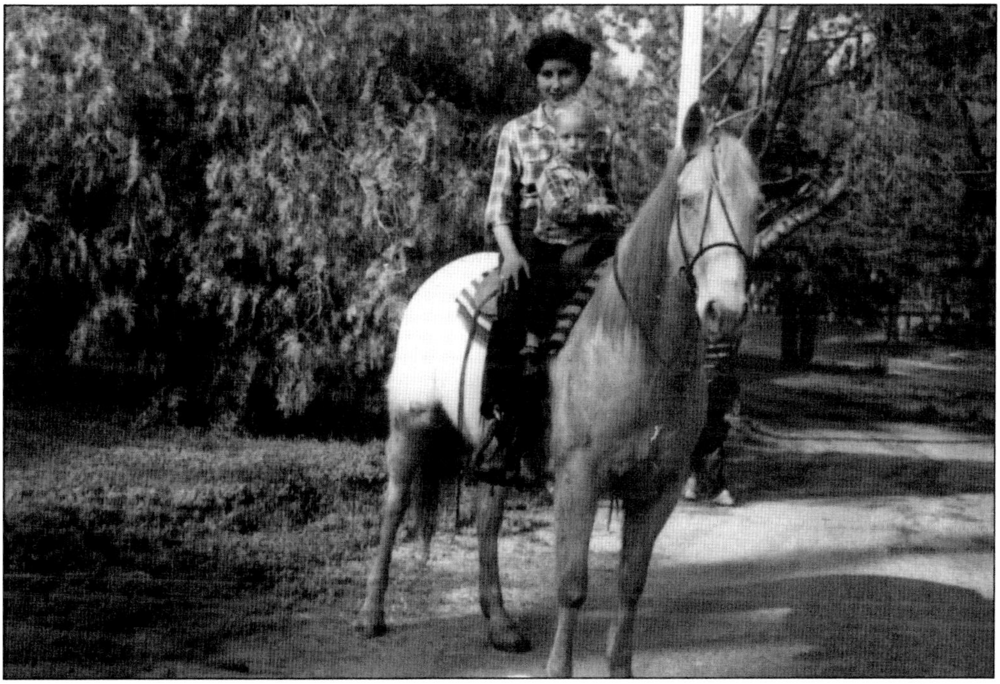

Barbara sits pretty in the saddle in the 1953 photograph above, taken on the west side of the road at Red Mountain. In the background to the right is the northern Foster Park Bridge, which passes over Coyote Creek and winds around to Santa Ana Road. The wee lad is Mike Neatherly, who was fortunate to have Barbara as a babysitter. (Courtesy of Barbara Turner Randall.)

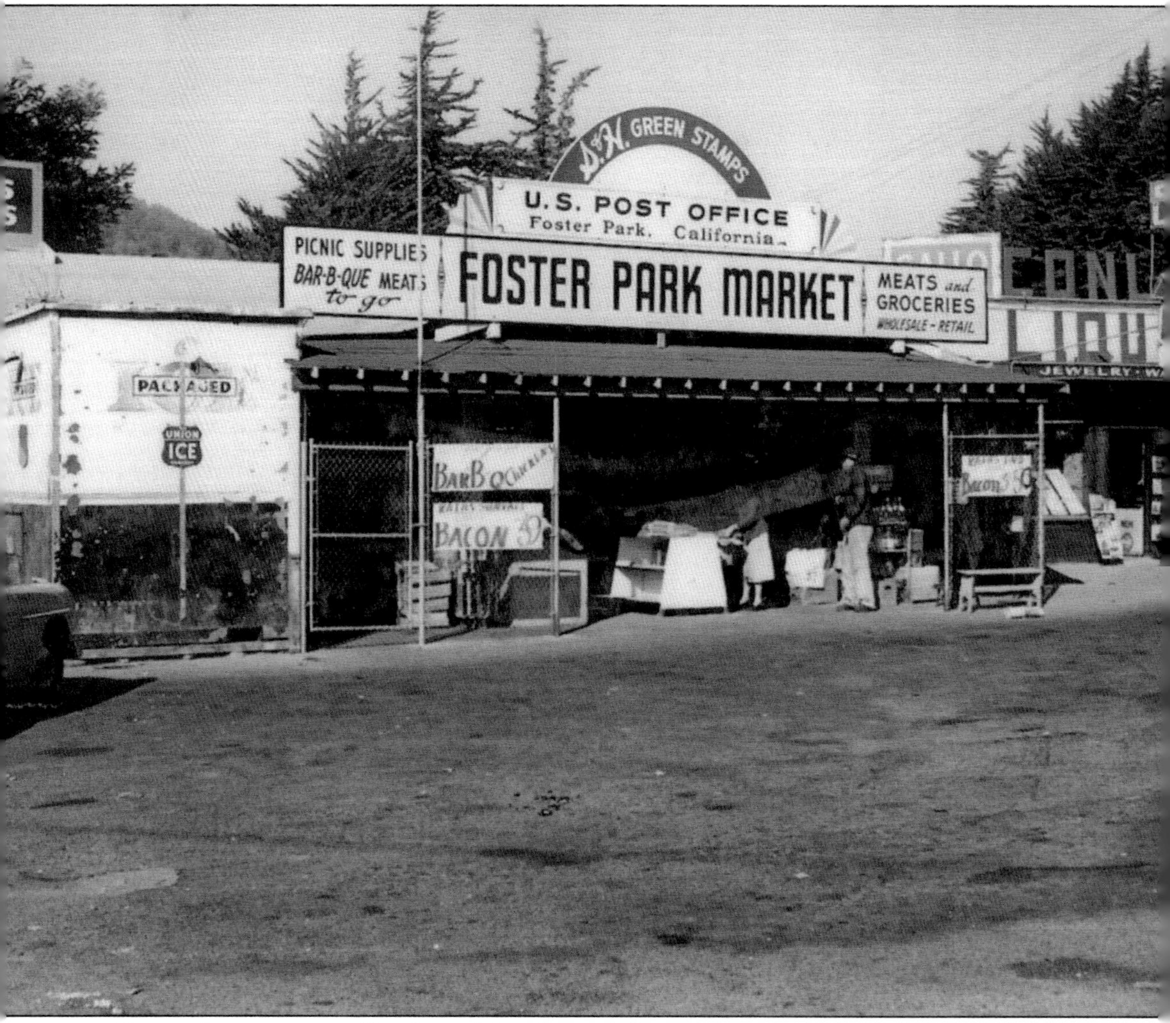

The market, now owned by Gene Boles, depicts a busy enterprise in the early 1950s. The Coca-Cola sign has been replaced by S&H Green Stamps. To the right is Conley's Liquor Store and jewelry pawn shop. Left of the open-air produce section is the Union Ice walk-in box, full of ice blocks to be chipped to order. Inside, among a variety of goods, sat wooden barrels of homemade sauerkraut and juicy pickles and a booth that offered postal services. Kit Mungo, the market's butcher, crafted colorful signs on white butcher paper announcing daily specials, as seen on the chain-linked gate. One sign he made that hung permanently behind the meat counter read, "Our Meat Can't Be Beat." As the aroma of roasting meat and fresh sawdust wafted throughout the market, folks could not help but make their way to the glass display case, so aesthetically arranged with an assortment of meats and side dishes, to see what was for dinner. But it was Mungo's real Western jerky that took center stage and put Foster Park Market on the map. (Photograph by Merrel C. Allyn, courtesy of Kit Mungo Jr.)

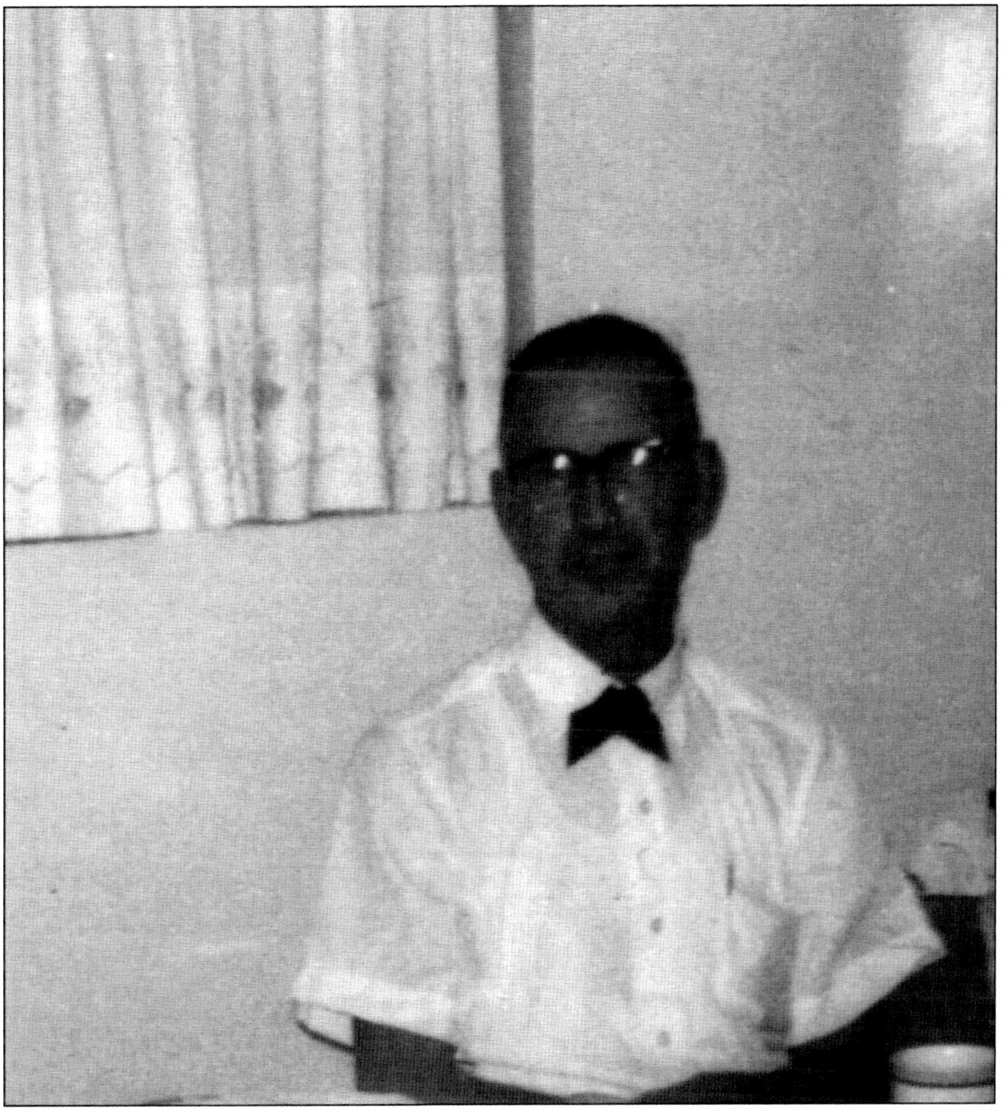

Walter Kitchen "Kit" Mungo was born in Charlotte, North Carolina, in 1908. In his memoirs of Foster Park, Rick Mungo wrote this about his father: "Kit Mungo's meat counter was his kingdom. His southern drawl, his Andy Griffith-Mayberry-like humor, smile and unpretentious casual style made everyone feel comfortable around him. He could peel the bark off the crustiest people. He served in the Navy during World War II as a commissary chef. At the war's end he was assigned at Point Mugu. After the war he spent the remainder of his years working and consulting where he was the happiest—commanding meat counters and businesses throughout Ventura County." His middle name, "Kitchen," Mungo explains, came from a wager between his father, who was a prominent judge, and his father's physician. "Should the man named Kitchen be elected governor, his new son's middle name would be Kitchen, should the man named Horn be elected, then Horn would be his middle name. Fate or electorate had a way of determining my father's profession—helping others with what they served in the kitchen." (Courtesy of Kit Mungo Jr.)

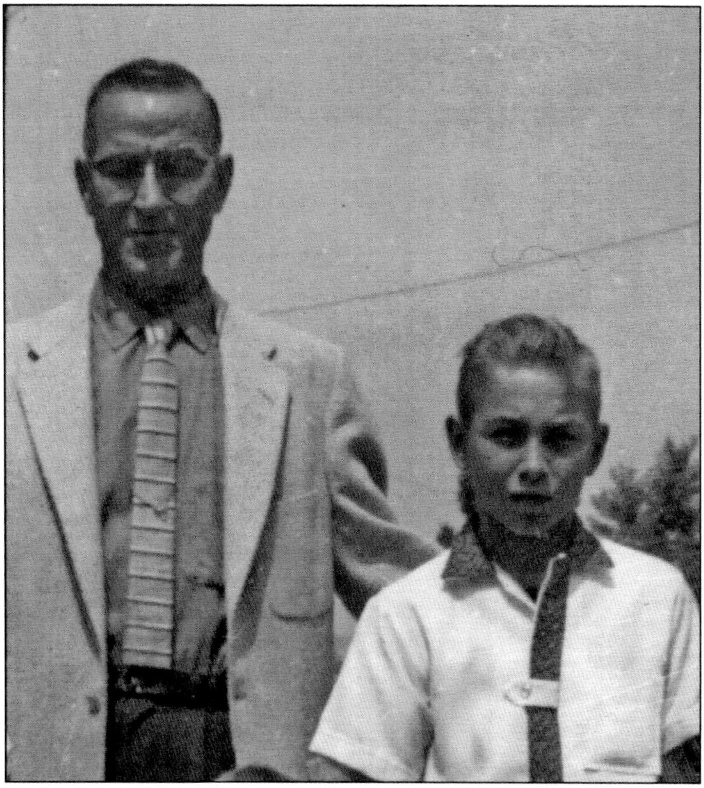

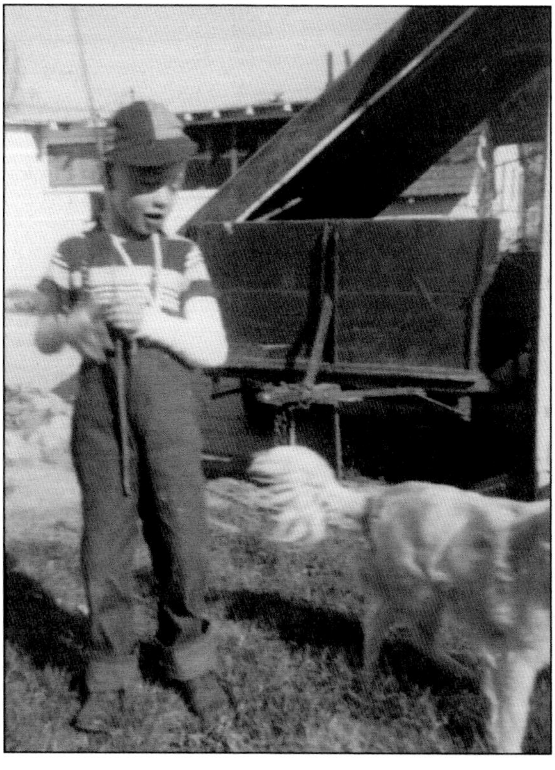

Rick Mungo (above) began working at the Foster Park Market with his father, Kit, at age six. Some of his duties included chipping ice, putting down sawdust behind the counter, splitting wood, and chasing the neighbor's mischievous monkey out of the produce section. Sometimes he helped his father make signs and deliver holiday dinner to patrons. Mungo describes these years as "something special . . . just a kid working with my father behind the meat counter, helping in the market, seeing the locals, travelers and celebrities, seeing it all—life was good." In 1952, while at the market, five-year-old Mungo (right) slipped away and crawled onto the back of a beer truck. The unaware driver took off down Highway 33, and Mungo panicked and jumped out of the truck, breaking his arm. The incident made headlines and young Mungo a hotshot at kindergarten. (Above, courtesy of Ruth Ball Rosemann; right, courtesy of Rick Mungo.)

Kit Mungo lived in Oak View with his wife, Delores "Dee," and sons, Rick and Kit Jr. At age six, Kit Jr. (right), too, was put to small tasks at the Foster Park Market. In his adult years during the mid-1970s, Mungo Jr. introduced his friend Jim Bach, an accountant who moved to Ventura from South Dakota, to his now-retired father. Through that fateful meeting came a union of Bach's ambition and Mungo Sr.'s know-how, creating a partnership that established the famous Pacific Coast Jerky Factory. Pictured below is 75-year-old Kit Mungo Sr., posing in front of the first Pacific Coast Jerky Factory, located on Front Street in Ventura. Before selling the business in 2005, Bach and his brother Rick continued to move into larger buildings to keep up with the volume. (Both, courtesy of Kit Mungo Jr.)

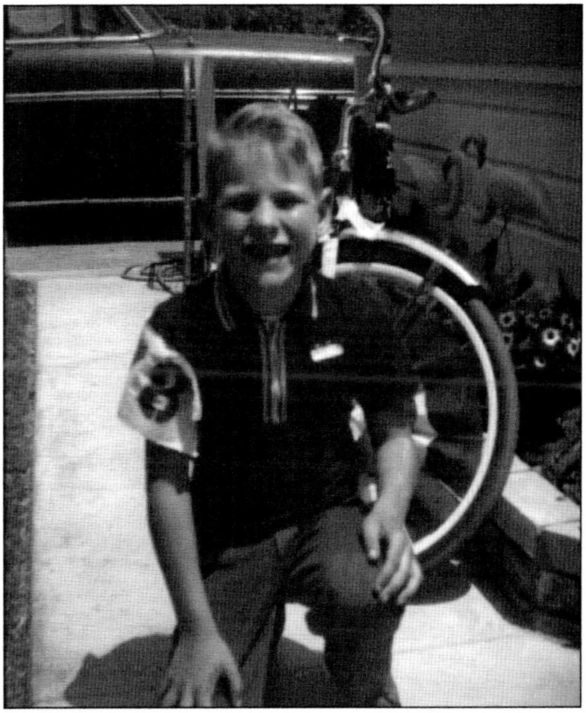

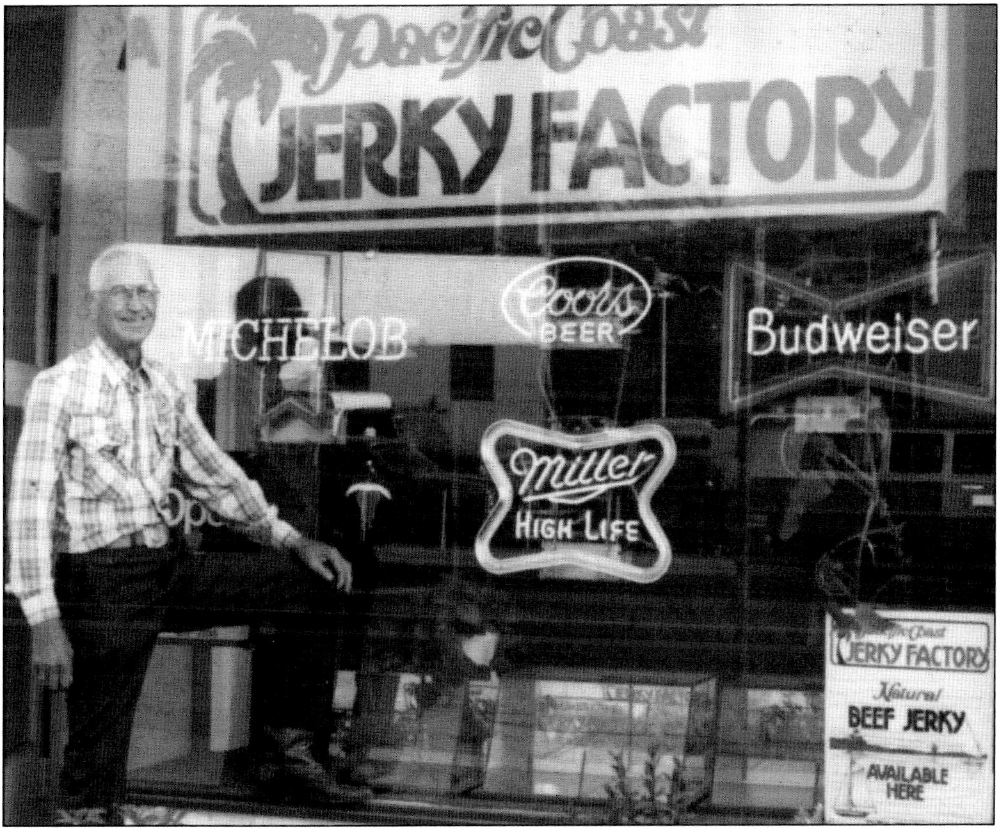

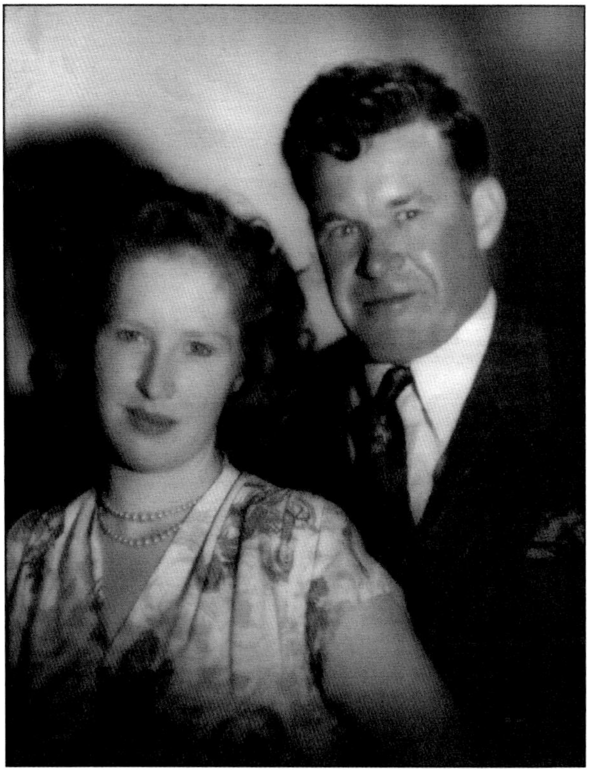

Weast Austin Keeter was the son of Kirk and Myrtle Keeter. The Keeters were sharecroppers from Yellville, Arkansas, who worked their way westward and settled in Foster Park. In this 1948 photograph, Keeter bears a proud countenance as he poses with his new bride, Patricia. The newlywed couple settled in Foster Park, and Keeter was employed as a construction laborer. (Courtesy of the Weast and Patricia Keeter family.)

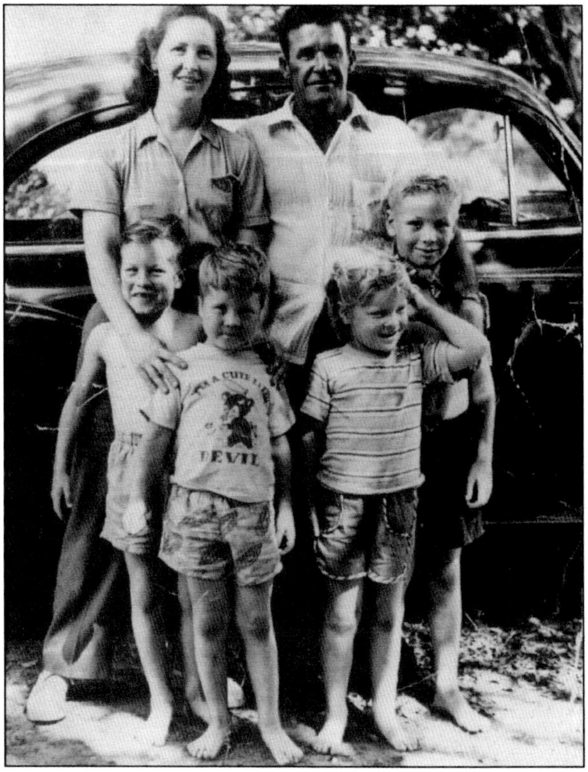

By the mid-1950s, the Keeter family had gained four new members. The Keeter children are, from left to right Kirk, Weast Jr., Gayle, and Rodney. After moving to Casitas Springs in 1957, the Keeters had two more children, Armand and Kathy. (Courtesy of the Weast and Patricia Keeter family.)

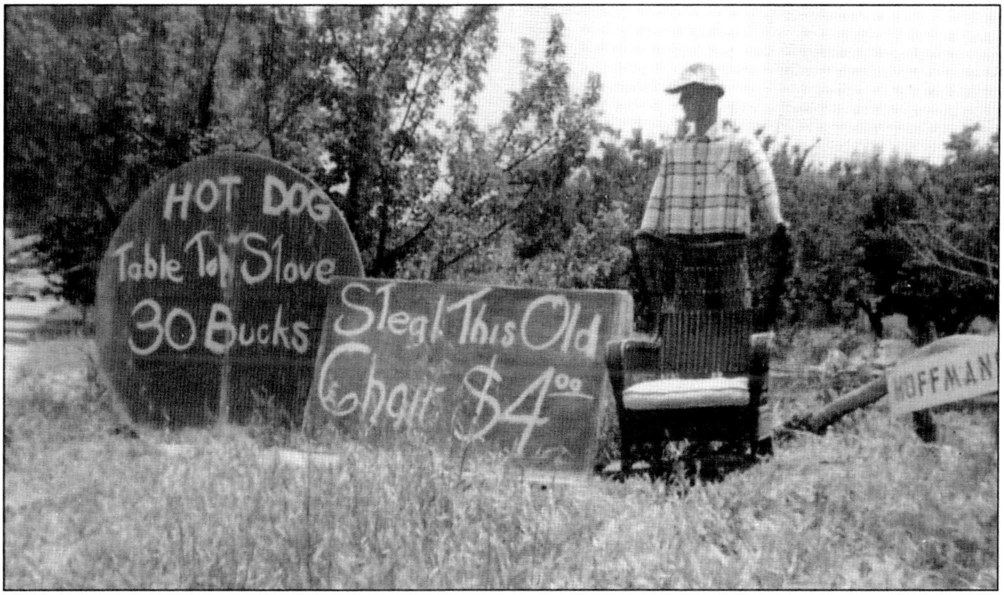

"Hot dog!" was a common expression used by second-hand dealer Charles "Charlie" Hoffman, who settled at the south end of Foster Park in 1950. He opened a second-hand store and displayed his merchandise to passersby on Highway 33. Items sold in the shop ranged from tea cups to this serving tray painted with an image of Napoleon Bonaparte and Beatles memorabilia. However, his eclectic inventory was not what put the retired tool grinder from Michigan on the map of Foster Park. (Above, courtesy of Jennifer Tidwell Kennedy; below, courtesy of KCBS-TV©.)

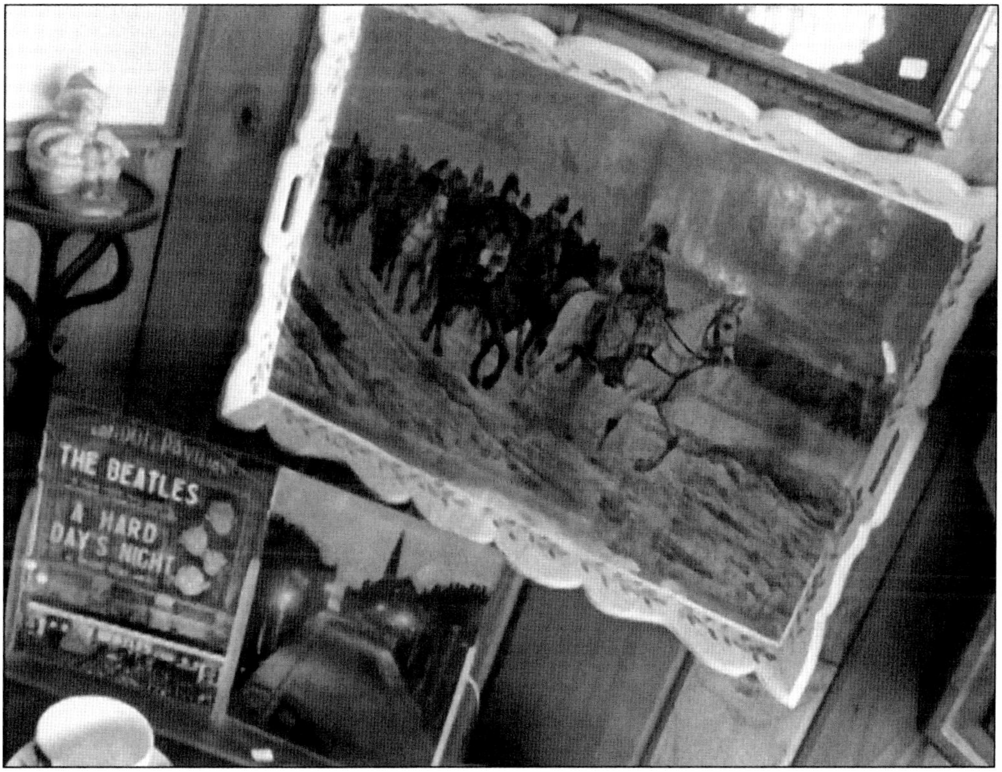

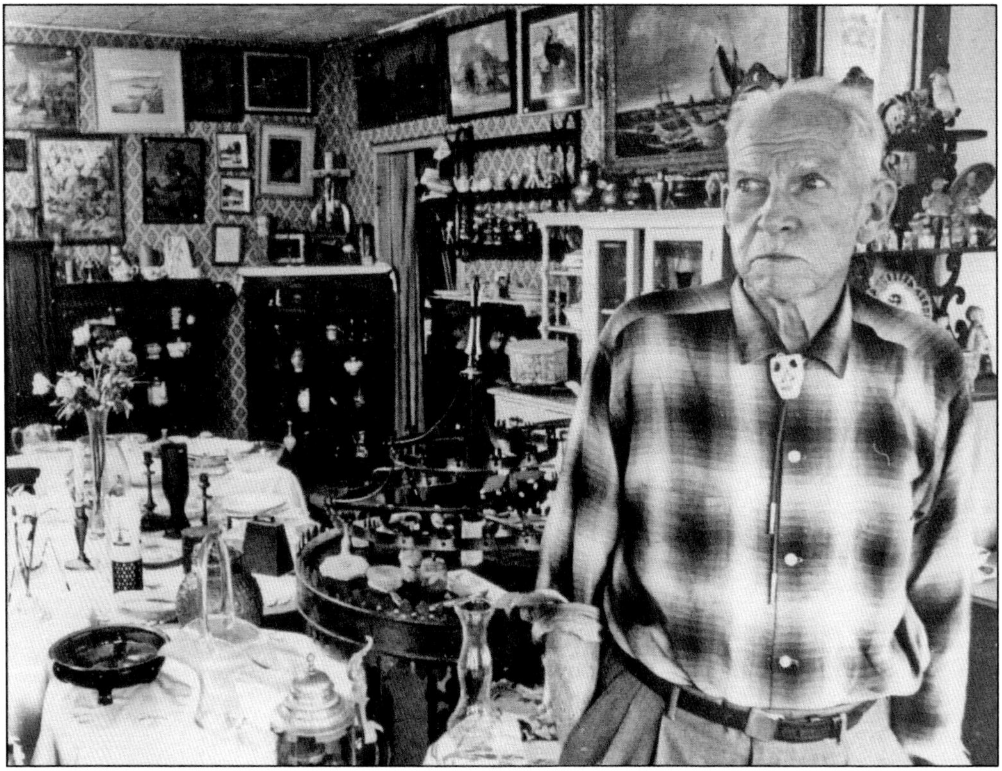

A large blackboard erected in front of his shop, inscribed with a daily message, is what made Charlie Hoffman so famous. Folks traveling along Highway 33 would slow down to see what bit of humor and wisdom the white-haired Hoffman had to offer for the day. He was known as the "Sage of Foster Park." Hoffman also wrote clever, humorous signs to draw attention to certain items; for an antique gramophone he wrote, "Portable juke box for sale cheep," and on an old stove the sign read, "When you buy this you can do no harm, it's just to keep your fanny warm." Pictured above, Hoffman poses in his shop. In the photograph below, Hoffman used this refrigerator to store his inventory of used paperback novels, which he sold for 5¢. (Above, from *Ventura-Star-Free-Press*, courtesy Jennifer Tidwell Kennedy; below, courtesy of KCBS-TV©.)

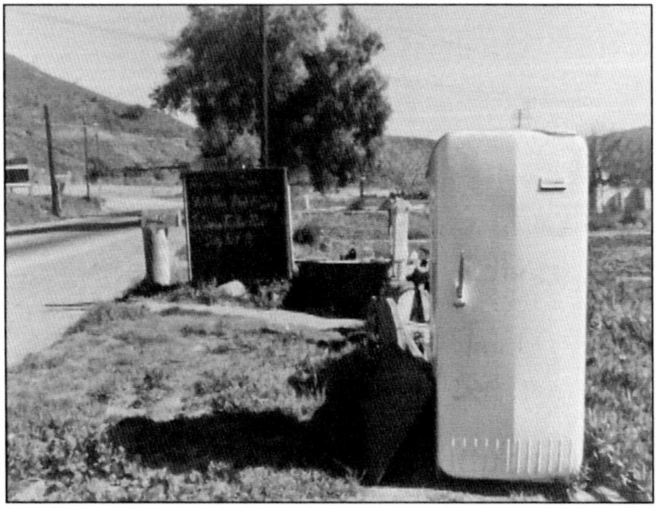

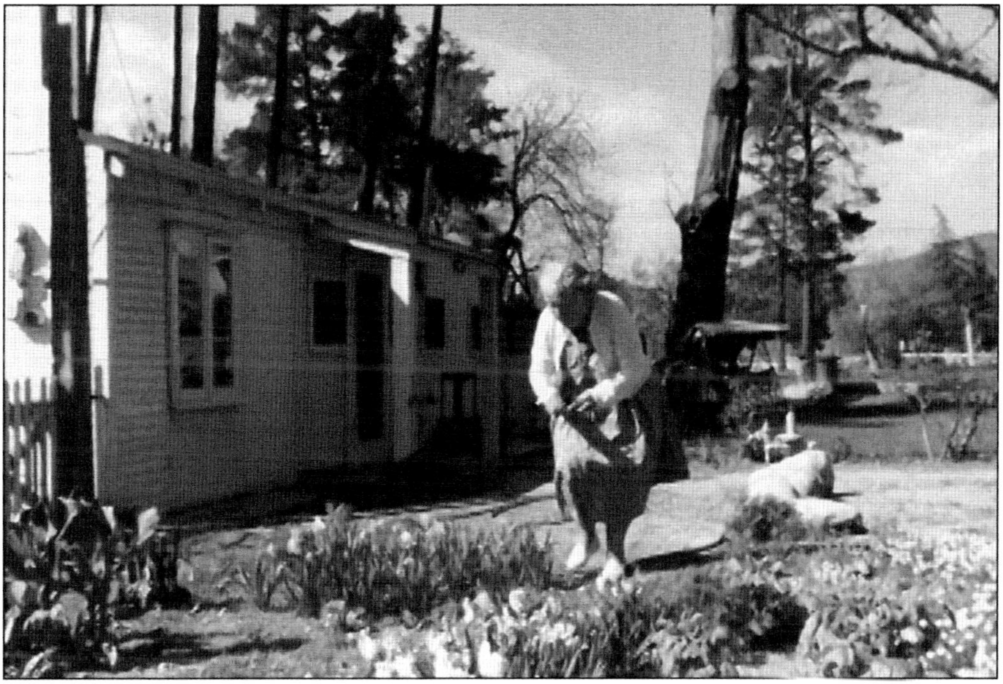

Towering pines and sycamore trees in the park stand like sentinels behind this humble home owned by longtime resident Ruby Combs, pictured above. It was the last house traveling northward, wedged in a small lot just a few yards from the railroad track and the highway. In the background beyond the swing lounge is the Foster Park horseshow arena. Despite her proximity to the clanking of the train and the roaring of traffic, Combs found a slice of serenity tending to her daffodils and roses. In the photograph below, Combs found the exposure to the highway had a monetary advantage, as she posted a sign offering her services. (Both, courtesy of KCBS-TV©.)

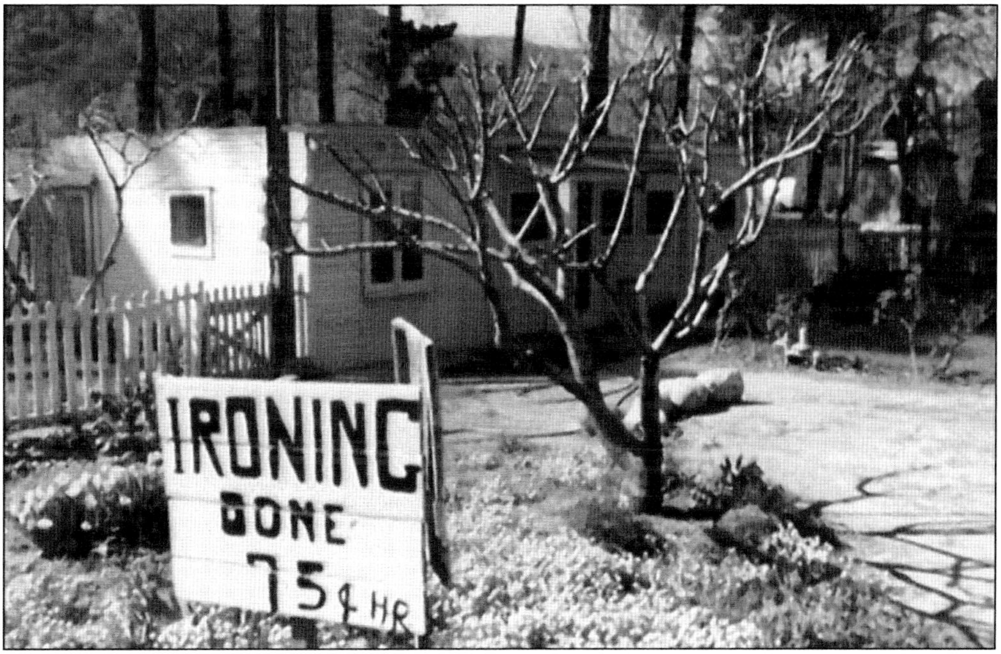

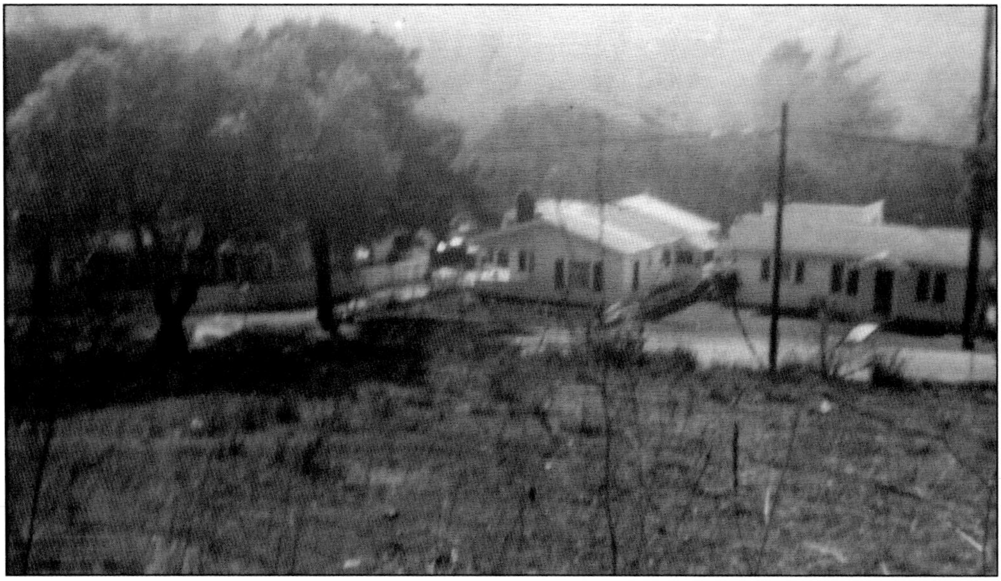

Facing west, this 1945 photograph was taken from the hillside above Highway 33 toward the north end of Foster Park. The house to the left was purchased by Joe and India Pluim in 1939. The Pluims sold the house to Glen Kieborz as an investment property in 1943. The Pluims purchased the house next door on the right, where they lived until 1965. The house on the far right belonged to Ray Barger. Pictured below is the Pluims' house as it appeared in the early 1960s. The home to the right, formerly owned by Barger, was the residence of Al and Josephine Herrera during this time. In the background, the tall pine trees of Foster Memorial Park give an idea of its proximity to the residential area. (Both, author's collection.)

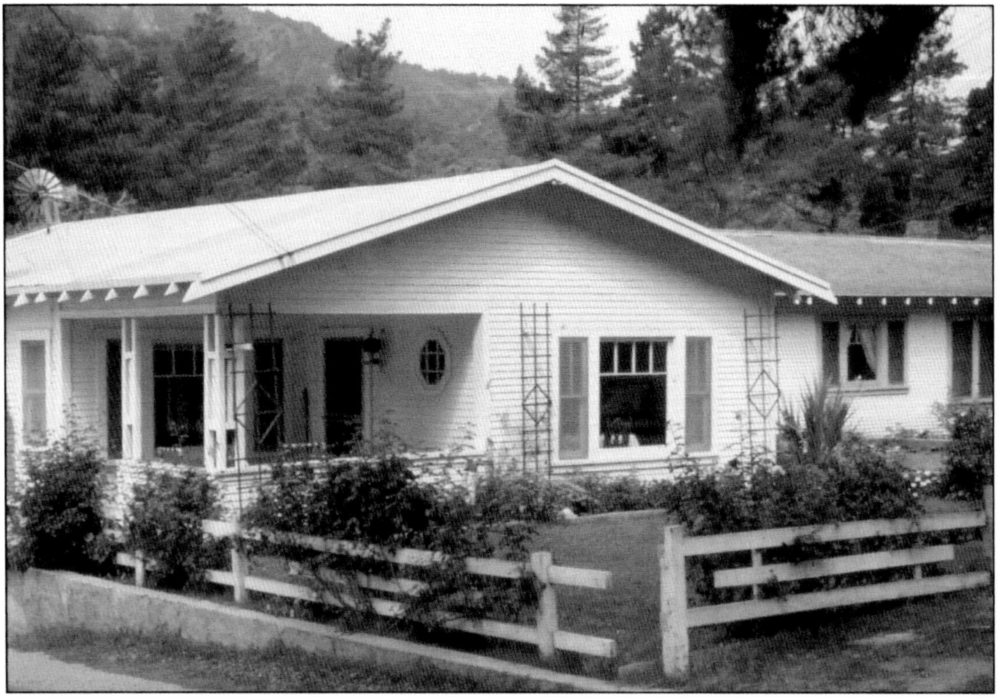

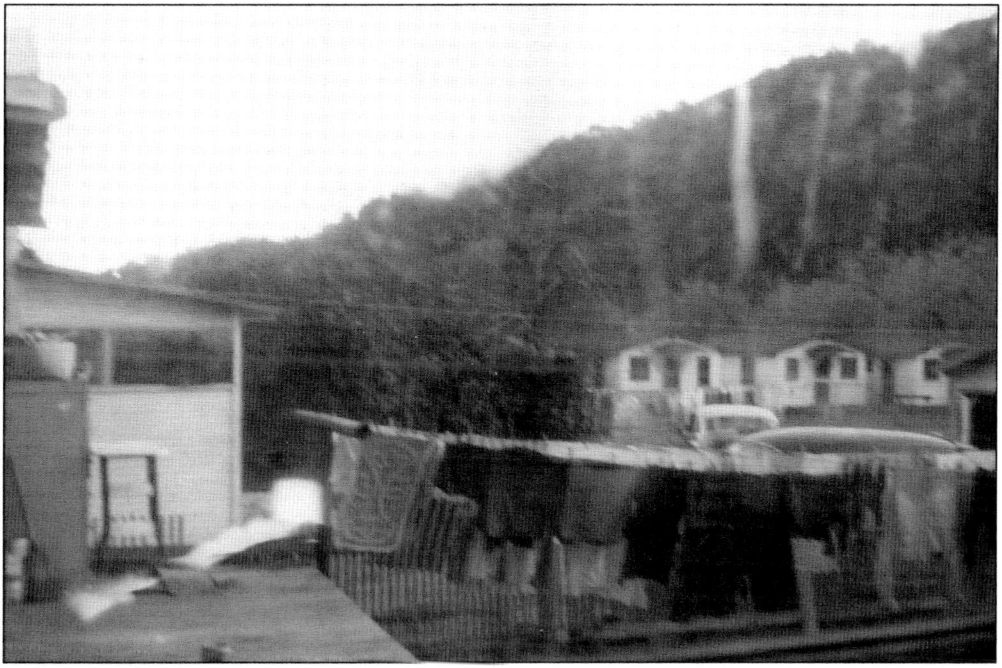

This haunting image captures life as it was in Foster Park. It was taken from a backyard at the north end of town as a breeze gently blows the drying clothes hanging on the line. The picket fence stands as boundary marker rather than a concern for privacy. In the background, Red Mountain appears to be closer than it really is to the bungalows at Jet's Motor Court beyond the fence. (Courtesy of Annie Cody.)

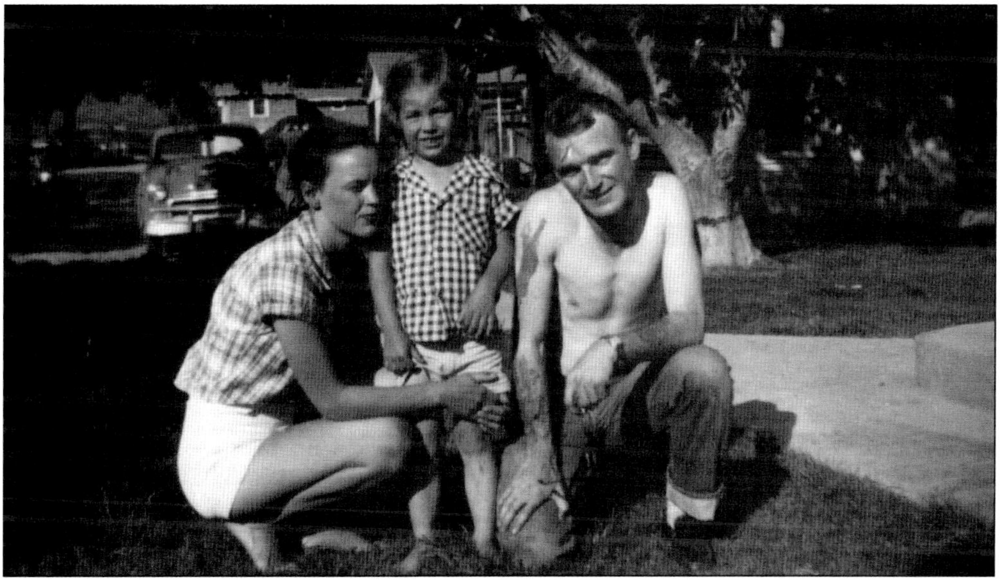

This photograph was taken from the west end of a lot owned by Glen Kieborz, which had three houses on it. Looking up the car-lined driveway is Highway 33. The driveway was shared with the Pluims, who lived next door on the left. The house where this family is sitting was the closest to the railroad track. Pictured are the Doty family, Lita, daughter Lonette, and James. (Courtesy of Naomi Guinn.)

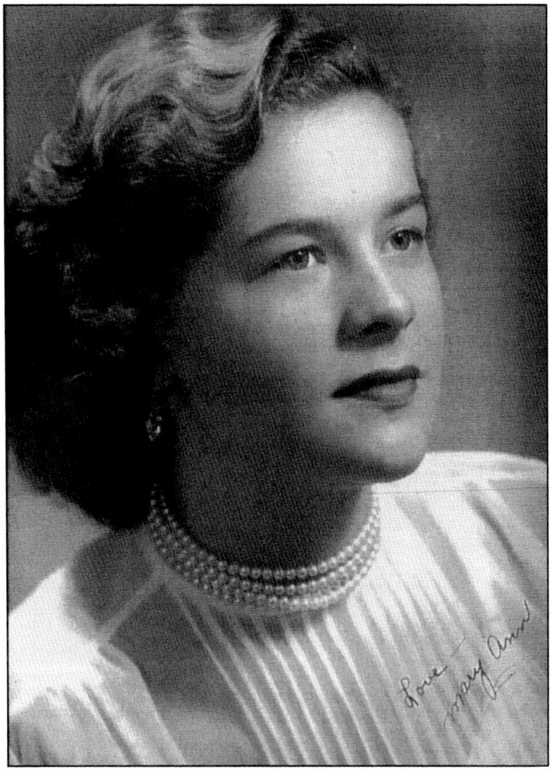

Mary Ann Pluim was the Ventura County New Year's baby of 1936. The announcement that ran in the newspaper was clipped and made into postcards and sent to family and friends. Many years later, while seeking a copy of her birth certificate, Pluim discovered her birth had never been recorded. A saved clipping of her birth announcement, along with family witnesses, were used as proof to acquire a delayed birth certificate. (Courtesy of Mary Ann Aguilar.)

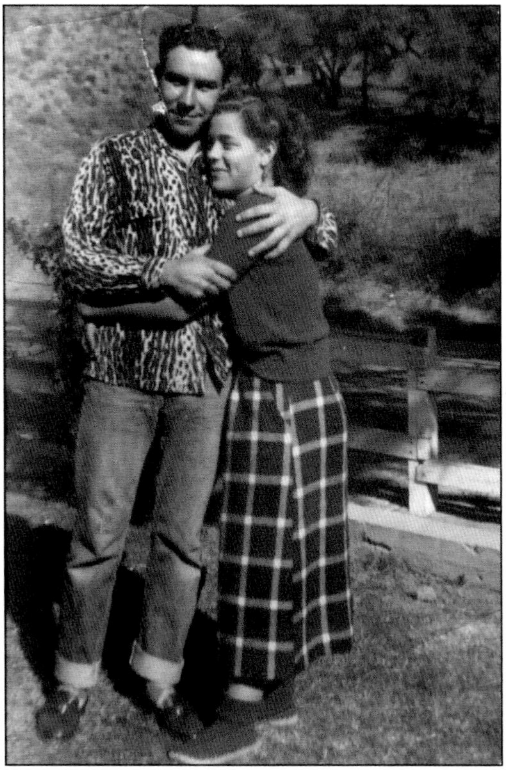

After graduating from a school of mechanics in New Bedford, Massachusetts, in 1948, Joseph "Joe" Alferes enlisted in the US Navy. He served as an engineman on the USS *Norton Sound* and was stationed at Port Hueneme. Alferes met Mary Ann Pluim at the Ventura skating rink in 1949, and the couple were married in 1951. After his service in the Navy, they settled in Foster Park. (Author's collection.)

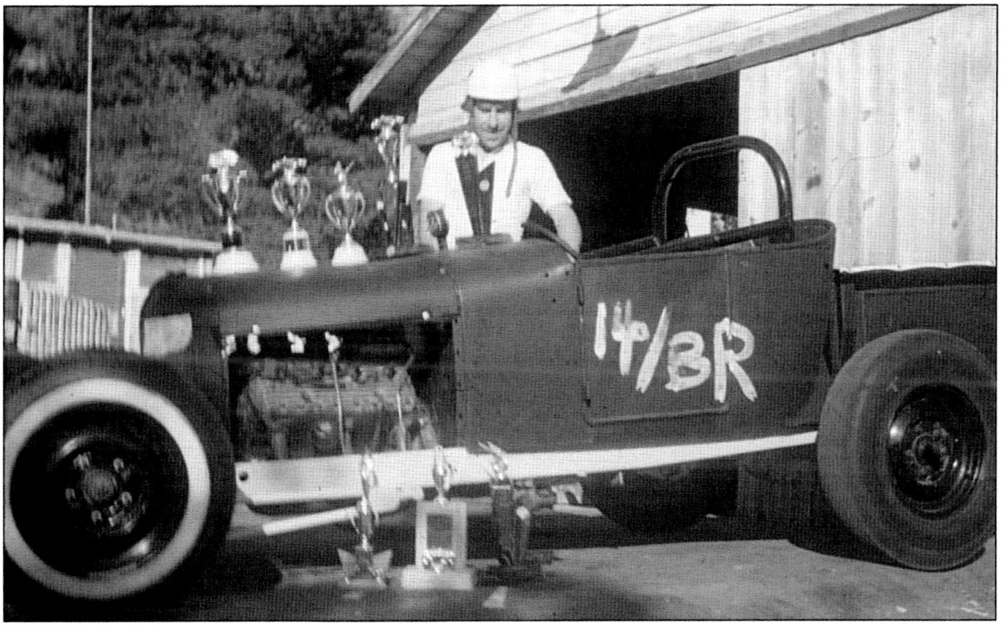

Joe Alferes had a profound interest in cars and racing, which lead him to becoming a member of the Ventura Kustomeers car club along with his brother-in-law, Jan Pluim, in the mid-1950s. Alferes was the main mechanic and keeper of the club's roadster, and he was employed by Southern Counties Gas Company. Pictured above, Alferes poses with the club roadster and trophies at his home in Foster Park. (Photograph by Joseph P. Pluim, author's collection.)

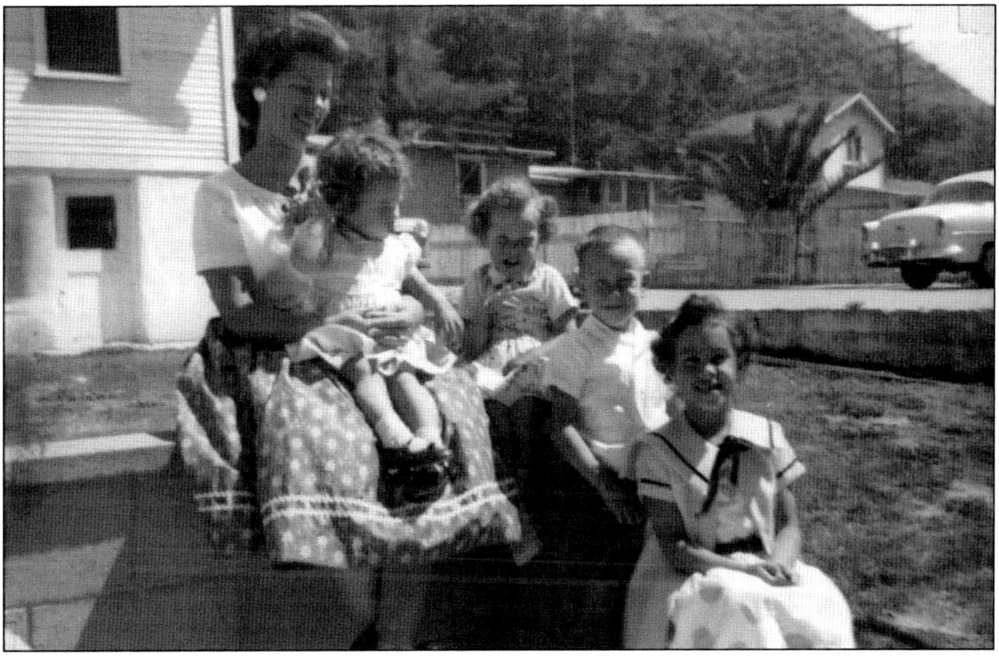

By 1957, Joe and Mary Ann Alferes had four children. Pictured in this 1959 Easter photograph are, from left to right, Mary Ann, Gwen (on lap), Annie, Joe Wayne, and Dora Lynn. The home in the center right with the palm tree is the Alferes residence. The palm tree presently stands at the end of the Ojai Freeway, west of the old Highway 33. (Author's collection.)

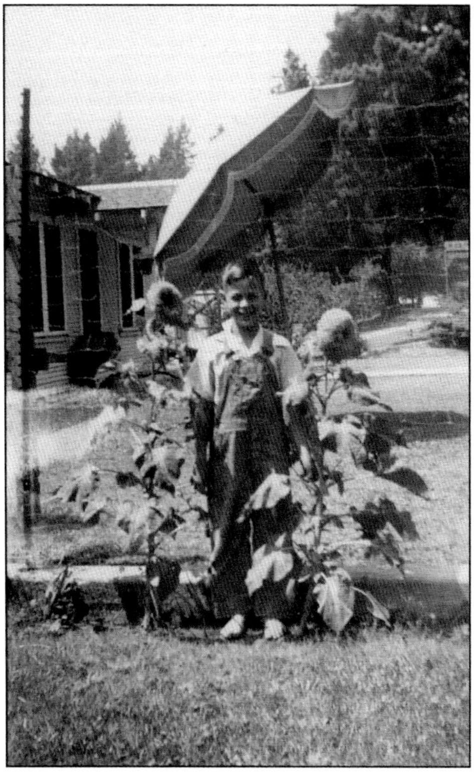

Jan Pluim, son of Joe and India Pluim, stands barefoot between the tall sunflowers growing along the wire fence in this 1943 photograph. In the background are rows of driveways that faced Highway 33. Property lots on the north side of Foster Park sloped downward from the highway to the Southern Pacific Railroad track. (Courtesy of Joan Du Four.)

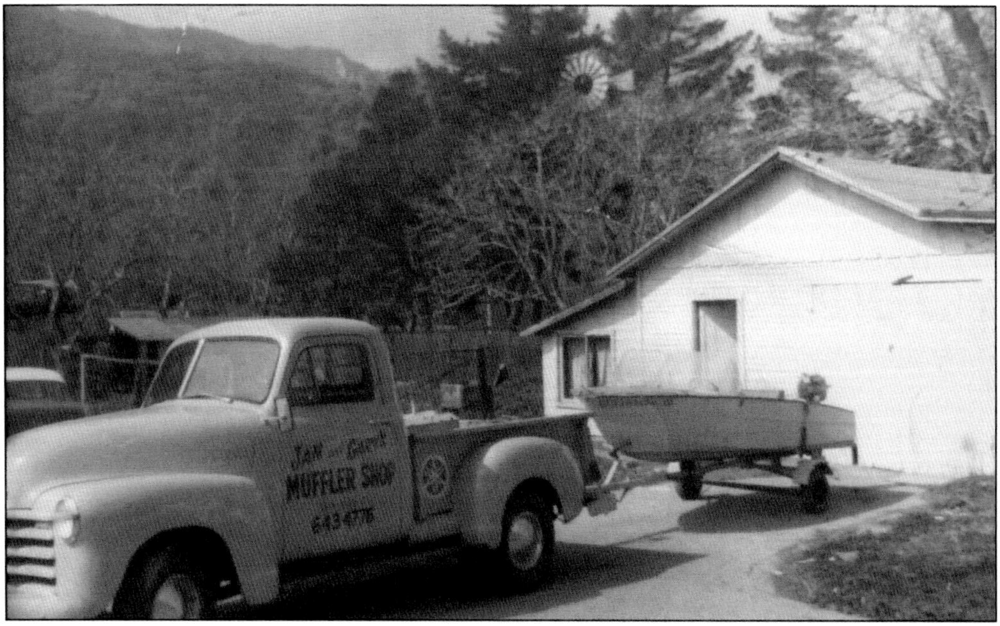

A windmill twirls among the distinguished pines of the park in the background. The building in the foreground is a garage with an attached studio apartment at the west end of the lot owned by Joe and India Pluim. During the 1960s, their son, Jan, and his friend Gary Kallusky owned and operated Jan and Gary's Muffler Shop. It was located at 113 East Main Street in Ventura. (Courtesy of Annie Cody.)

Even as a girl, Naomi Pluim possessed a charm and beauty that continues to linger in the memories of those who knew her. She married high school sweetheart William "Billy" Lee Hale in 1954. The couple made their home in Foster Park, but tragedy struck. In 1957, Billy lost his life in an automobile accident on Highway 33, leaving Naomi a widow with three children, Gene, Robin, and Teresa, who was born after Billy's death. (Courtesy of Teresa Ross.)

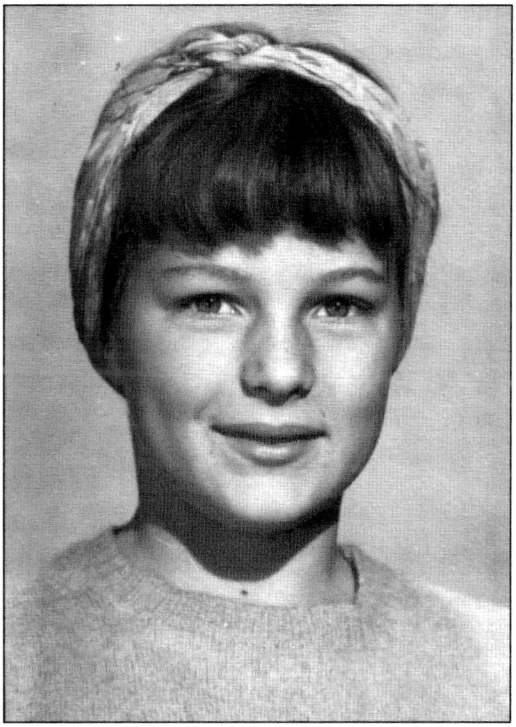

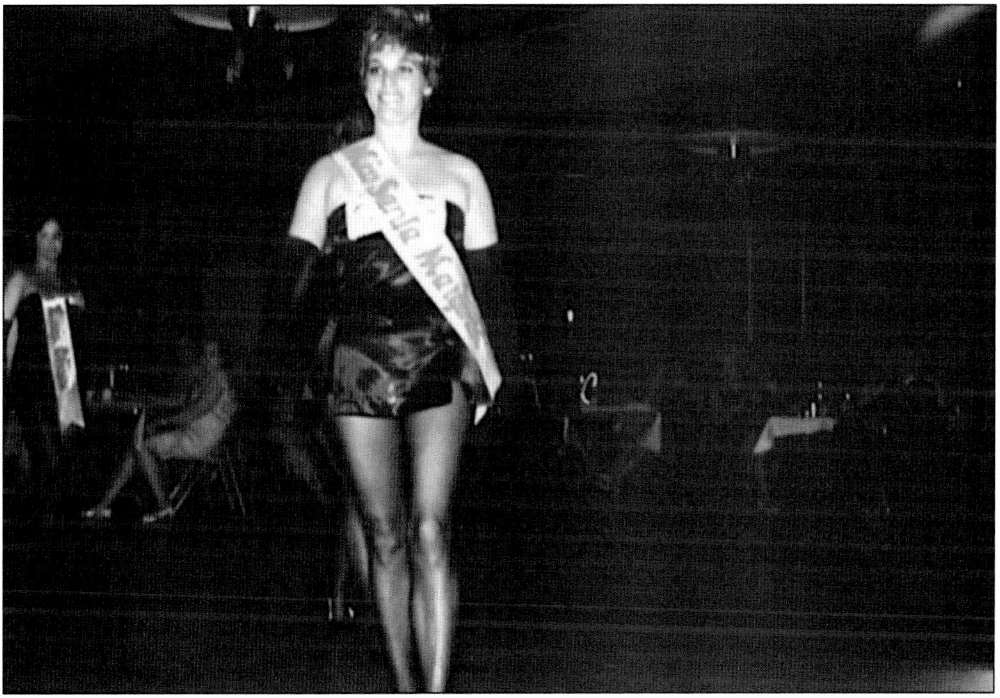

Although her beauty rivaled any Hollywood starlet, she never aspired to the silver screen. Naomi did, however, appear on popular game shows of the 1960s. As a widow she appeared on *Queen For A Day*; and as a newlywed to second husband Charles Guinn, she appeared on *It Could Be You*. In this image, Naomi performs in a dance revue at an Elks Club. (Courtesy of Robin Young.)

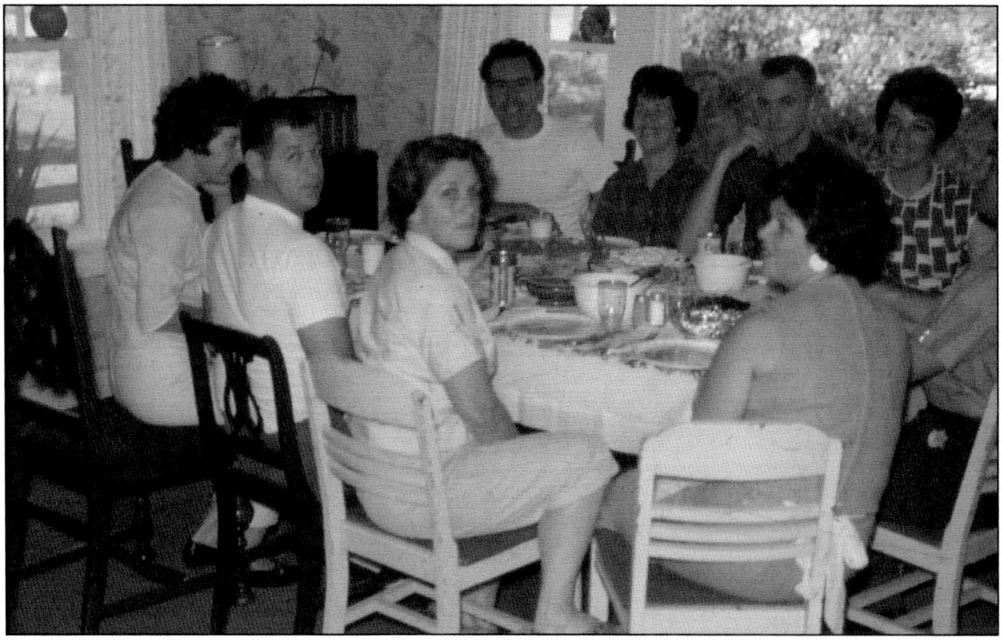

During election season, the dining room where the Pluim family gathered for a Thanksgiving feast was transformed into a voting place for folks in the community. Seated around the table clockwise from front center are India Pluim, Jan Pluim, Barbara "Babs" Pluim, Joe Alferes, Mary Ann Pluim Alferes, Chuck Guinn, Naomi Pluim Guinn, Jack Dale, and Jeannie Pluim Dale. (Photograph by Joseph Pluim, author's collection.)

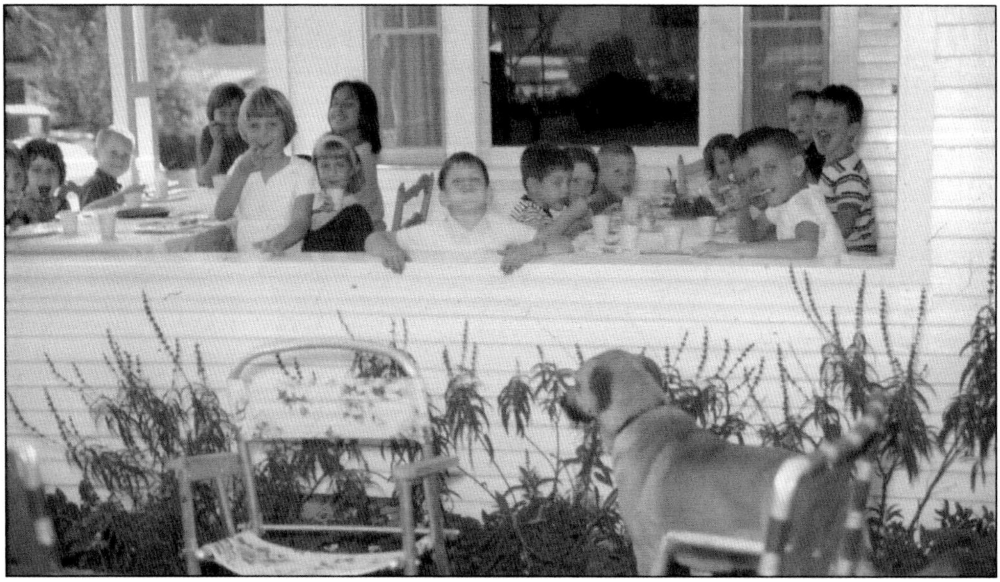

Outside, the Alferes family dog Rex longingly waits for a scrap of food as the third Pluim generation gobbles turkey on the front porch. Around the left table are, clockwise from bottom left, Teresa Hale, Gwen Alferes, Joel Pluim, Annie Alferes, Dora Lynn Alferes, Brenda Dale, and Robin Hale; around the right table are, clockwise from bottom left, Mike Dale, Mark Dale, Jill Pluim, Jeff Pluim, Janelle Pluim, Steve Dale, Brian Dale, Joe Wayne Alferes, and Gene Hale. (Photograph by Joseph P. Pluim, author's collection.)

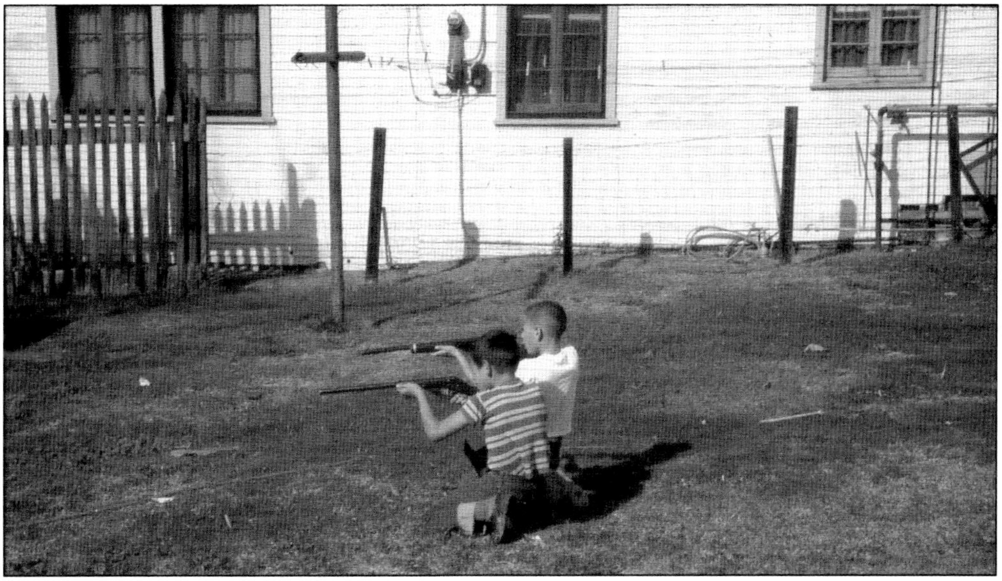

Cousins Joe Wayne Alferes (left, wearing striped shirt) and Gene Hale take to the backyard of their grandparent's house for some target practice with their new Red Rider BB guns. The boys affixed a target to the brick wall that surrounded the patio without a thought of a ricochet. Fortunately for them and the neighbors, there were no casualties. (Photograph by Joseph P. Pluim, author's collection.)

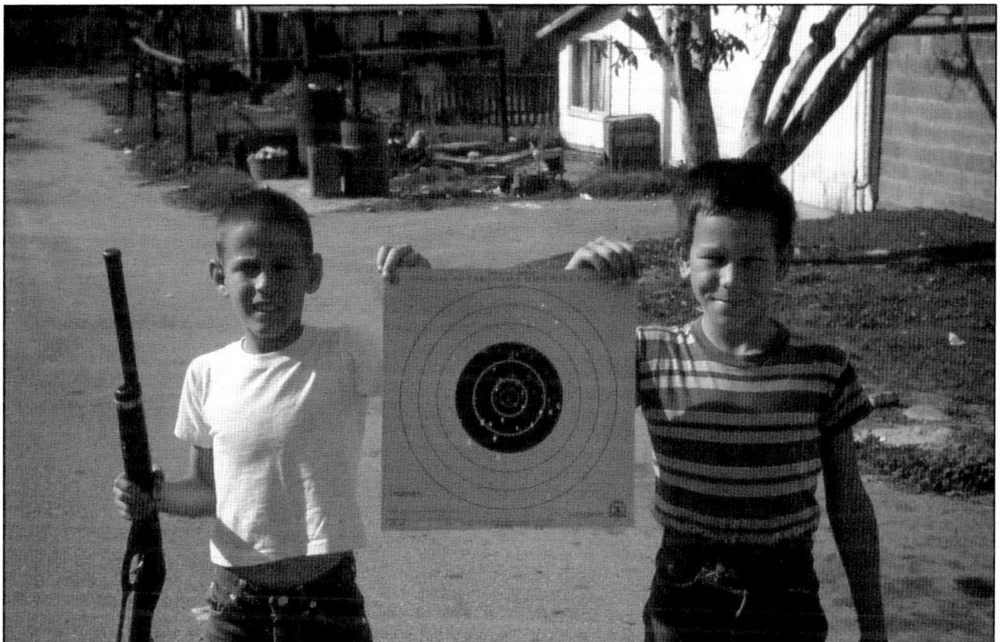

With their guns in one hand and target in the other, the budding sportsmen proudly display their shooting pattern. A westerly view looking down the throat of the Pluims' driveway depicts an era long past. The barrels in the background were used to dump garbage in, then incinerated. This was a common form of waste management used during that time. Note the Coca-Cola cooler to the right. (Photograph by Joseph P. Pluim, author's collection.)

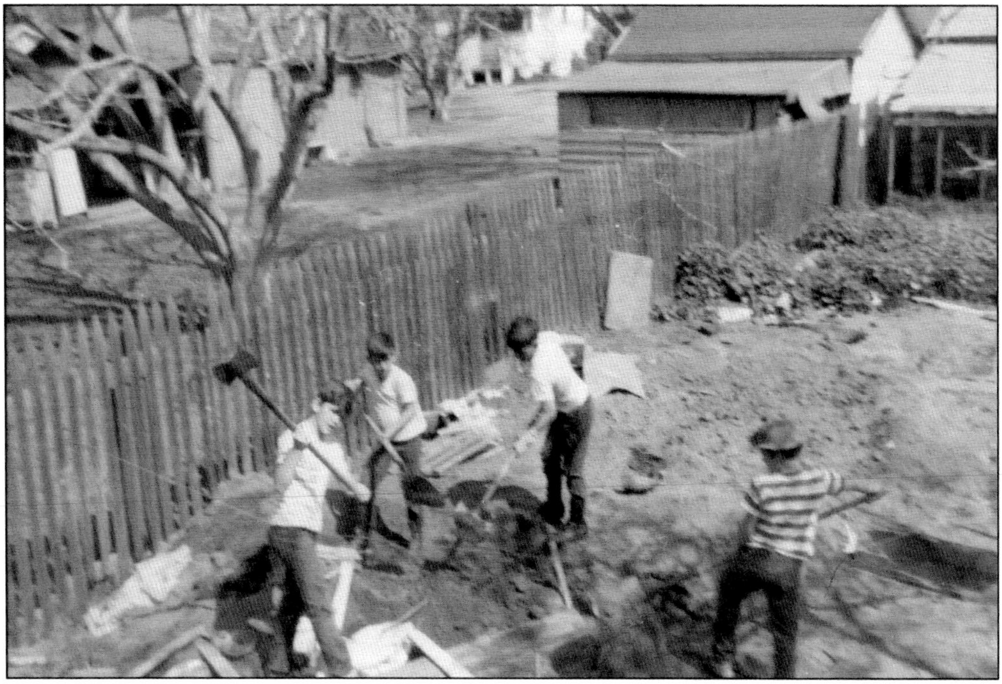

An old door placed in the branches of a walnut tree made the perfect platform for a bird's-eye view of these young laborers working as a team to build an underground fort in the mid-1960s. The fort's location was at the end of a lot owned by Joe and India Pluim. With ax and shovels, the Pluims' grandsons, along with their neighborhood buddies, take liberties with the open space. (Courtesy of Annie Cody.)

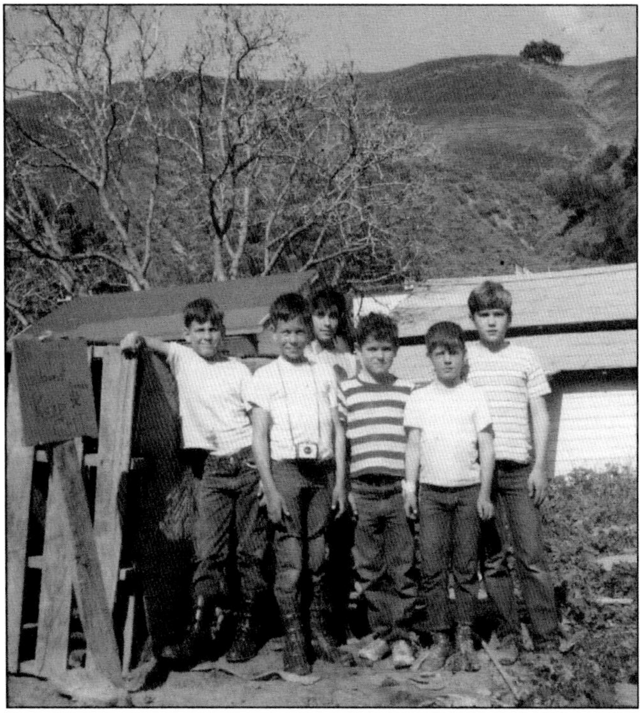

After a hard day's work, this crew takes a break to pose for this photograph outside their newly constructed underground fort. Pictured here from left to right are Gene Hale, Joe Wayne Alferes, Dora Lynn Alferes, Danny Lee, Mike Dale, and Gary Lee. Note the sign to the left, "No girls allowed, KEEP OUT." It certainly did not stop Joe Wayne's older sister Dora Lynn from getting into the action. (Photograph by Joseph P. Pluim, author's collection.)

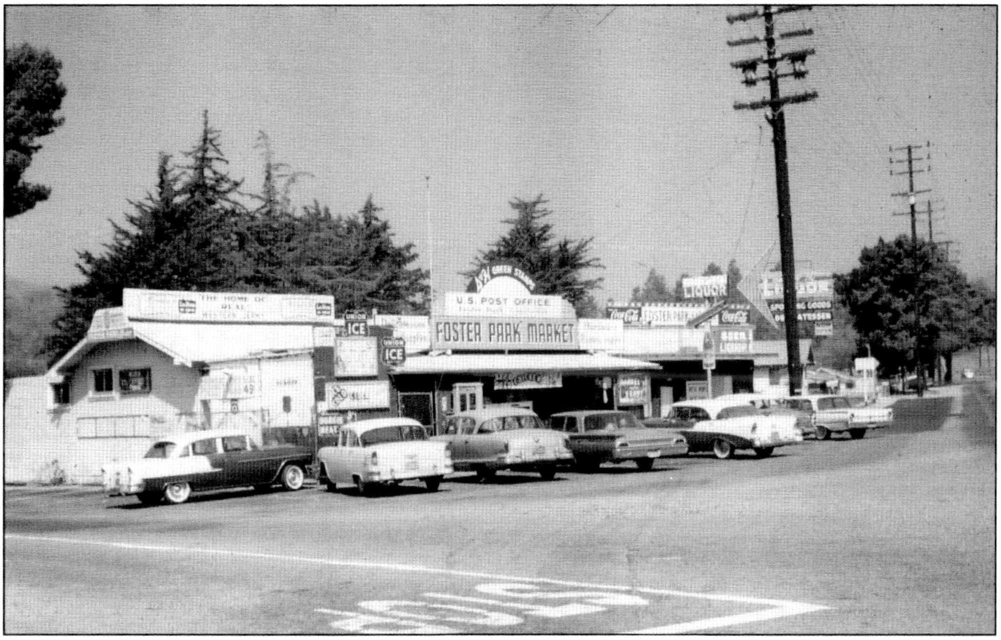

At the intersection of Highway 33 and Casitas Pass Road, a few more changes are revealed in this 1960 northwesterly image of the Foster Park Market. On the left, a new sign atop the store announces "Home of Real Western Jerky" and advertises Knudsen products. A phone booth and a red-and-blue drop-off mailbox now stand at the store's entrance. While Kit Mungo's tinseled signs remain, Conley's Liquor Store sign now reads "Foster Park Liquor," with a sign in the window that reads "moved next door," as seen in the photograph below. The sight of the former Young's Barber Shop and the Foster Park Motor Courts gave way to this modern building that was erected as the new home of the Foster Park Liquor store, now owned by Chuck Eaton. (Both photographs by Joseph P. Pluim, author's collection.)

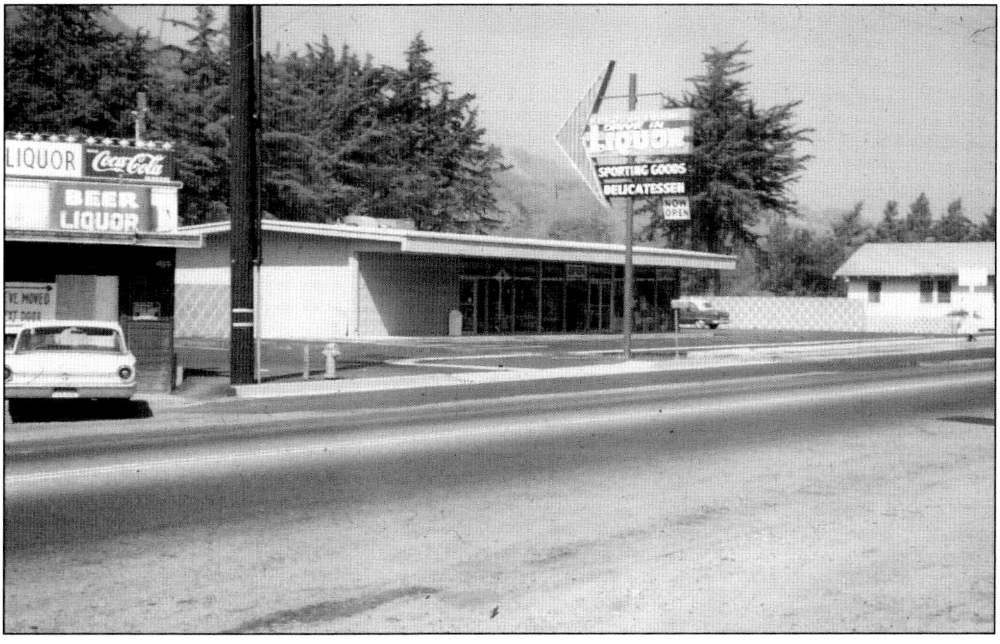

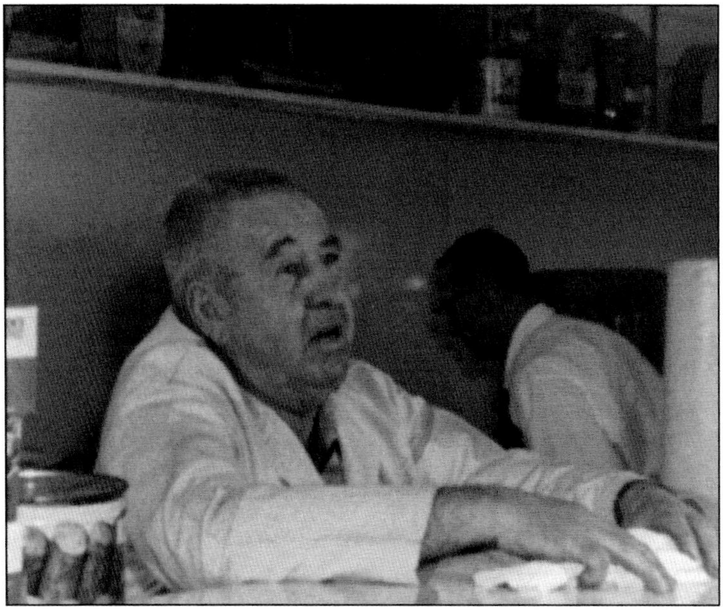

Gene Boles, owner of the Foster Park Market, runs the meat counter while Kit Mungo busily continues his work behind the scene in this 1965 photograph. Boles and his wife, Virginia, had been in the grocery business for many years. The couple owned Foster Park Market from 1951 to 1966 and worked together in the store. (Courtesy of KCBS-TV©.)

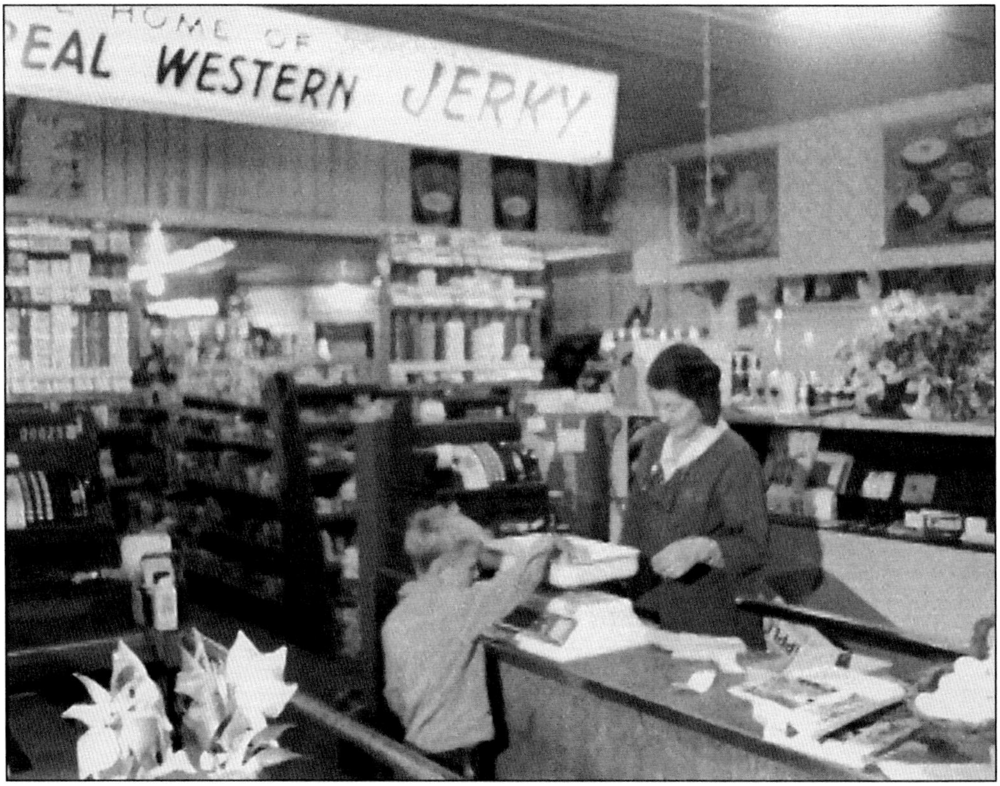

Inside the market, beyond the open-air fresh produce section, the "Home of Real Western Jerky" sign blares overhead, facing the entrance. In this nostalgic scene, owner Virginia Boles stands behind the check-out counter reading the weight of an apple placed in the produce scale by this young local boy, Mike Brown. To the left is another check-out stand; note the dated cash register. (Courtesy of KCBS-TV©.)

One of the best features of the market next to the meat counter was the addition of the US Post Office substation. It was put in after the Boleses took ownership in the early 1950s. To the left along the wall are mailboxes, and on the right of the wrought-iron window hangs the schedule of postal services. (Courtesy of KCBS-TV©.)

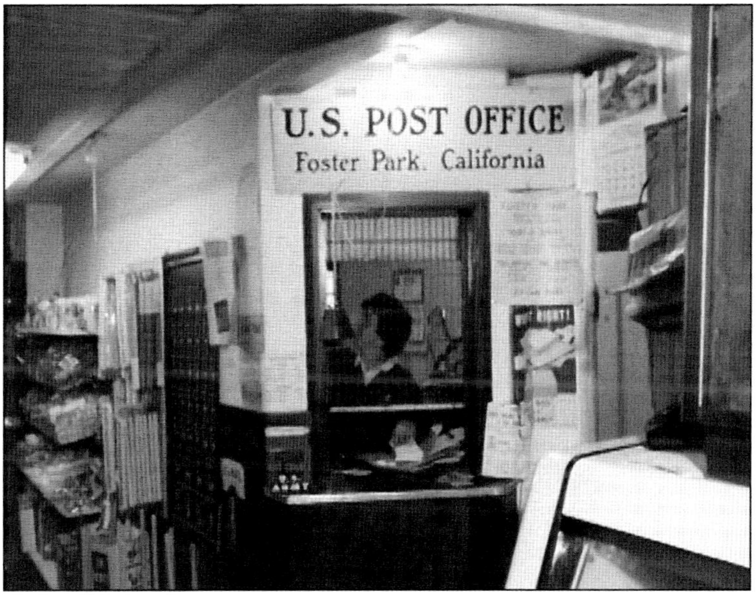

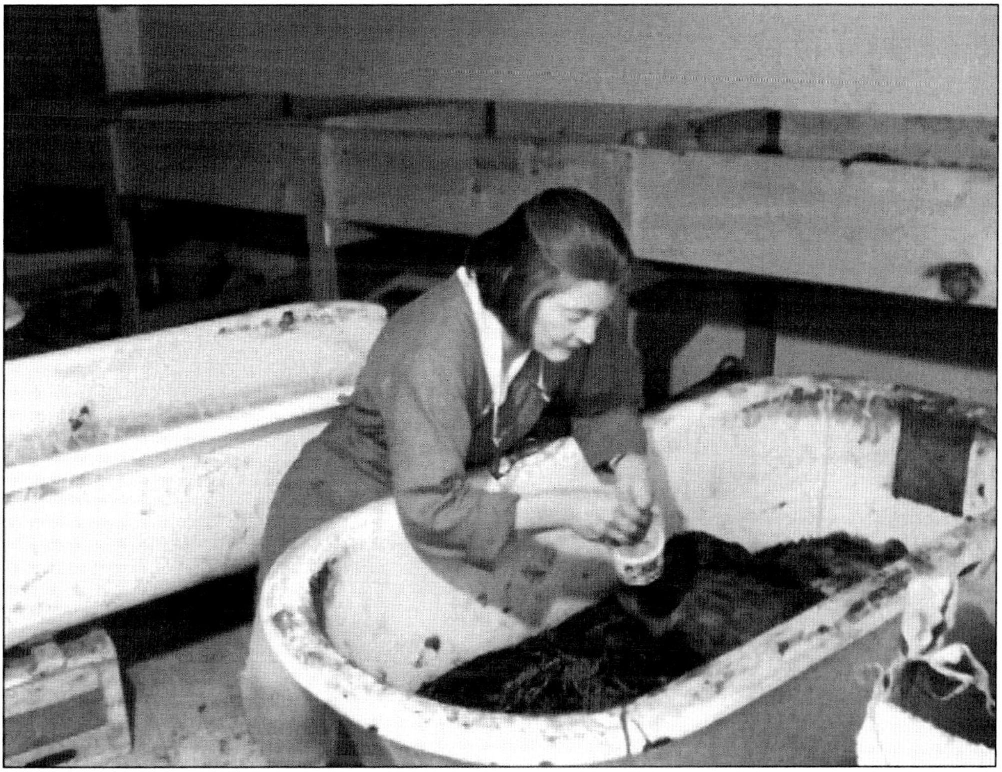

After the construction of Lake Casitas, the demand for fishing supplies increased the market's inventory along with the size of the market. The Boleses took over the adjacent space formally occupied by the liquor store to install this live bait hatchery. The vintage bathtubs were stocked with African nightcrawlers bedded in a peat moss mixture. Since this particular breed of worm thrives best in warm temperatures, the hatchery was electrically heated. Virginia Boles scoops up a container of live bait. (Courtesy of KCBS-TV©.)

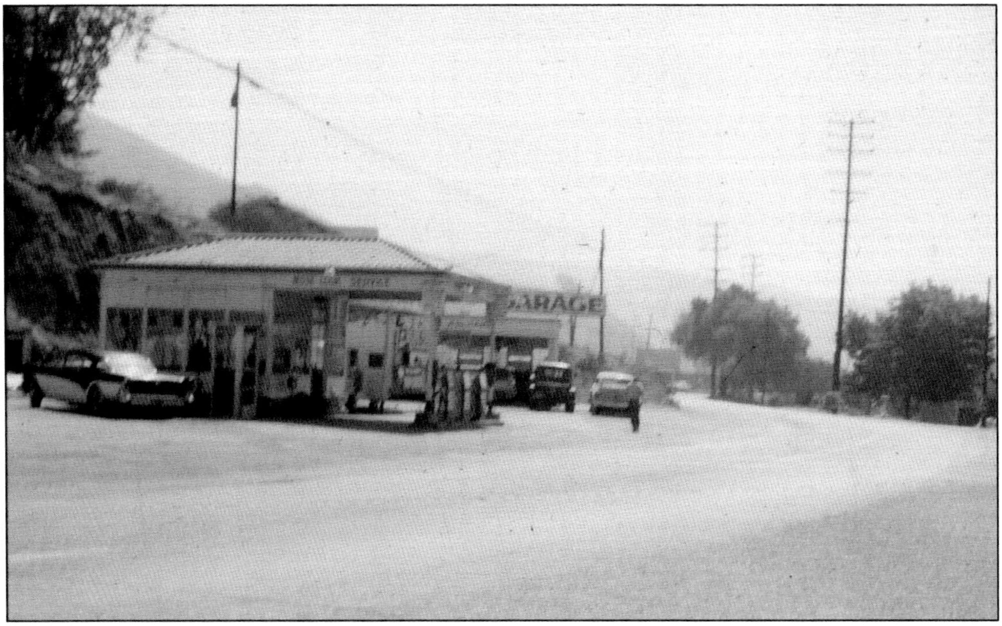

A traveler stopping at the Foster Park Service Station on a cloudy day may have heard the attendant give this observation: "Looks like it's gonna clammer-up and spurt a might." Longtime Ojai resident Neil Mashburn recalls his late mother, Arlou Mashburn, relaying such a story about her visits to the station. In the 1960 photograph above, the gas station has a more modern look on this day of clement weather. (Photograph by Joseph P. Pluim, author's collection.)

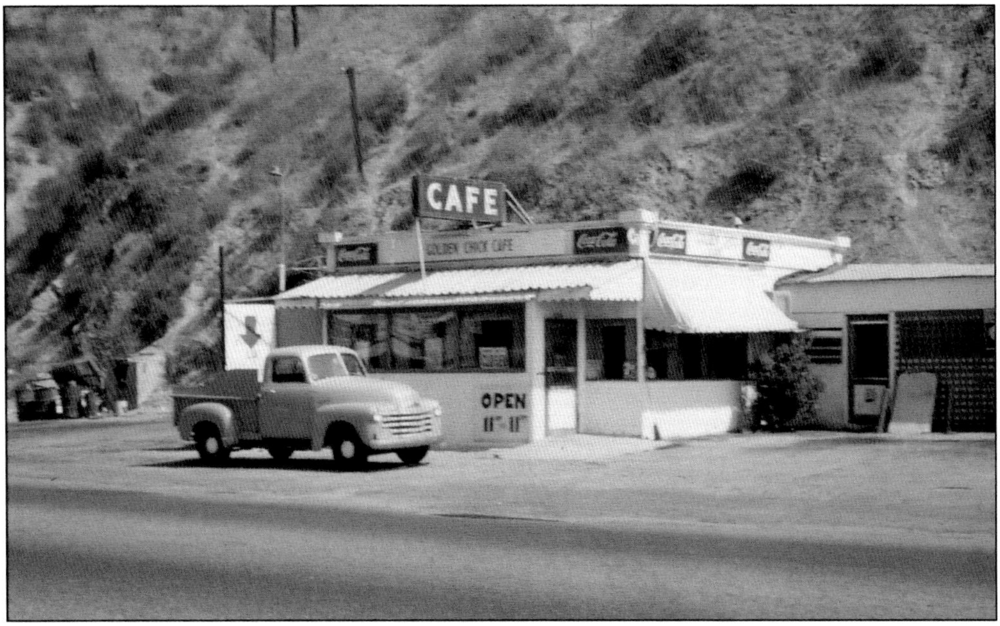

In this 1960 photograph, the Foster Park Café is now the Golden Chick Café. The section to the right is the storage room. As supplies were moved from the right to the café, the waste was disposed of in the incinerators to the left. Though it is gone today, a remnant of its back wall is still visible from the highway at the end of the Ojai Freeway. (Photograph by Joseph P. Pluim, author's collection.)

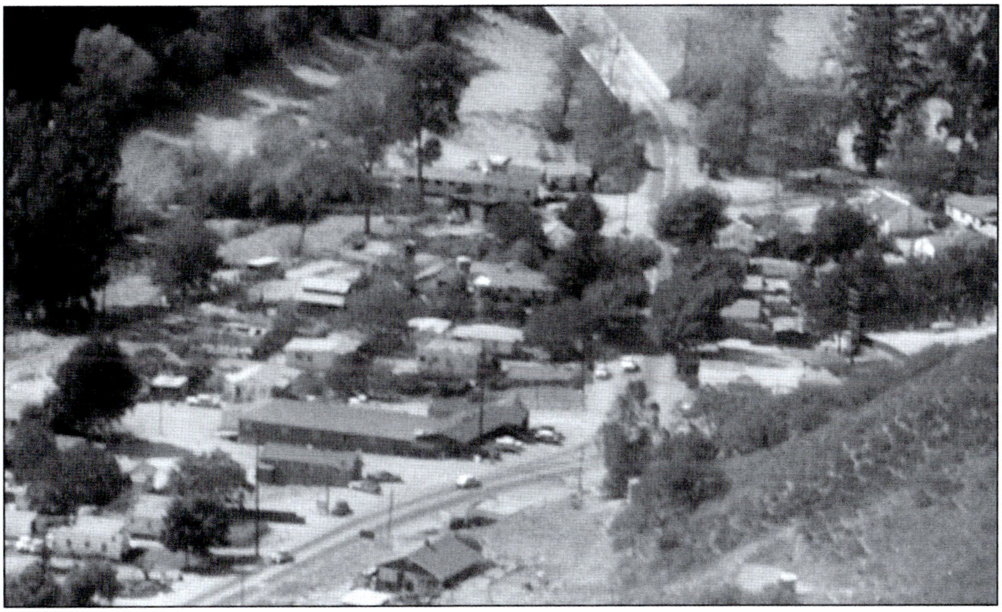

Facing west is a view of the south end of town. The large T-shaped building in the foreground, across Highway 33, is Okie's Tavern, formally the Moose Hall, with a new look but still booking big-name performers. One such performer was Jerry Lee Lewis. Jim Capito, a lifelong Ventura resident and budding musician, (below with guitar) remembers that evening. It was around 1958 when he and some buddies tried to catch the show, but it was full to capacity with no more admittance. So the determined young men climbed in a vulnerable window. When the blond, curly-haired performer showed up, the crowd went wild. Before Lewis could finish his third ivory-pounding number, he was escorted out the door into the safety of a waiting Cadillac. "Before you knew it, it was over and he was gone," recalls Capito. (Above photograph by Walt Dibblee©, courtesy of Steve Dibblee; below, courtesy of Jim Capito.)

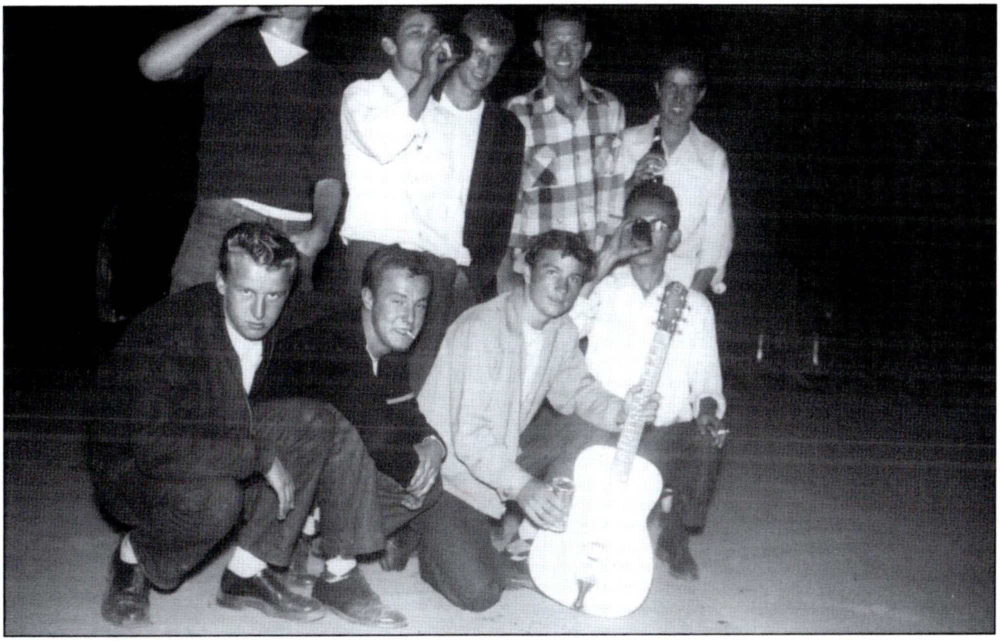

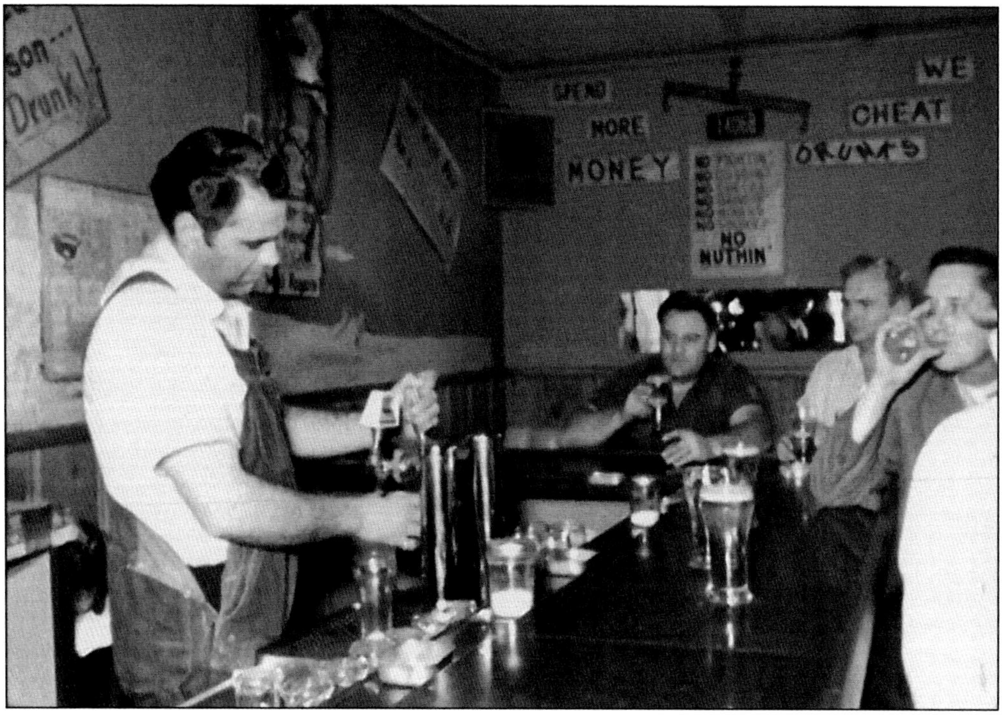

Part of the draw to Okie's Tavern was the owner himself, Fred "Okie" Leaf. Leaf was an Oklahoma native and proud of it. He had a wry sense of humor and played up the stereotypical Oklahoma dust-bowler image. He wore bib overalls and posted humorous misspelled signs inside and outside of the tavern. One sign in the bar read, "Jist Plane Folk tryin' to make enuff to git back to OKLAHOMA." Another sign gives a warning, "We never cheat a sober person, so don't get drunk!" Other gag signs offered contest prizes such as an all-expenses-paid trip to Casitas Springs and free parking at Okie's for a year. Pictured above, Leaf tops off a frothy brew. For the wives of male patrons Okie offered membership in the "Okie Widows' Club" and issued the certification below. (Above, courtesy of KCBS-TV©; below, courtesy of Vicky Beria-Jefferson.)

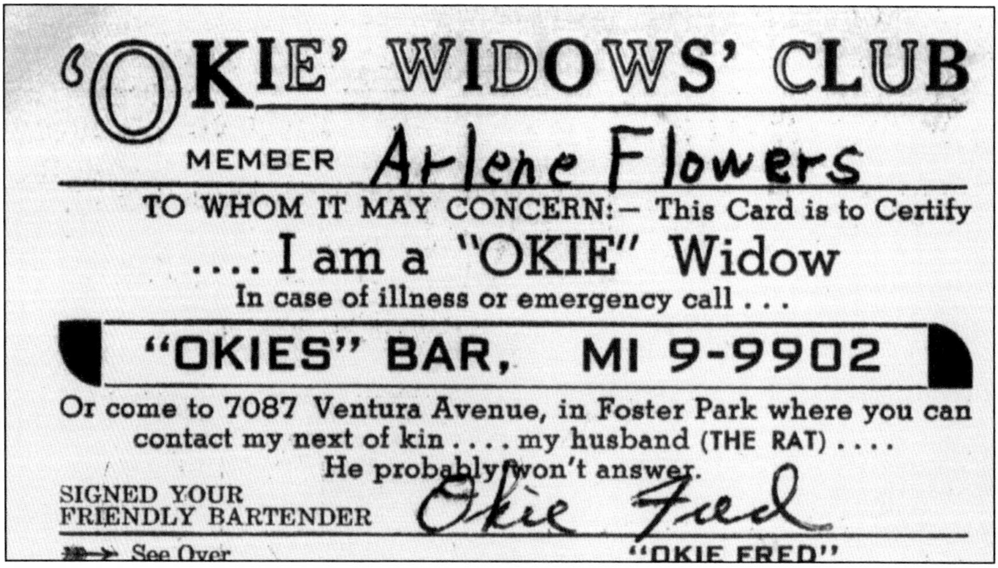
'OKIE' WIDOWS' CLUB

MEMBER Arlene Flowers

TO WHOM IT MAY CONCERN:— This Card is to Certify

.... I am a "OKIE" Widow

In case of illness or emergency call . . .

"OKIES" BAR, MI 9-9902

Or come to 7087 Ventura Avenue, in Foster Park where you can contact my next of kin . . . . my husband (THE RAT) . . . . He probably won't answer.

SIGNED YOUR FRIENDLY BARTENDER Okie Fred

"OKIE FRED"

→ See Over

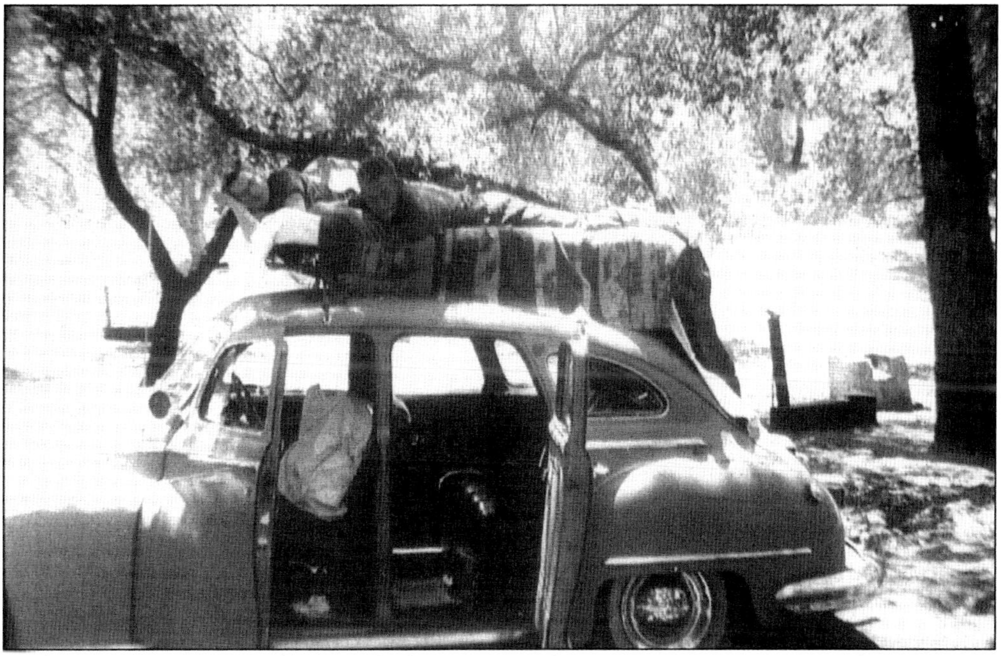

Fred Leaf's signature misspellings made their way into the *Star Free-Press* newspaper advertisements. His advertisements often included sound advice to prospective patrons such as "Don't Forgit, tonite's Satiday nite so be shere and take yer bath," and warnings, "ATTENTSHUN!! Please take yer mattresses of 'n the car before comin' to the dance!! We had 2 stolen last week!" Hopefully Arlene and Nelson Flowers (pictured above napping at Foster Memorial Park) read the advertisement before joining their friends (below) at Okie's. Patrons crowd around the table inside Okie's in 1962; from left to right are Dot Finch, Allen Finch, Arlene Flowers, Barney Sparks, Joe Wishart, Joann Kirksey, Wayne Kirksey, unidentified, Nelson Flowers, Margret Wilson, and unidentified. (Both, courtesy of Vicky Beria-Jefferson.)

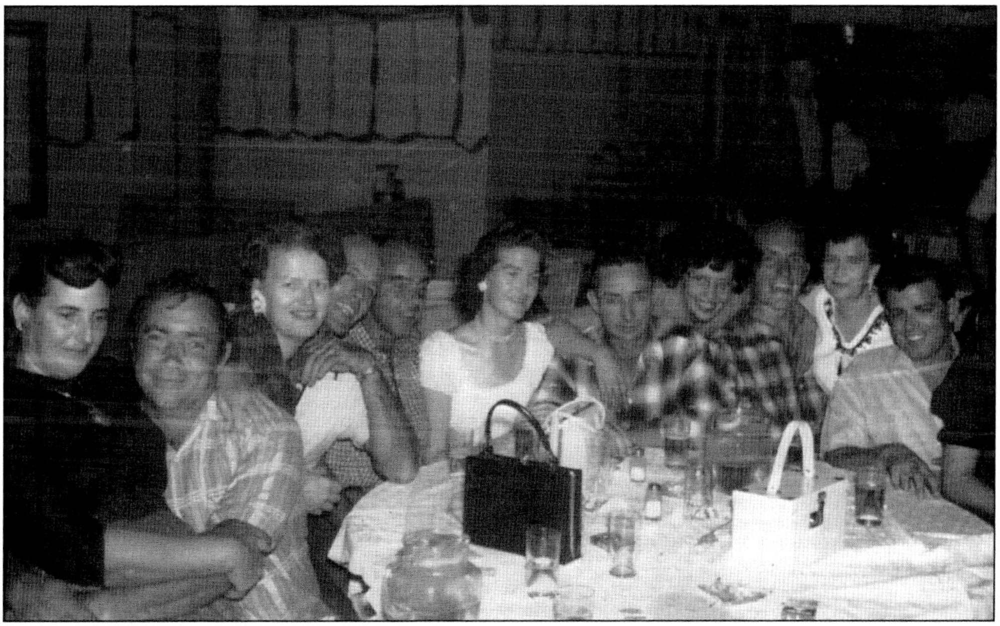

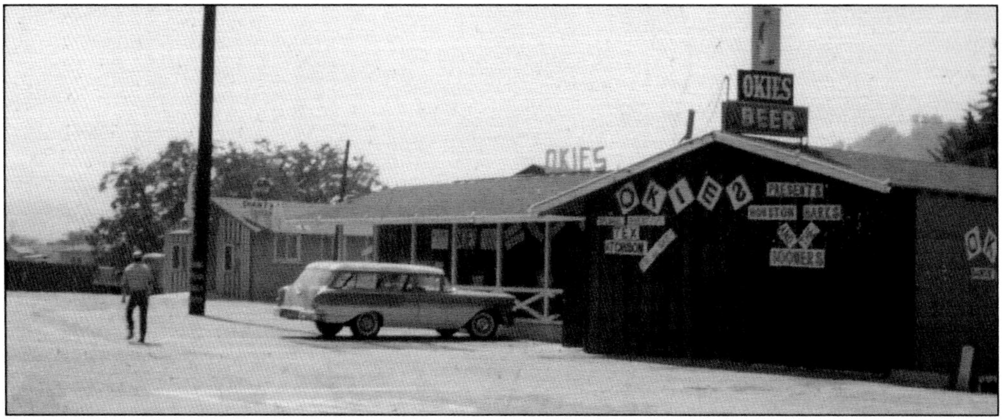

Outside, atop the tavern sits a caricature sign of a man wearing bib overalls. Exterior signs include gag advertising offering "Champunship" Bowling, free coffee, easy credit, and valet parking for $1. One sign that read more fact than fiction was, "Floor Show At Anytime." While Okie's was known as a fun place to go, it was not uncommon to watch more than one fight break out a night. It was nicknamed the "Bucket of Blood." The small striped building next door was another tavern called the Shanty. As one former resident put it, "If you got 86ed from one place you could go to the other." One could also take his hostility to the ring at the boxing gym that was installed at Okie's in the early 1960s. "Indian" Joe Castro, a former boxer and trainer, offered free lessons for all. (Above, photograph by Joseph P. Pluim, courtesy of the author; below, courtesy of Vicky Beria-Jefferson.)

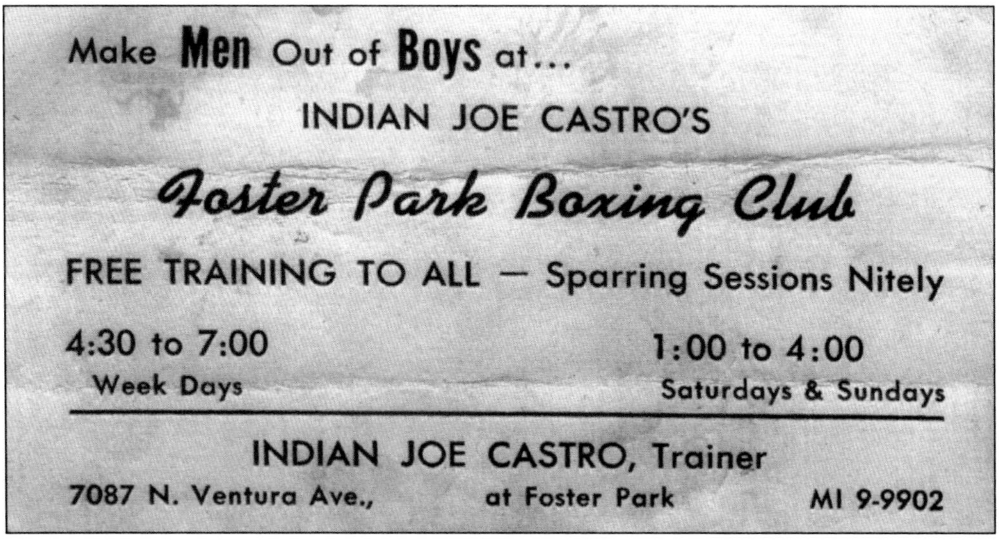

Ray "Windmill" White delivers a ferocious punch to opponent Terry "Irish" Lee, defending his title in this 12-round California state championship fight in 1971. White held the state title from 1970 to 1974. During the 1960s, he was a Foster Park resident and sparred at the Foster Park boxing gym owned by his friend Okie Leaf. (Courtesy of Ray "Windmill" White.)

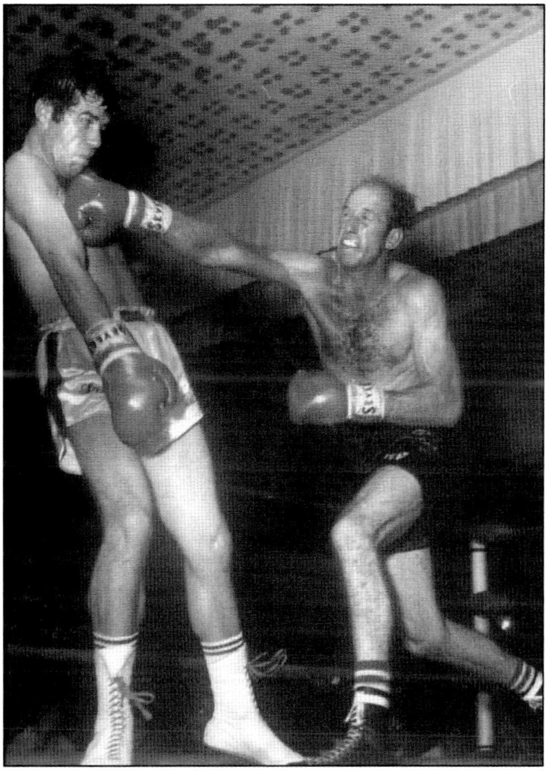

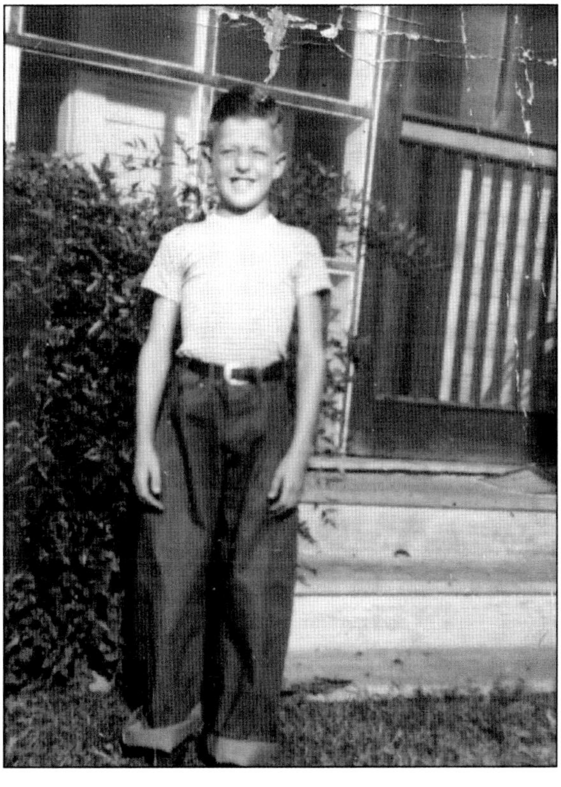

White was born to Dewey and Claire White on August 3, 1938, in Rochelle, Georgia. He came into the world weighing nearly nine pounds and a lengthy 24 inches. In this 1946 photograph taken at his family's new home in Monroe, Louisiana, eight-year-old White displays a lanky physique—a physique that would direct the course of his life. At age 16, White took an interest in boxing after watching a live match in Monroe and started training. (Courtesy of Ray "Windmill" White.)

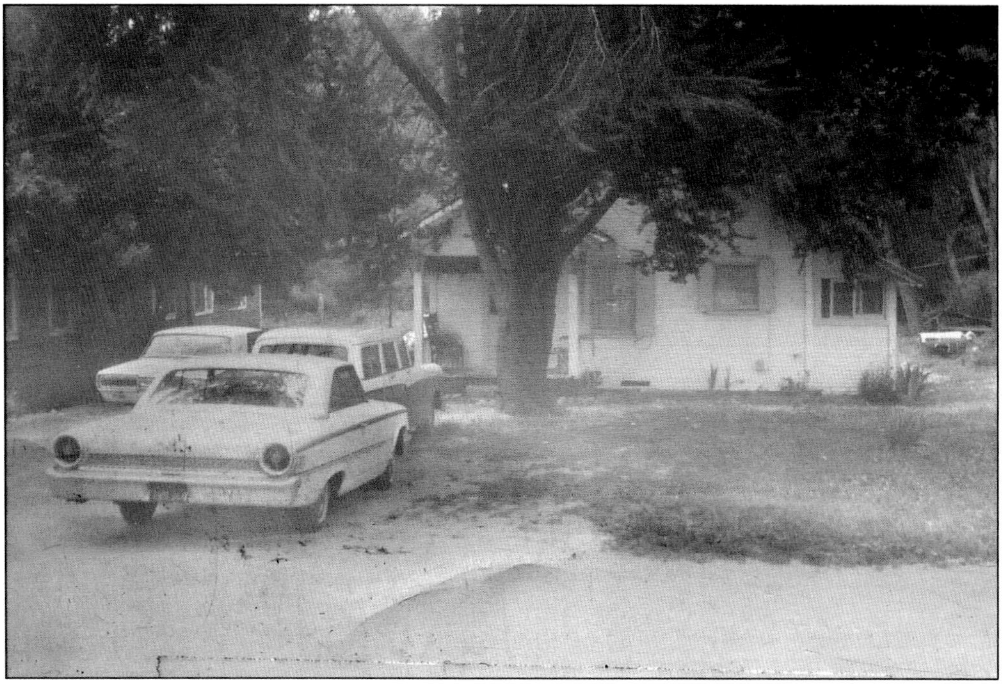

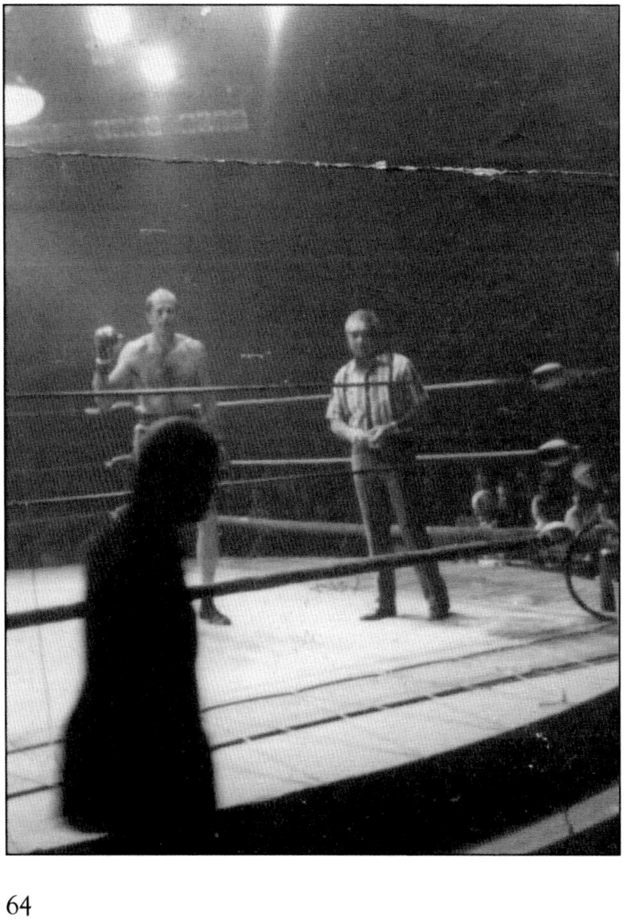

After joining the Navy Seabees in 1957, Ray White continued to train, and he fought his first professional fight in Monroe in 1958. He was later stationed at Port Hueneme, remaining in the area after his discharge in 1961 and earning a contractor's license from Ventura College. Eventually, he moved into the house above in Foster Park behind Okie's Tavern. There, he conveniently trained at the new boxing gym. His dedication to the sport gained him the California Light Heavyweight Championship from 1970 to 1974, but it was his fighting style that made him a legend in the world of boxing. In the photograph at left, White stands in the ring with former boxer, and trainer Indian Joe Castro during a match at the Cabrillo Hotel in Ventura in the late 1960s. (Both, courtesy of Ray "Windmill" White.)

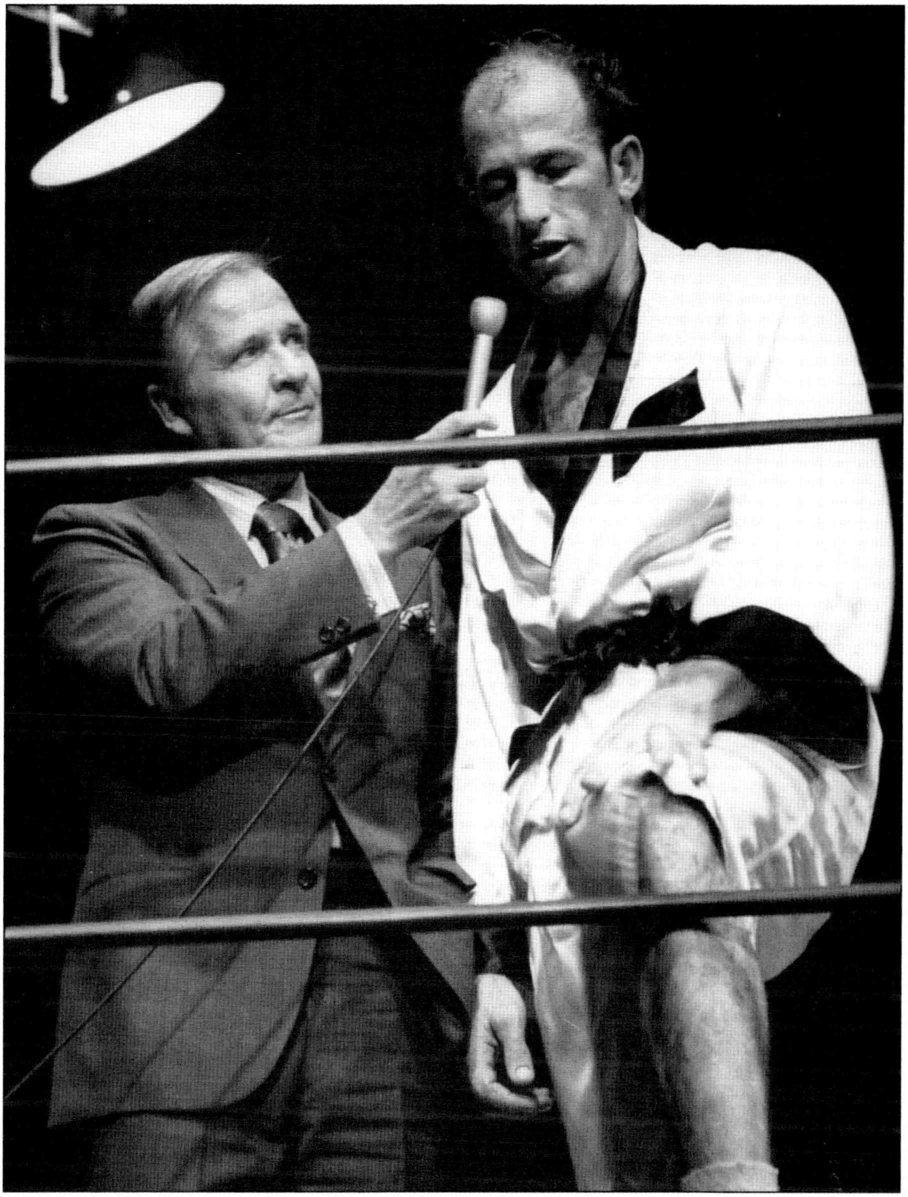

Determined to go to the distance, win or lose, Ray White did what he could to survive in the ring, developing a comical fighting style. The six-foot-four-inch lanky boxer had a pocketful of unpredictable antics, vexing opponents and wildly entertaining the crowds. In her memoirs, the late Clair White wrote this about her son: "Ray was so tall and had such a long reach that he could do some unique things, like a behind-the-back punch." During the 1960s and early 1970s, his fights were televised nationally and he developed a large following as Windmill White. His popularity gained him guest appearances on the talk shows of Merv Griffin and Mike Douglas. After watching White defeat Charles Atlas in Monroe, his mother said she was proud but could hardly watch. "That was my baby boy out there!" Mixing humor with sports, he was also known as the "Clown Prince of Boxing" and the "Harlem Globe Trotter of the Boxing Ring." White gives a ring-side interview with boxing matchmaker Mickey Davies at the Los Angeles Olympic Auditorium in this 1967 photograph. (Courtesy of Ray "Windmill" White.)

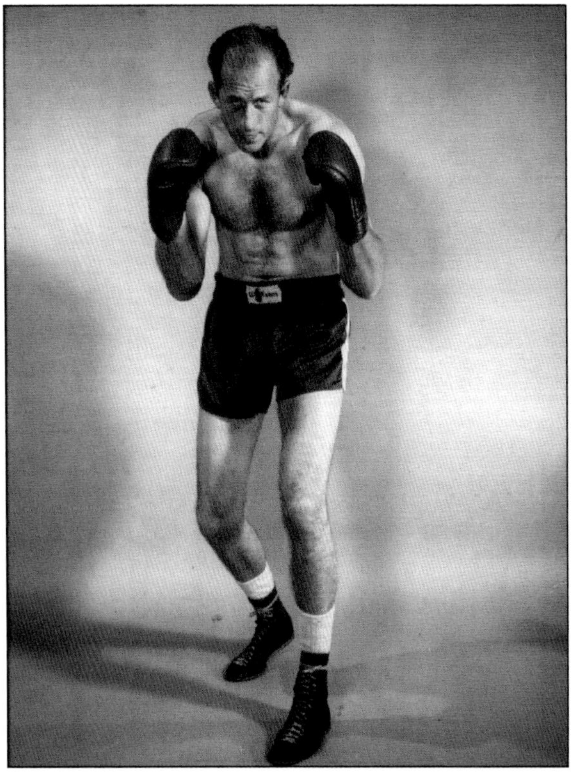

Often criticized and called an embarrassment to the sport, White proved himself worthy in the ring as he fought many heavy hitters of that era. He retired in 1974 with a record of 41 wins, 14 losses, and 5 draws. In *The Ultimate Boxing Book of Lists*, authors Bert Randolph Sugar and Teddy Atlas ranked Windmill as the seventh most awkward boxer. He remained involved in the boxing world as an instructor, training professional and amateur boxers in Ventura County. In 2011, White was inducted into the Ventura County Sports Hall of Fame. With his gloves off, a gentler Windmill coddles newborn Chihuahua puppies at his Foster Park home in this 1962 photograph. (Both, courtesy of Ray "Windmill" White.)

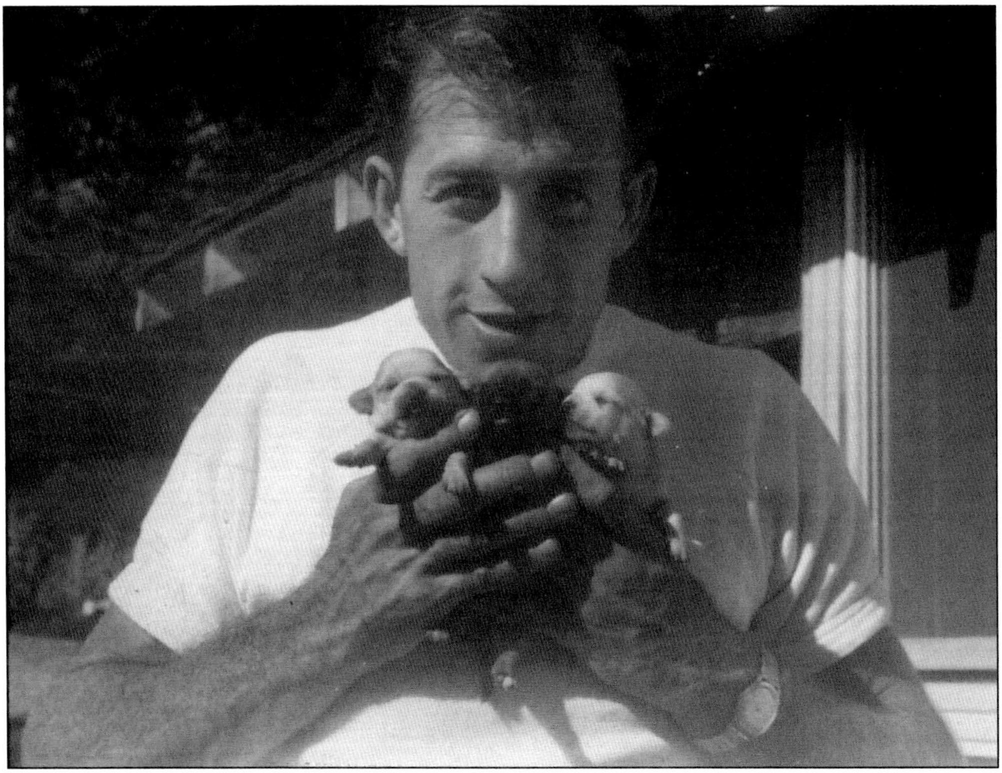

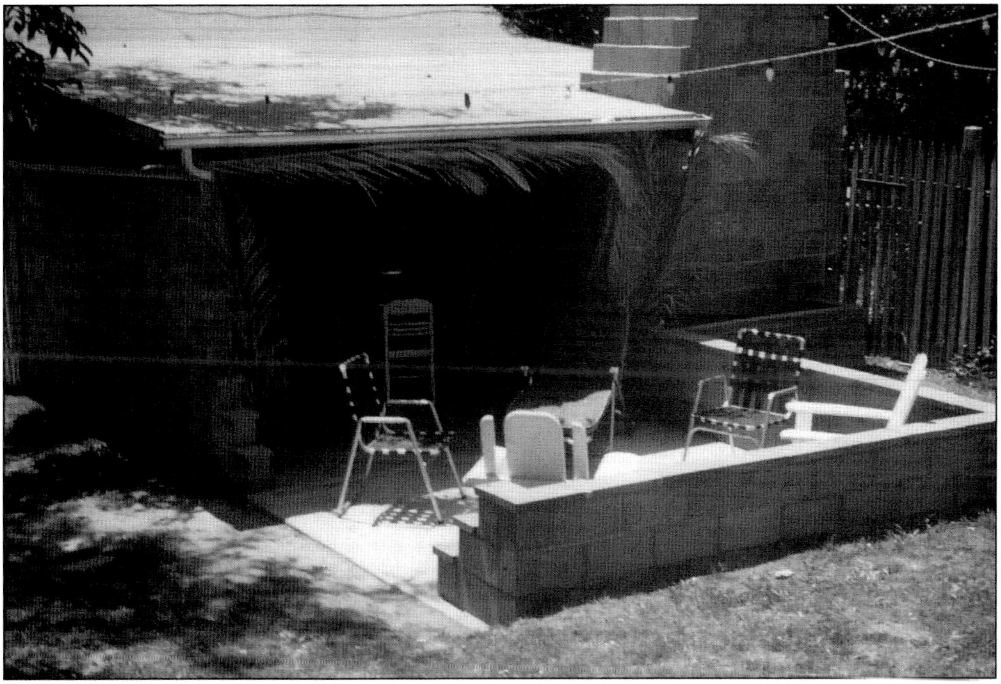

Okie's was not the only hotspot for entertainment in town. In the mid-1950s, Joe Pluim erected this indoor-outdoor patio, fully equipped with a kitchen, indoor barbecue pit (note the chimney to right), restaurant-type seating with checkered tabletops, and interior walls wrapped with scenic murals. In this 1959 photograph, the patio entrance is decorated with a string of lights and palm branches to set a tropical mood for the evening's event. (Photograph by Joseph P. Pluim, courtesy of Annie Cody.)

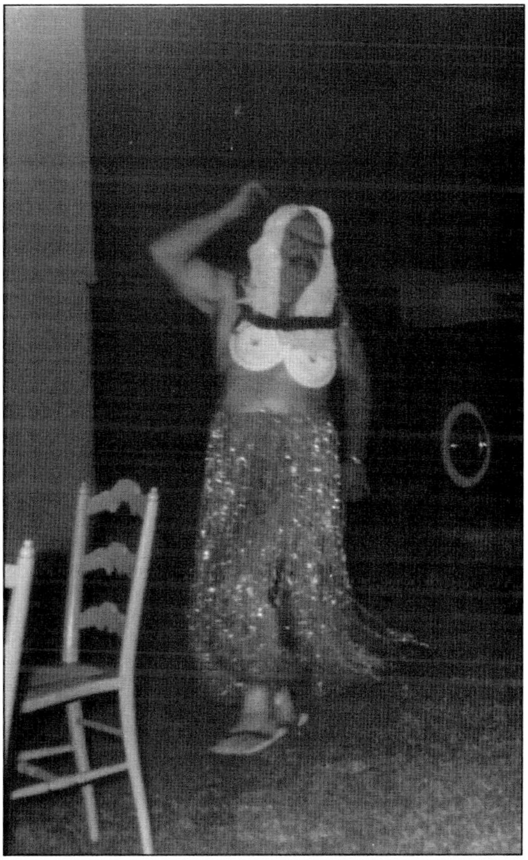

After the sun set and local guests arrived, Joe Pluim posed for this photograph wearing a string-mop wig, paper-plate chest coverings, and a Hawaiian lei and grass skirt while making his way to entertain party guests. As the portly Pluim rolled his belly in his best attempt at hula dancing, his guest burst with belly-rolling laughter. (Courtesy of Teresa Ross.)

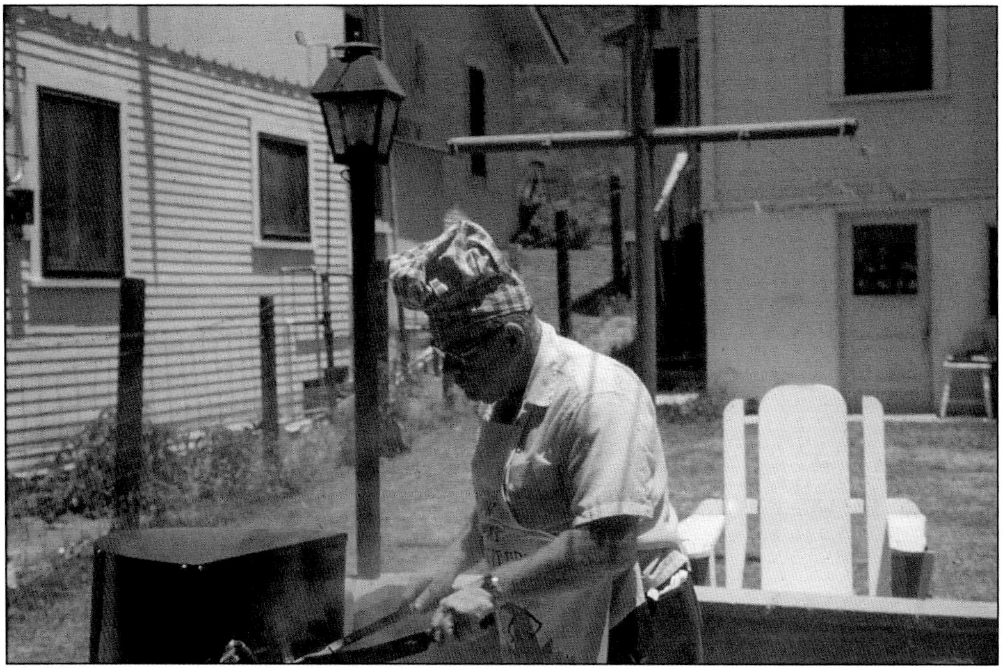

In this 1960 photograph, a less glamorous Joe Pluim is seriously involved with what he liked doing best—backyard barbecuing. As an employee for Southern California Gas Company, Pluim was also one of the designated cooks for the company's picnics. The two houses in the background sit along Highway 33, and the house to the left was the residence of Josephine and Al Herrera. (Courtesy of Robin Young.)

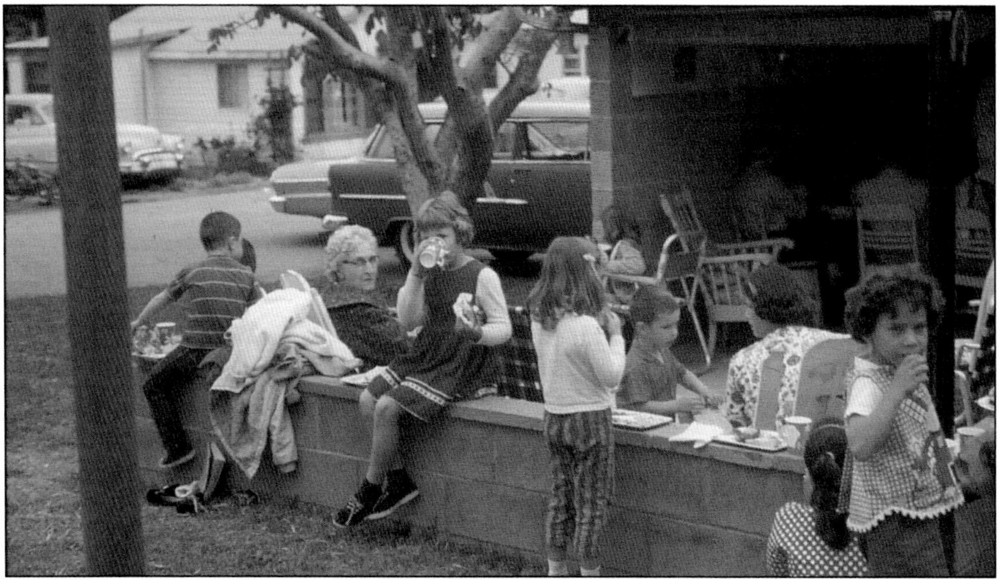

With the population of the Joe and India Pluim family rapidly multiplying, the indoor-outdoor patio was perfect for accommodating their hungry generational horde. The patio was situated near the end of a lot with a shared driveway. The houses in the background are on a lot owned by Glen Kieborz. In the foreground, young Pluim offspring feed while adults gather around a table for a game of cards inside in 1963. (Courtesy of Robin Young.)

Three

THE CANET RANCH AND ITS FAMILIES

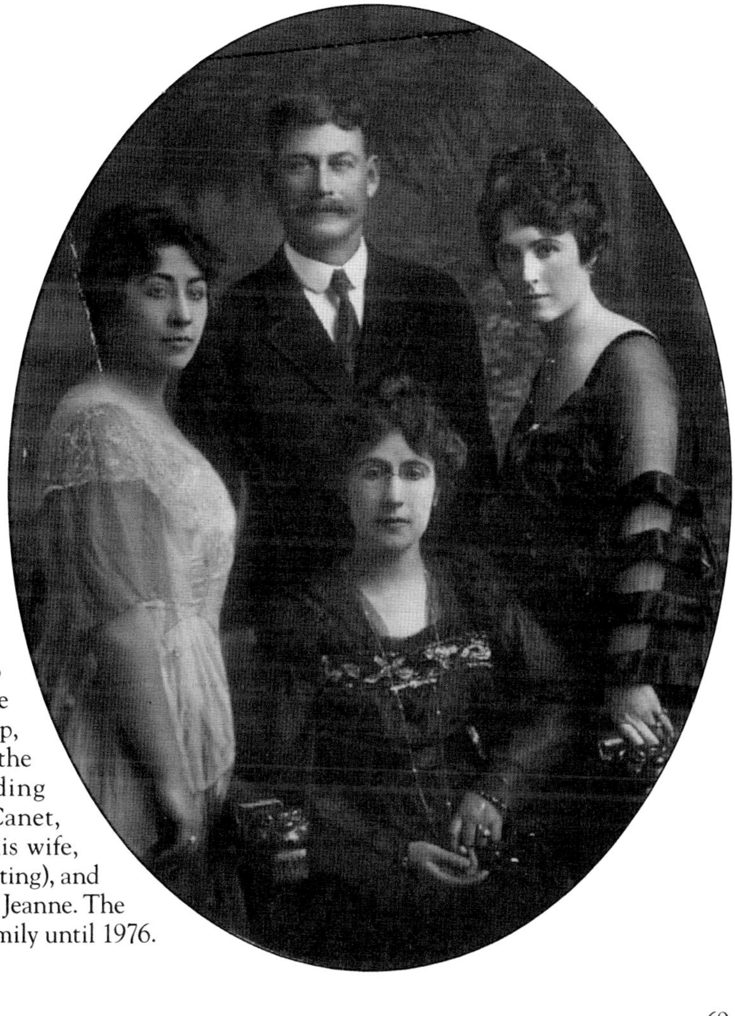

Anselmo Canet was born in 1833, came to New York from France, and married Catherine Brannigan in 1863. Canet eventually moved to Ventura and purchased property at the Rancho Cañada Larga in 1874. He started out raising sheep, then branched out into the cattle business. Standing is Edouard Constant Canet, son of Anselmo, with his wife, Marie-Louise Sentous (sitting), and daughters Renee (left) and Jeanne. The ranch belonged to the family until 1976. (Courtesy of JiJi Lee.)

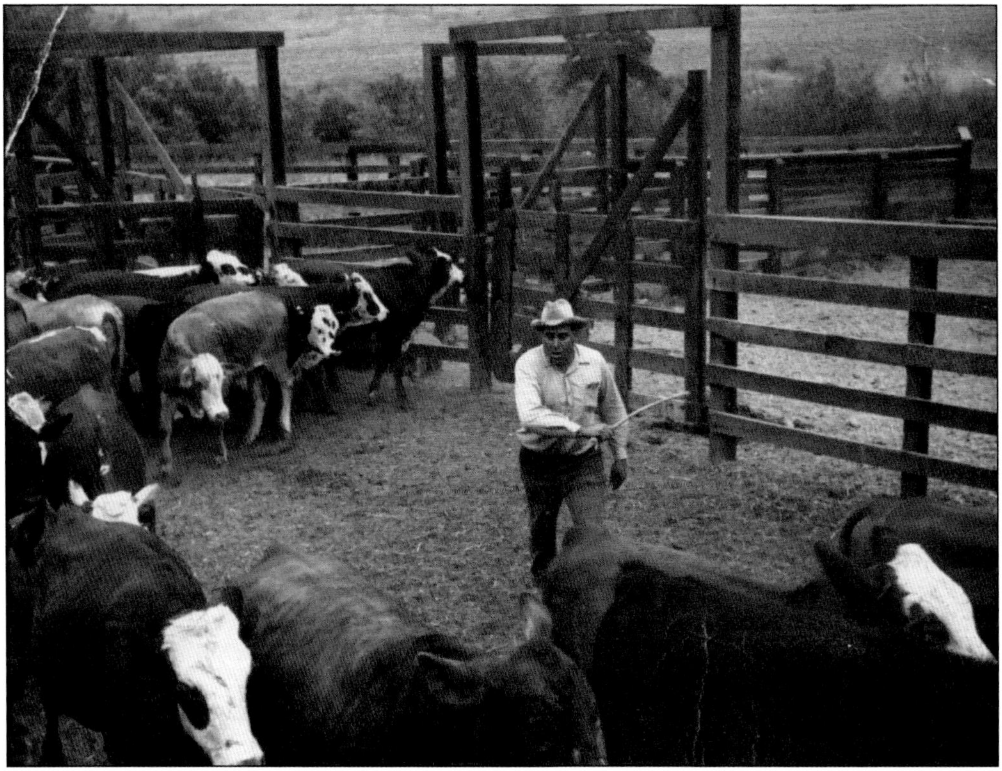

On this round-up day at the Canet Ranch, Mike Pulido, the head ranch foreman, herds cattle into the corral to hold until being sorted for shipping. Pulido worked his way up from a laborer to head foreman. He was the last foreman to work on the Canet Ranch. (Photograph by C. Robert Lee©, courtesy of C. Robert Lee.)

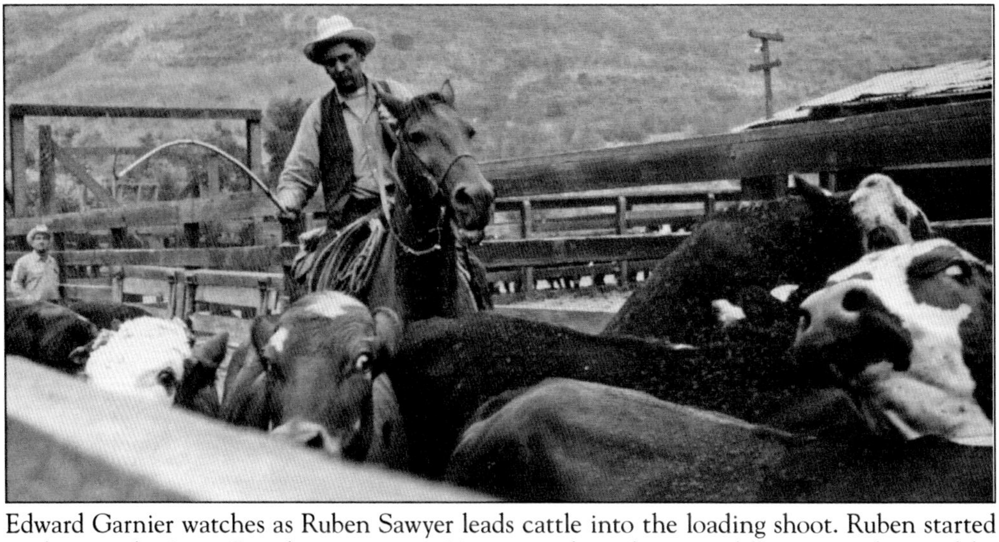

Edward Garnier watches as Ruben Sawyer leads cattle into the loading shoot. Ruben started working on the Canet Ranch as a teenager. He was ranch cattleman and foreman in charge of the health and wellbeing of the cattle. While attending Holy Cross Catholic School in Ventura, he met his future wife, Thelma. They had three children, Joan, Ernie, and Mary Jane. (Photograph by C. Robert Lee©, courtesy of C. Robert Lee.)

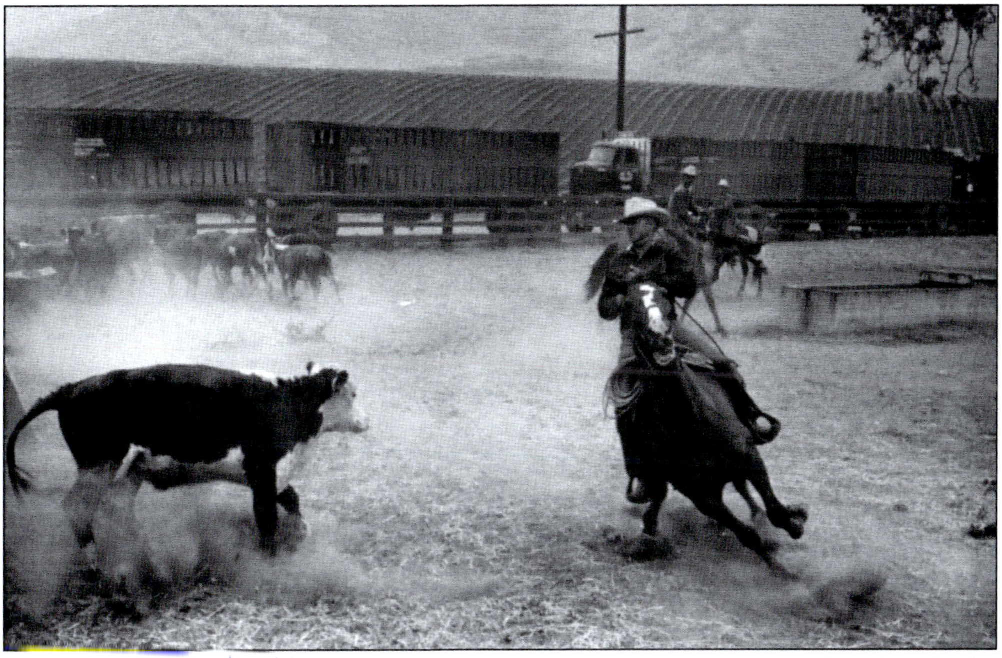

George Randall displays his expertise as cow-horseman as Juan Manriquez (right) and John Lorenzana (left) are poised to make their next moves. Randall, an Ojai resident and seasoned cow-horseman, would come to the ranch to help during round-up. In the background, the rolling hillside along Cañada Larga Road is striped with rows of lima beans. (Photograph by C. Robert Lee©, courtesy of C. Robert Lee.)

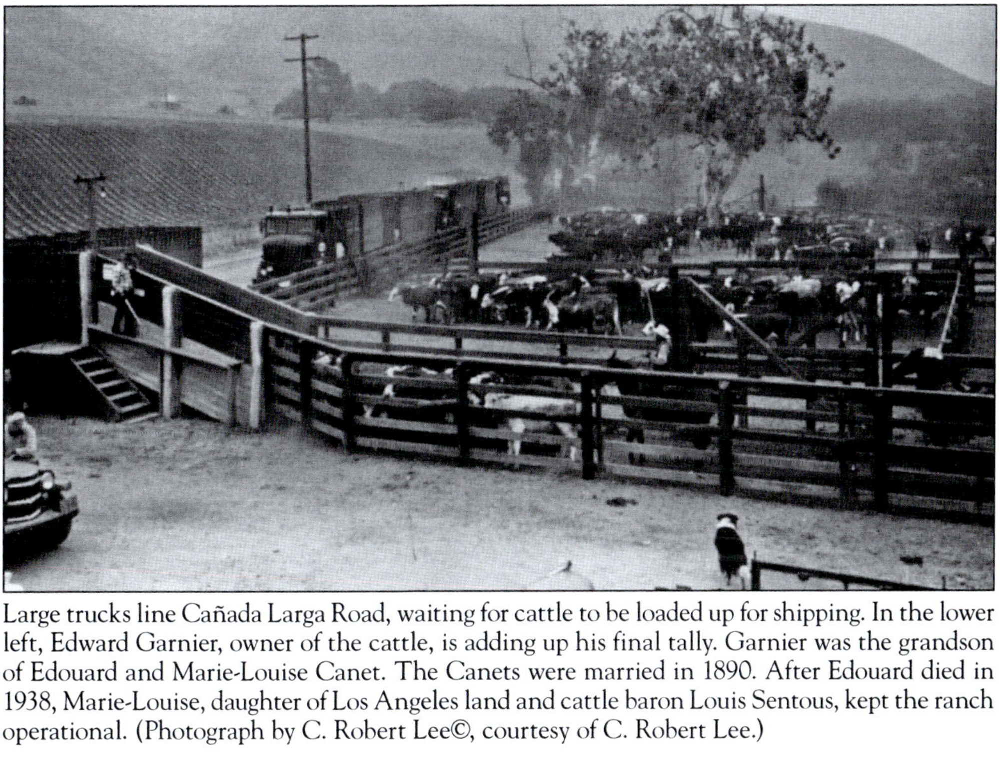

Large trucks line Cañada Larga Road, waiting for cattle to be loaded up for shipping. In the lower left, Edward Garnier, owner of the cattle, is adding up his final tally. Garnier was the grandson of Edouard and Marie-Louise Canet. The Canets were married in 1890. After Edouard died in 1938, Marie-Louise, daughter of Los Angeles land and cattle baron Louis Sentous, kept the ranch operational. (Photograph by C. Robert Lee©, courtesy of C. Robert Lee.)

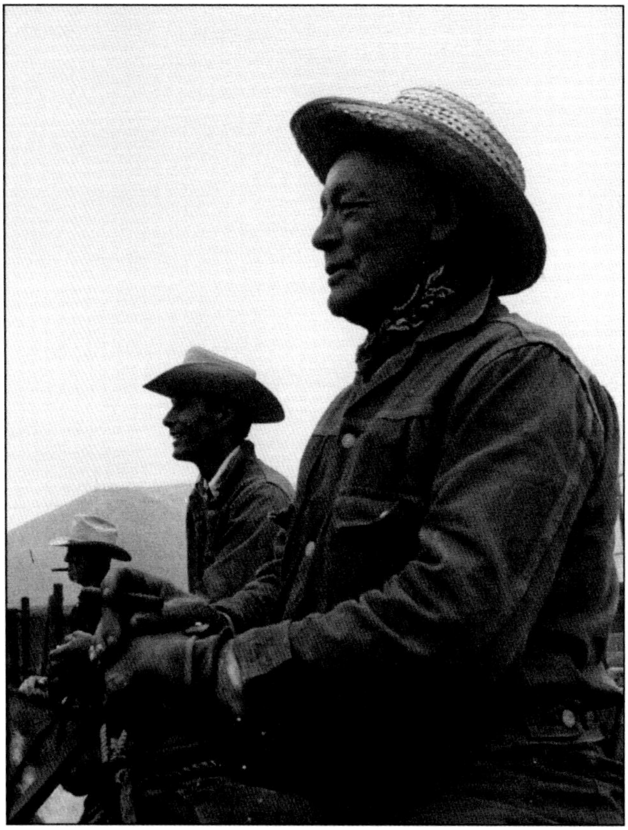

These cattlemen stop for a well-deserved break after a job well done. In the foreground is Juan Manriquez, who lived and worked on the ranch for many years. Sitting in the middle is John Lorenzana. Though he worked on the ranch, he lived on the Avenue. Lorenzana eventually married Erma Pulido, the daughter of foreman Mike Pulido. On the end, George Randall enjoys a smoke with Manriquez. (Photograph by C. Robert Lee©, courtesy of C. Robert Lee.)

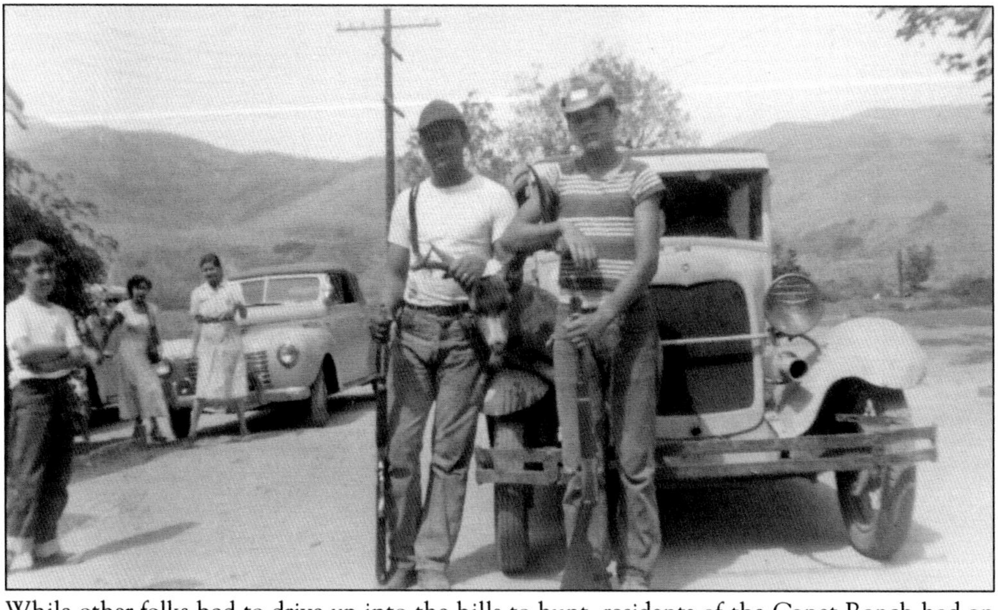

While other folks had to drive up into the hills to hunt, residents of the Canet Ranch had an abundance of game in their own backyard. Kelly Felix (left) and cousin Ernie Sawyer pose with a buck bagged on the ranch. The women in the background are Tilly Felix (left) and Thelma Sawyer. The boy to the left is unidentified. (Courtesy of Ernie Sawyer.)

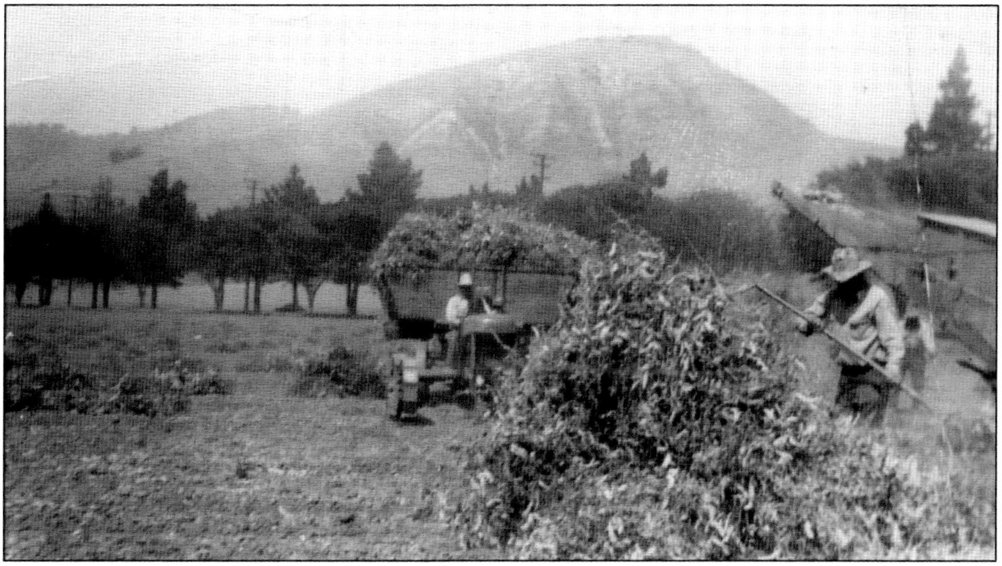

Harvest time at the Canet Ranch is captured in this photograph of field laborers threshing lima beans. Red Mountain stands as a prominent backdrop in this view facing west. To the left, lofty pine trees line Highway 33 as a single car makes its way southward. The Canet Ranch was located about half a mile from downtown Foster Park. (Courtesy of John and Erma Lorenzana.)

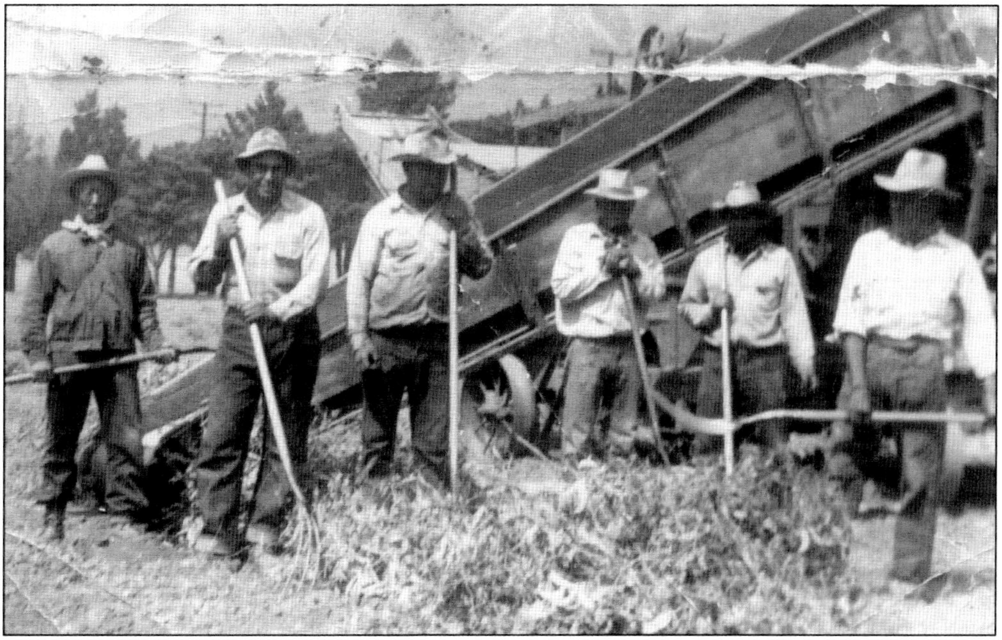

The western border of the Canet Ranch stretched across Highway 33, beyond the Southern Pacific Railroad track and to the banks of the Ventura River. The lima bean threshing crew takes a break for this early-1950s photograph. Pictured here from left to right are Juan Manriquez, Mike Pulido, Johnny Orr, Francisco "Poncho" Duran, Ruben Sawyer, and Larry "Lauro" Delgadillo. (Courtesy of John and Erma Lorenzana.)

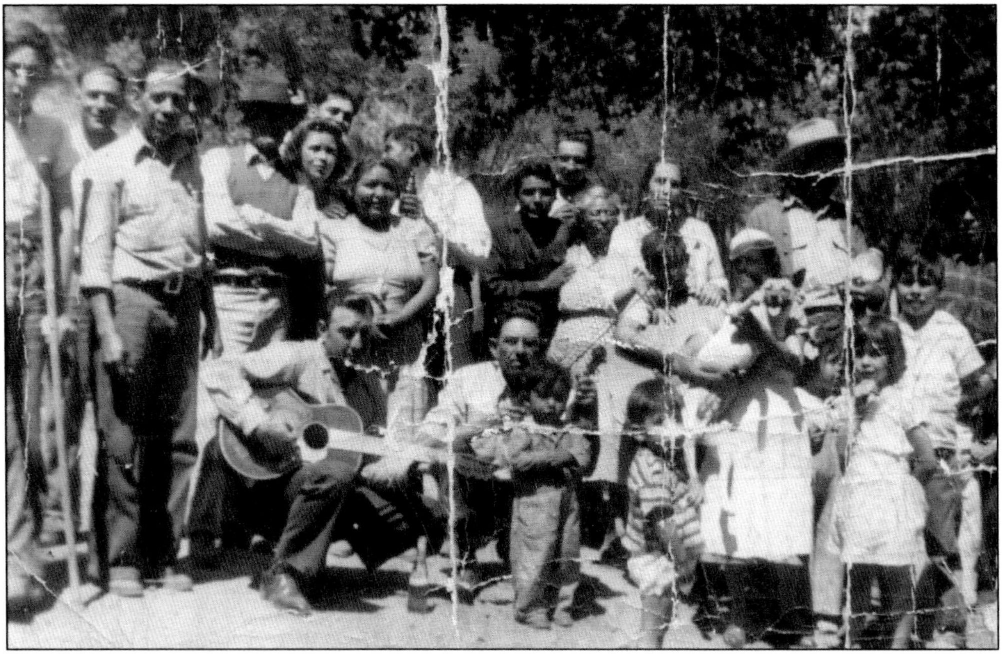

Many families lived and worked on the Canet Ranch over the years. This group gathers for a photograph before it loads up into a flatbed truck to take a ride to Wheeler's Gorge for a picnic. Pictured here are members of the Pulido, Duran, Valencia, Delgadio, Arellanes, Tumimait, Sawyer, and Melendrez families. (Courtesy of Gracie Duran Varela.)

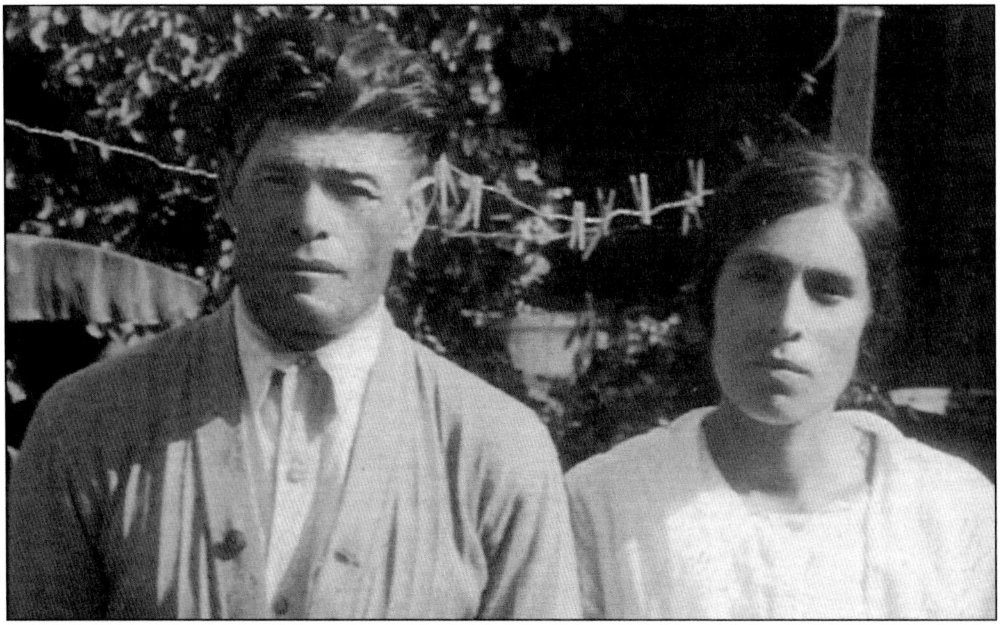

Francisco "Poncho" Duran and his wife, Soledad Pulido Duran, came to the Canet Ranch around 1925. The Durans lived on the ranch, where they raised their eight children, Adam, Teresa, Conrad, Pete, Frank, George, Gracie, and Billy. Poncho worked as a laborer on the ranch, and Soledad was a woman of many talents. She could farm, hunt and clean her own game, and chop wood for the stove to cook it on. (Courtesy of Pete Duran.)

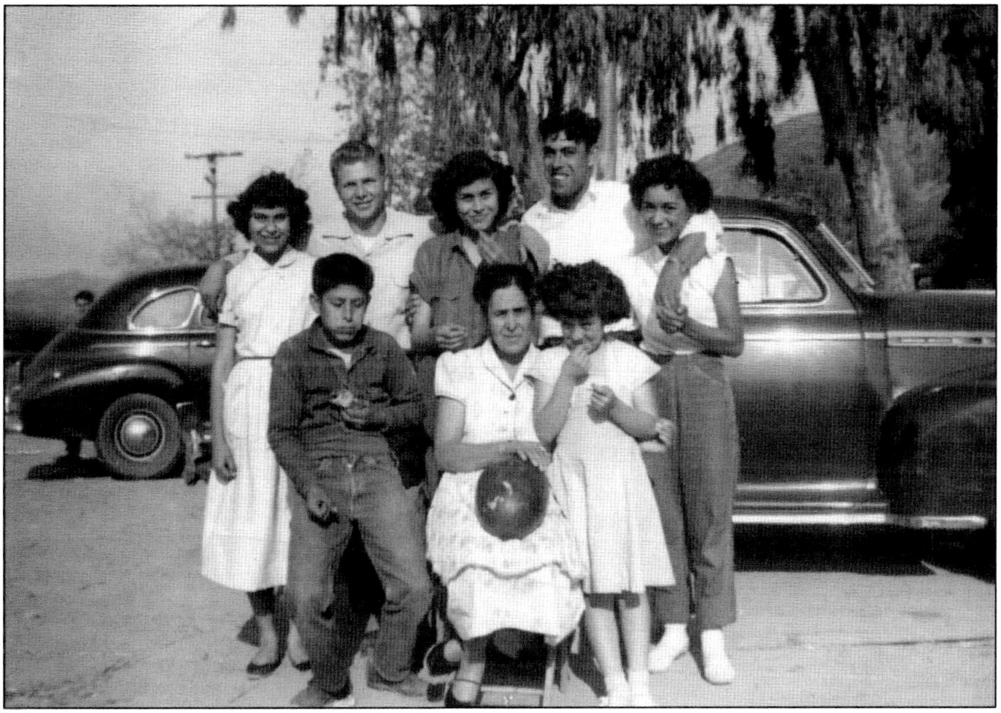

Among her other talents, Soledad Duran was a fantastic storyteller, particularly of scary ones. Her son Pete recalls the story of "La Llorona," a tale of Mexican folklore about a weeping spirit searching for her lost children. It has been told over the years to keep children close to home. Duran said it worked; even as an adult returning from the Navy, he never liked walking the canyon road alone at night. Pictured above are, from left to right (first row) Billy Duran, Soledad Duran, and Elvira Valencia; (second row) Gracie Duran, Albert Fountain, Erma Pulido, Pete Duran, and Angie Pulido. On the right is handsome Frank Duran, pictured here in Seoul, Korea, in 1952. Frank was the fourth son of the Durans, and he was drafted in 1952 and served in the Korean War. While there, Duran was wounded and awarded the Purple Heart. (Both, courtesy of Gracie Duran Varela.)

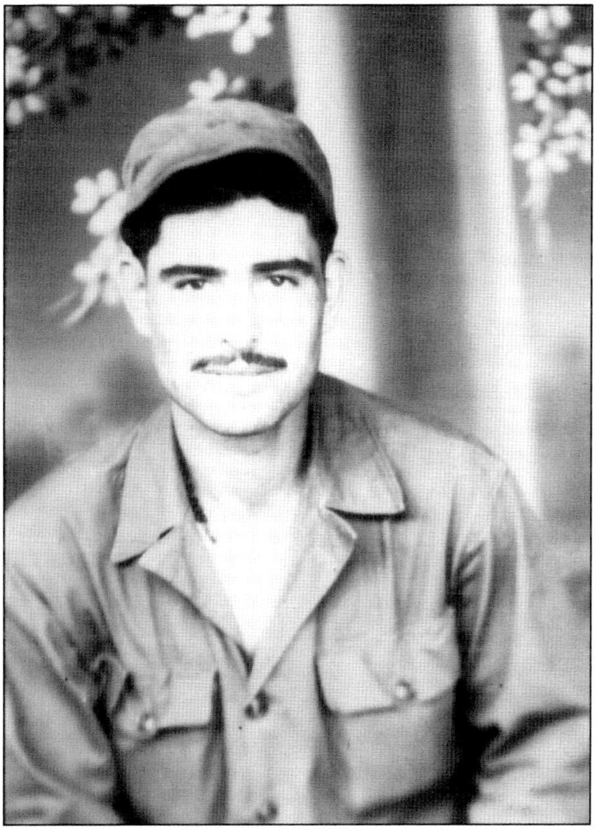

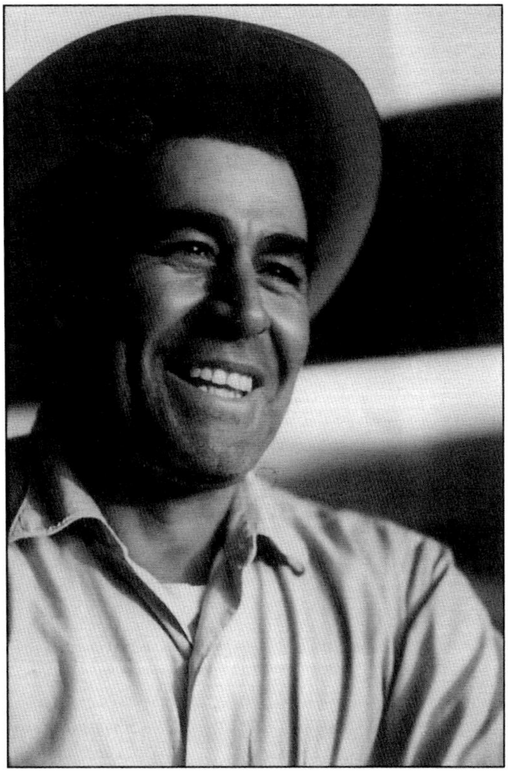

When Miguel Flores Pulido came to work at the Canet Ranch, he and his family lived with his sister and brother-in-law Soledad and Poncho Duran. Eventually, he moved the family into a house of their own. Pulido worked as a laborer and ran the farm equipment, plowing the fields, threshing the lima beans, and baling hay. He and his wife, Maria "Carmen" Moreno Castro Pulido (below), had four children, Alex, Erma, Angie, and Mike Jr., whom they raised on the ranch. Pulido was highly respected in the area, always willing to help others in need, and he never forgot where he came from. The Pulido family lived in different homes on the ranch, including a two-story house in the bean field. He lived and worked on the ranch until his death at age 65. (Left, courtesy of Alex Pulido; below, courtesy of Erma Lorenzana,)

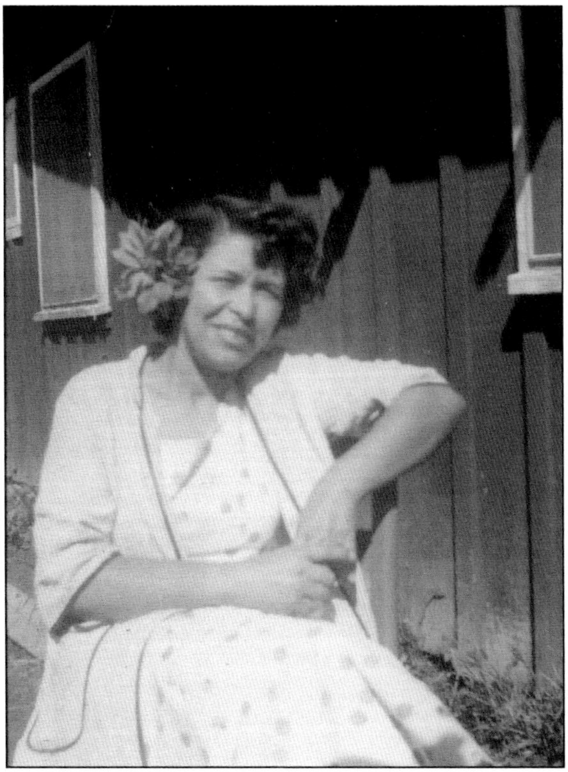

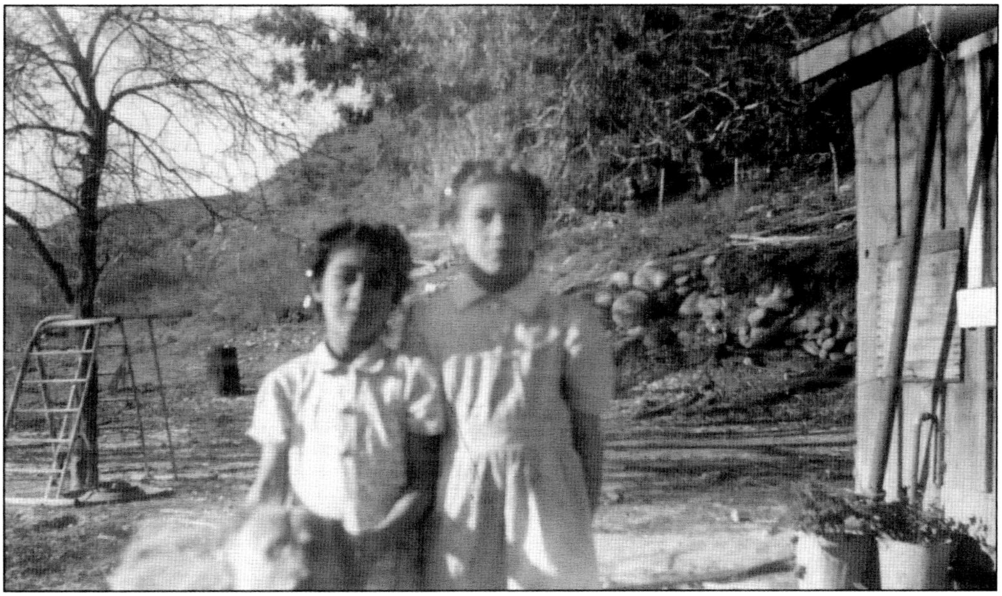

Angie (left) and Erma Pulido stand with their dog Topo in the yard of their house in the bean field, which faced Highway 33. Erma has many fond memories of growing up on the ranch. She recalls that every New Year's Day, Marie Louise Canet would drive to the houses on Cañada Larga Road and bring all the ranch children stockings full of candy and a silver dollar. (Courtesy of Erma Lorenzana.)

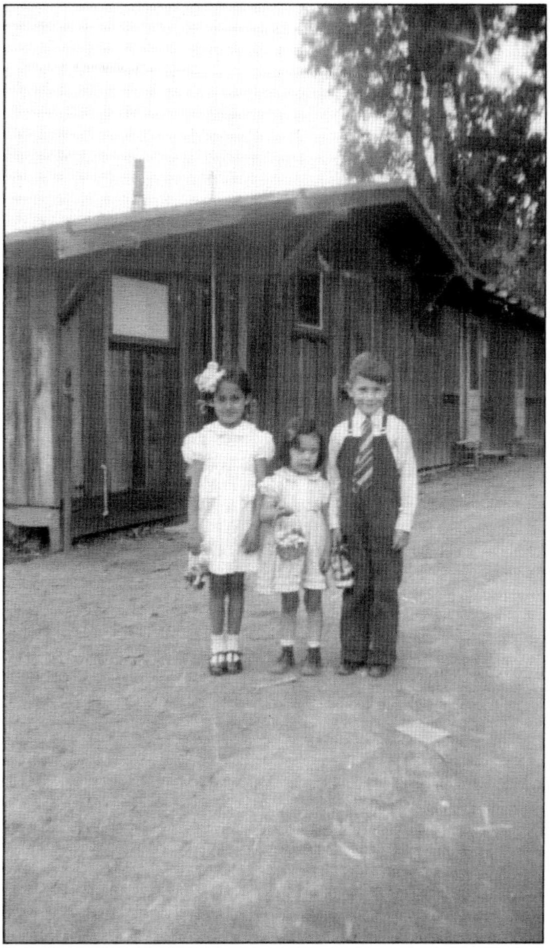

Joan (left), Mary Jane, and Ernie Sawyer pose with their Easter baskets in front of their house, which was located on the west side of Highway 33. They are the children of Ruben and Thelma Sawyer. (Courtesy of Ernie Sawyer.)

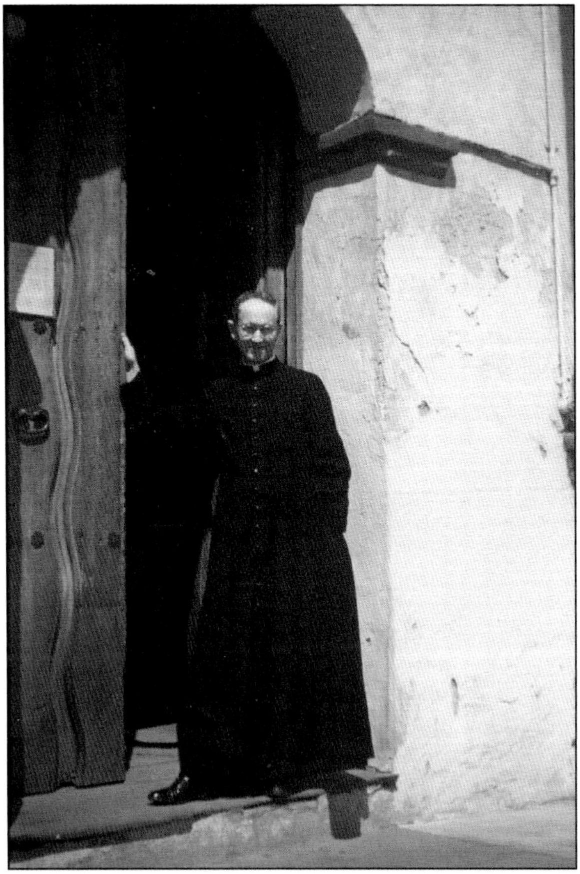

The children of the ranch and surrounding areas could not always make it to the Ventura Mission for catechism classes, so Fr. Daniel Hurley would make the trip up the Avenue to teach classes at the Canet Ranch. Ernie Sawyer recalls the times when Father Hurley would come to the ranch. After class was over, the boys would jump on top of his car and not let him leave. Hurley wised up, and he would throw handfuls of rock candy out the window and drive off as the children jumped off to get it. Below, catechism children from the ranch and Foster Park pose for this photograph as the truck in the background travels up Cañada Larga Road. Pictured here are, from left to right, (first row) Billy Duran, Mary Arellanes, Erma Pulido, Nellie Arellanes, and Mary Ann Pluim; (second row) unidentified; (third row) unidentified and Jeannie Pluim; (fourth row) Alex Pulido and unidentified. (Left, courtesy of San Buenaventura Mission; below, courtesy of Mary Ann Pluim.)

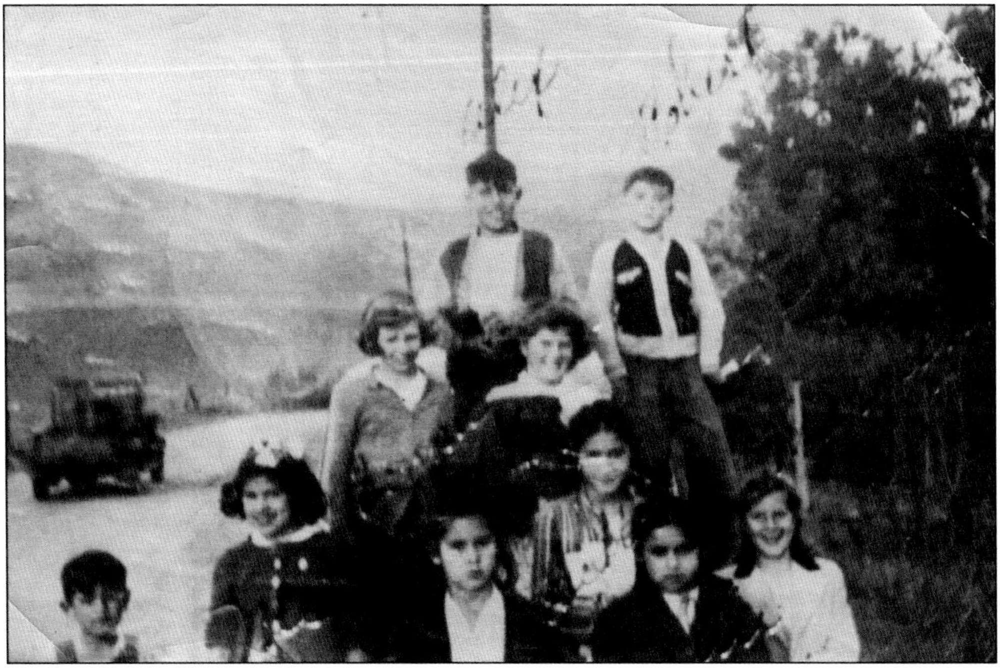

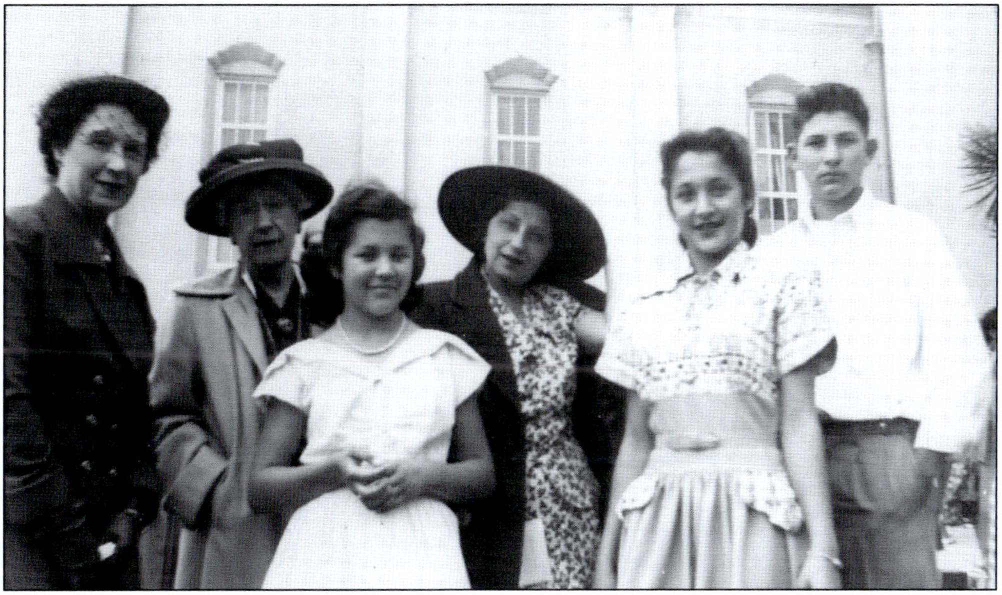

It was not uncommon for Marie Louise Canet to attend graduation ceremonies of the children of resident ranch employees. This photograph was taken at Mary Jane Sawyer's graduation in 1954. Pictured here from left to right are Jeanne Canet Gurnier, Marie Louise Canet, Mary Jane, Natalia "Netty" Faraud, Joan Sawyer, and Ernie Sawyer. Faraud was the owner of Faraud's Bakery on Main Street and cousin to Thelma Sawyer. (Courtesy of Ernie Sawyer.)

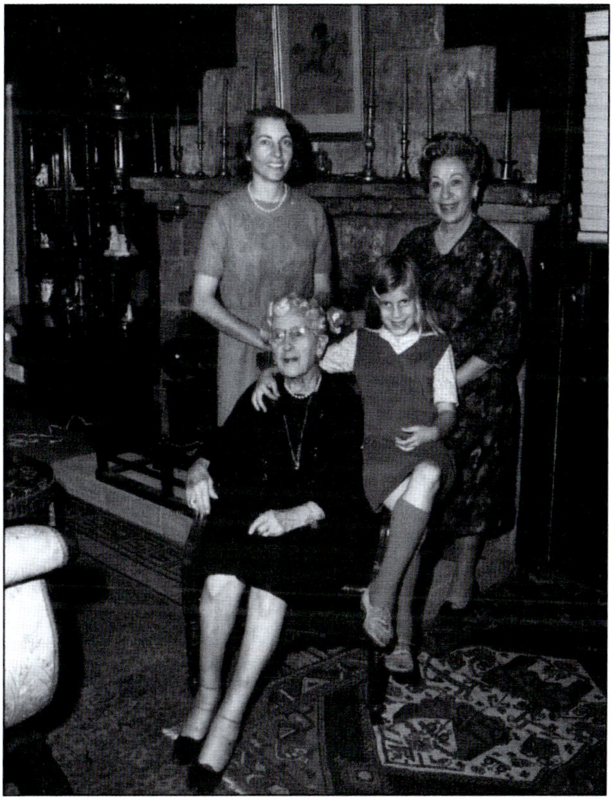

Four generations of Canets pose by the fireplace in the front family room of the ranch house. Pictured here from left to right are (first row) Marie Louise Canet and great-granddaughter JiJi Lee; (second row) granddaughter Ileana Lee and daughter Renee Pezzi. The fireplace was faced with bricks from the Ventura Mission. One of the bricks was chiseled with the date 1874. (Photograph by C. Robert Lee©, courtesy of C. Robert Lee.)

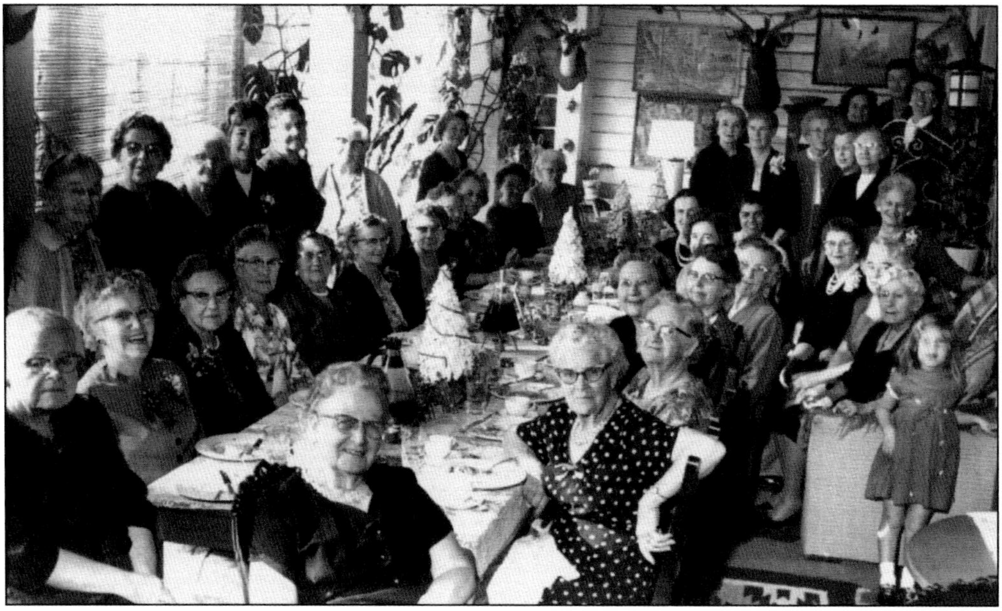

Part of a tradition at the Canet Ranch was the annual Casa De Rosas Christmas Party, hosted by Marie Louise Canet. Casa De Rosas was a North Ventura Avenue social club to which she belonged with other prominent local women. In the far right, young JiJi Lee stands at the end of the couch next to Canet, her great-grandmother. (Photograph by C. Robert Lee©, courtesy of C. Robert Lee.)

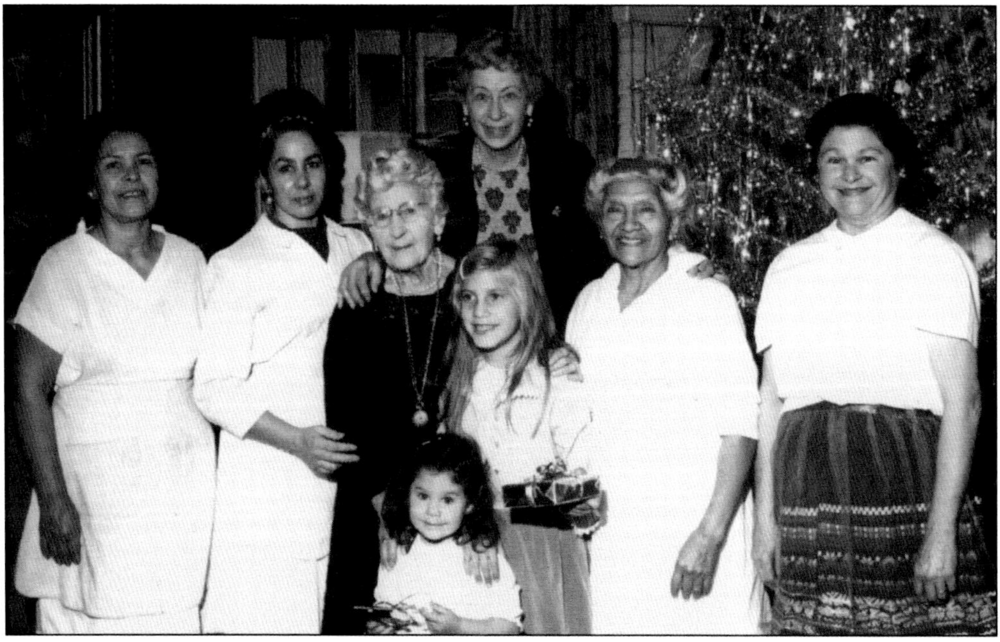

In this photograph, Canet family members pose with the party's helpers. From left to right are (first row) Traci Langbecker (granddaughter of Thelma Sawyer); (second row) Carmen Pulido, Gloria Valenzuela, Marie Louise Canet, JiJi Lee (great-granddaughter of Canet), Concha Cerna, and Thelma Sawyer; (third row) Rene Pezzi (daughter of Canet). (Photograph by C. Robert Lee©, courtesy of C. Robert Lee.)

Four

Old Mill School Days

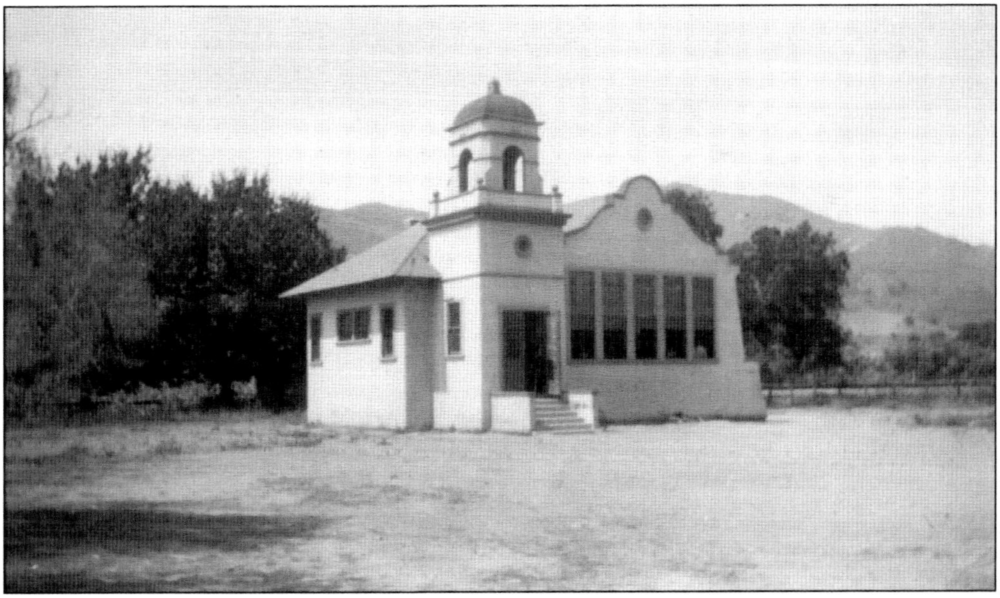

After a flood destroyed the original Mill School, built around 1875, a new site was chosen to erect this schoolhouse in 1884. The one-room schoolhouse, located on North Ventura Avenue, had a belfry and a wood-burning stove used for heat. The schoolhouse also served as a social meeting place and Sunday school for the small agricultural community. A teacher appears to be standing in the window on the right. (Courtesy of the Museum of Ventura County.)

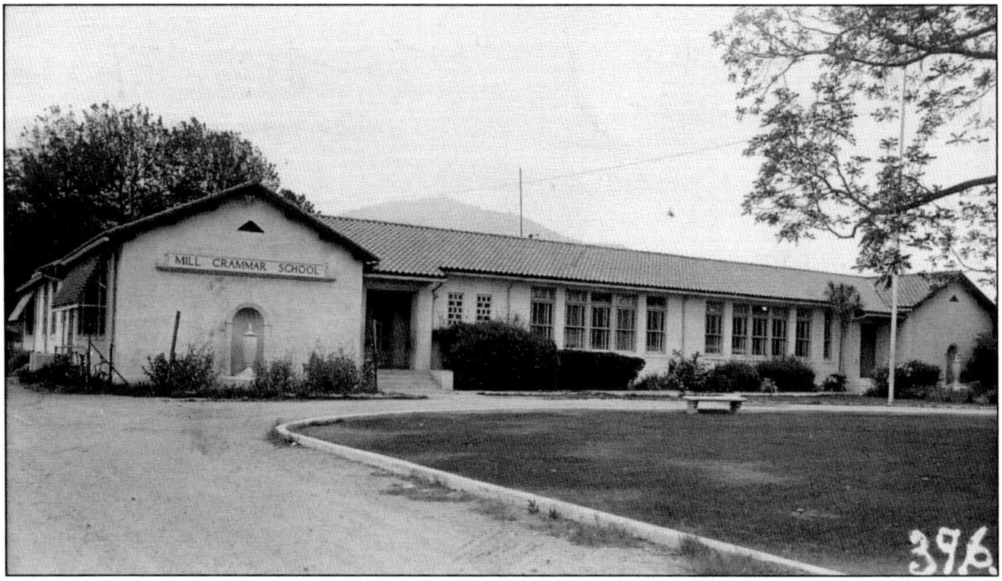

The school district for the area was originally established as the Cañada Larga School District in 1885. A year later, after the completion of the Ventura Flour Mill, the name was changed to Mill School District for easier pronunciation. The population growth that resulted from the Ventura Avenue oil boom of the 1920s presented a need for more classrooms. Construction of this larger building began in 1926. By the early 1950s, more classrooms were added to keep up with the growing student body. During this time, Mill and Santa Ana School Districts united, creating the Mill Union School District. In 1953, a swimming pool was put in and opened to the public for recreation during summer months. Below is a photograph of the Santa Ana School playground, taken in the early 1950s. It is now under Lake Casitas. (Above, author's collection; below, courtesy of Jeff Mulhardt.)

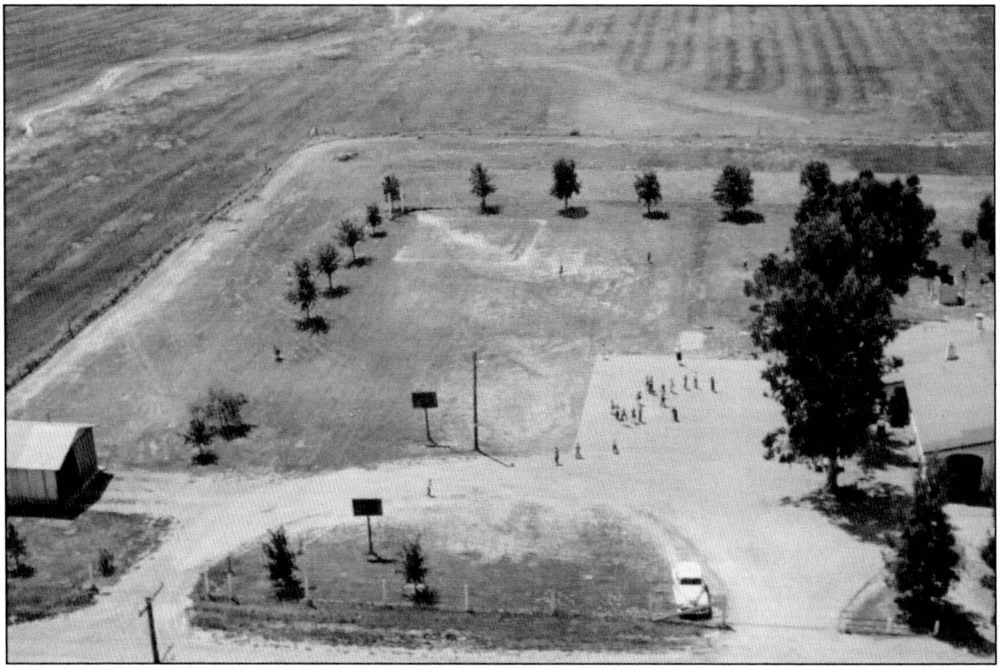

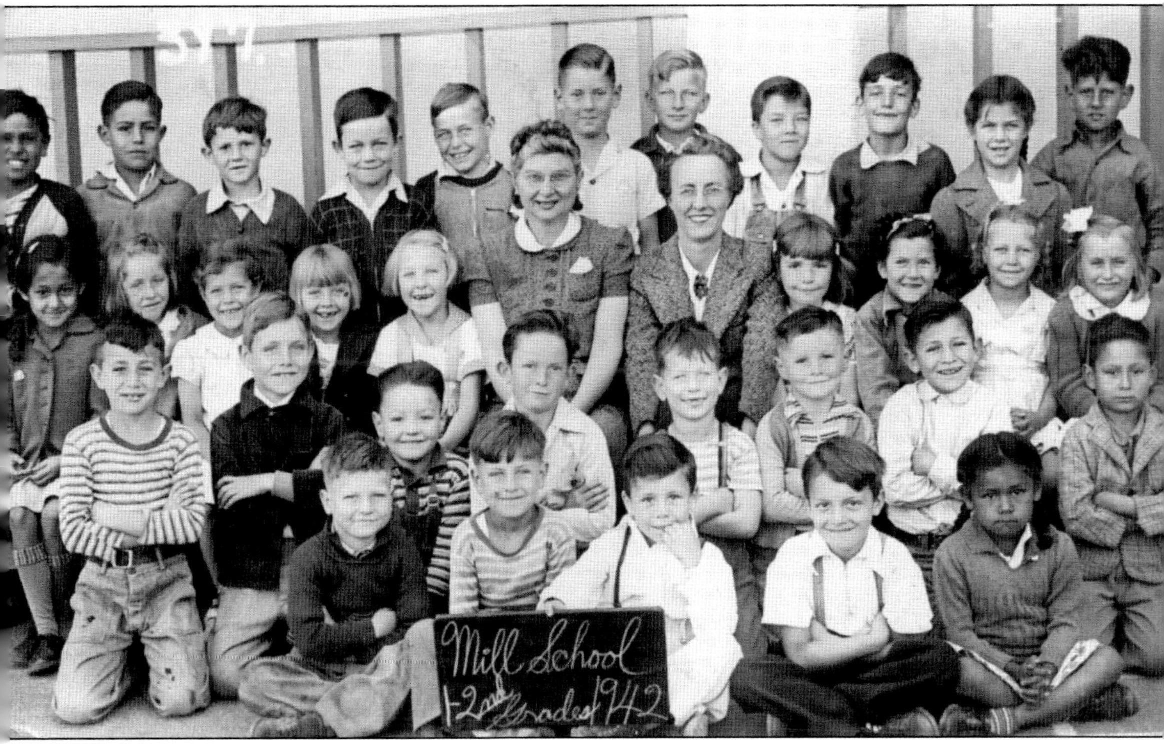

In February 1879, the *Ventura Signal* reported that the Mill District Schoolhouse had an average attendance of 15 pupils, and Kate Dunning was the teacher. Ruth Parker began her teaching career in that one-room schoolhouse in 1927, with an average of 40 students. In a 1989 *Star-Free-Press* interview, Parker recalled a problem with the overcrowding: "I asked the principal if some of the big boys could roll in some tree stumps for seats." A few years later, Parker moved into the new schoolhouse, where she taught for another 20 years. Parker sits with students in this 1942 class of first- and second-graders. From left to right are (first row) two unidentified children, Gary ?, Charlie Greathouse, and Nellie Arellanes; (second row) two unidentified children, Jackie Young, three unidentified children, Ernie Sawyer, and one unidentified child; (third row) Joan Sawyer, Geraldine Reynolds, Mary Ann Pluim, unidentified, Joyce Kimbrough, unidentified teacher, Ruth Parker, Ethel Kenney, Patty ?, Marilyn Kimbrough, and unidentified; (fourth row) Benny Arellanes, Frank Duran, unidentified, David Adamson, Bill Drennon, Billy Fraser, unidentified, Wilford Davis, Howard Mettin, Virgina Pluim, and Roger Belvins. (Courtesy of Ethel Marie Mullikin.)

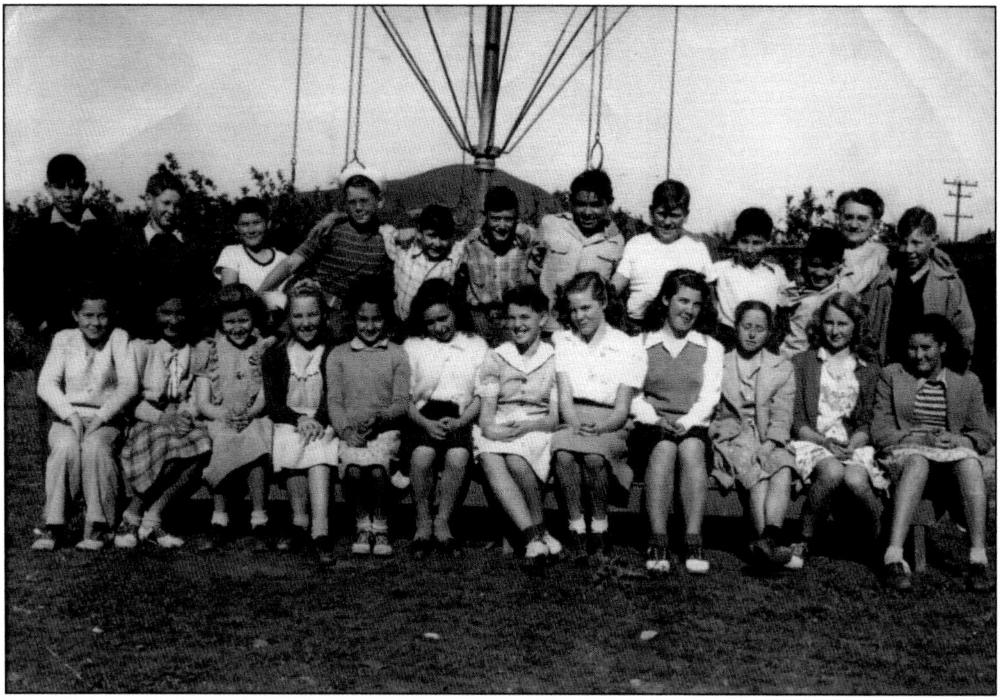

This class of 1945 fourth- and fifth-graders pictured here are, from left to right, (first row) Mary Ann Pluim, two unidentified students, Joyce Kimbrough, Joan Sawyer, unidentified, Virgina Pluim, two unidentified students, Geraldine Reynolds, and two unidentified students; (second row) Alex Pulido, two unidentified students, Billy Fraser, unidentified, Howard Mettin, Benny Arellanes, three unidentified students, unidentified teacher, and unidentified. (Courtesy of Mary Ann Aguilar.)

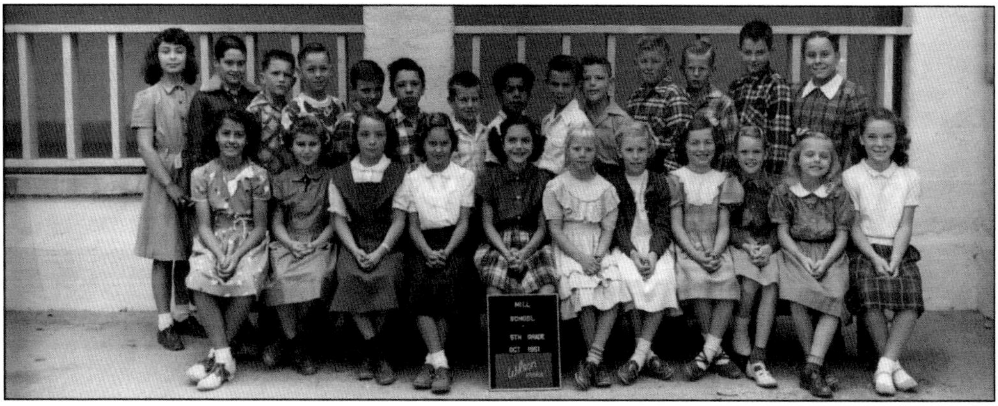

In this fall 1951 photograph, teacher Francis Page is absent. Her fifth-grade students pictured here are, from left to right, (first row) Mary Etta, Annette Richardson, Susan Shelby, Sue Bruce, Nancy Kull, Betty Bein, Lauretta Duncan, Carol Dodds, Carole Heffron, Barbara Gallinger, and Patty Austin; (second row) Norma Cline, Forrest Rockhold, James Leak, Richard Hatcher, Clyde Hewitt, Freddie ?, Charlie Eskew, Larry Delara, Bobby Miles, Ted ?, Craig Skinner, Errol Werre, Tom Siemenski, and Annette Helton. (Courtesy of Charlie Eskew.)

Mill School had many fine teachers over the years, most notably Ruth Parker. For Alex Pulido, a young boy growing up on the Canet Ranch, she played an inspirational part in his academic and professional life. Pulido, the son of ranch foreman Mike Pulido, recalls Parker visiting his mother, Carmen, at their humble home on the ranch to offer accolades for her son. It was this initial encouragement that put Pulido on a path of success. Pulido earned a bachelor's degree and teaching credentials at San Jose University in 1962, a master's degree in counseling from Texas Technical University in Lubbock, Texas, and a doctorate from the University of California Santa Barbara in 1984. During his career, Pulido was an educator, counselor, principal, and district superintendent, and he retired as a university professor from UCLA in 2008, always adopting Parker's philosophy of encouraging and supporting students. (Right, courtesy of the Leslie Ray Moore family; below, courtesy of Gracie Duran Varela.)

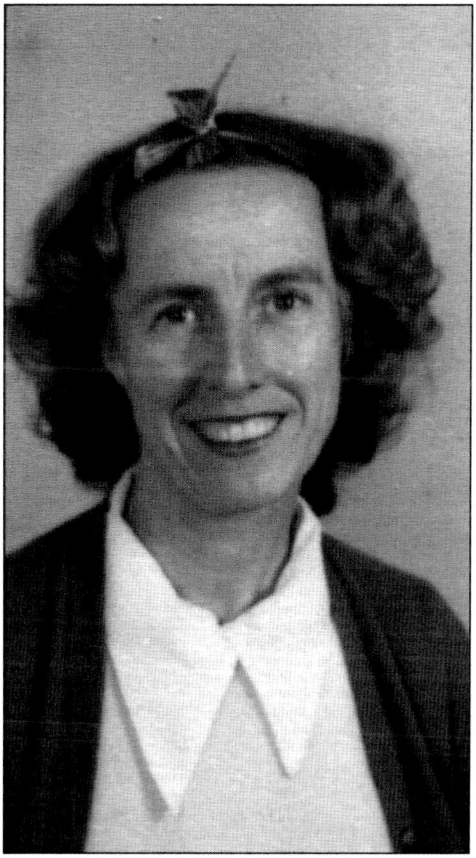

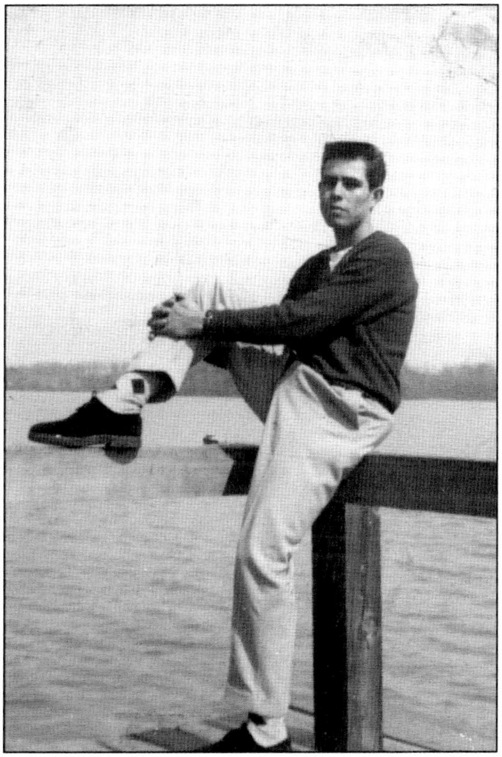

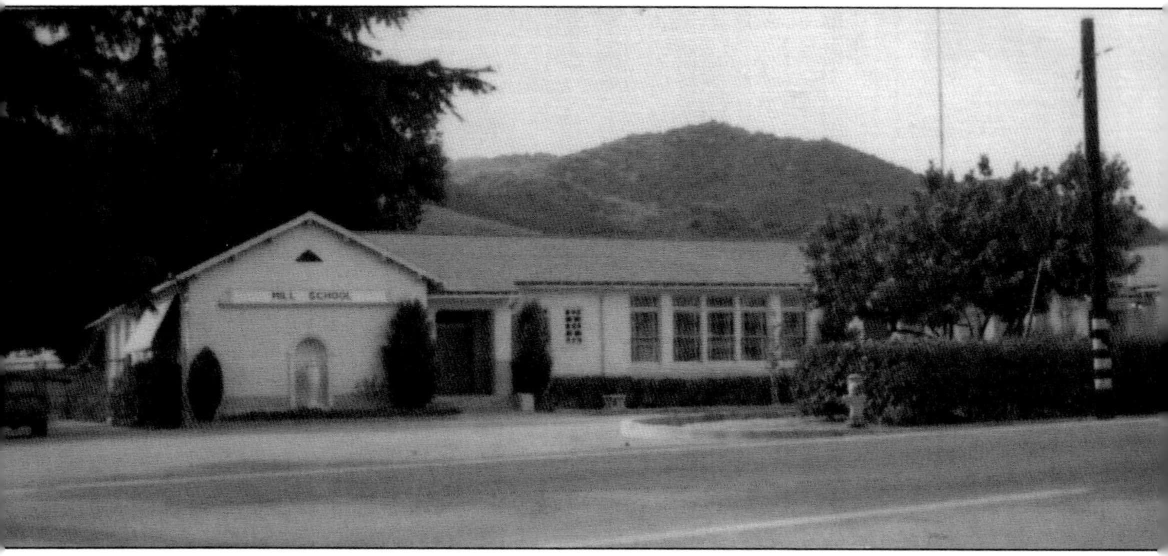

Mill School became part of the Ventura Unified School District in 1966. Due to low enrollment, the school closed its doors in 1981. After its closing, buildings and rooms were rented out to various businesses over the years. Santa Ventura Studios leased the property in 1997. It was a fully equipped production studio that produced films such as *The Prophet's Game*, starring Dennis Hopper, in 1999, and *Erin Brockovich*, starring Julia Roberts, in 2000. The studio also produced the television series *Mike Hammer, Private Eye*, starring Stacy Keach, from 1997 to 1998 and *Air America*, starring Lorenzo Lamas, from 1998 to 1999. In 2002, the former Mill School opened its doors once again as an institute for learning. The prestigious Brooks Institute found the eight-acre former production studio the perfect spot to open its new campus, which offers baccalaureate programs in professional photography, film, graphic design, and visual journalism. Pictured above is how Mill School appeared shortly before its closing in 1981. (Courtesy of Pete and Barbara Duran.)

Five

Eugene Cheney Foster Memorial Park

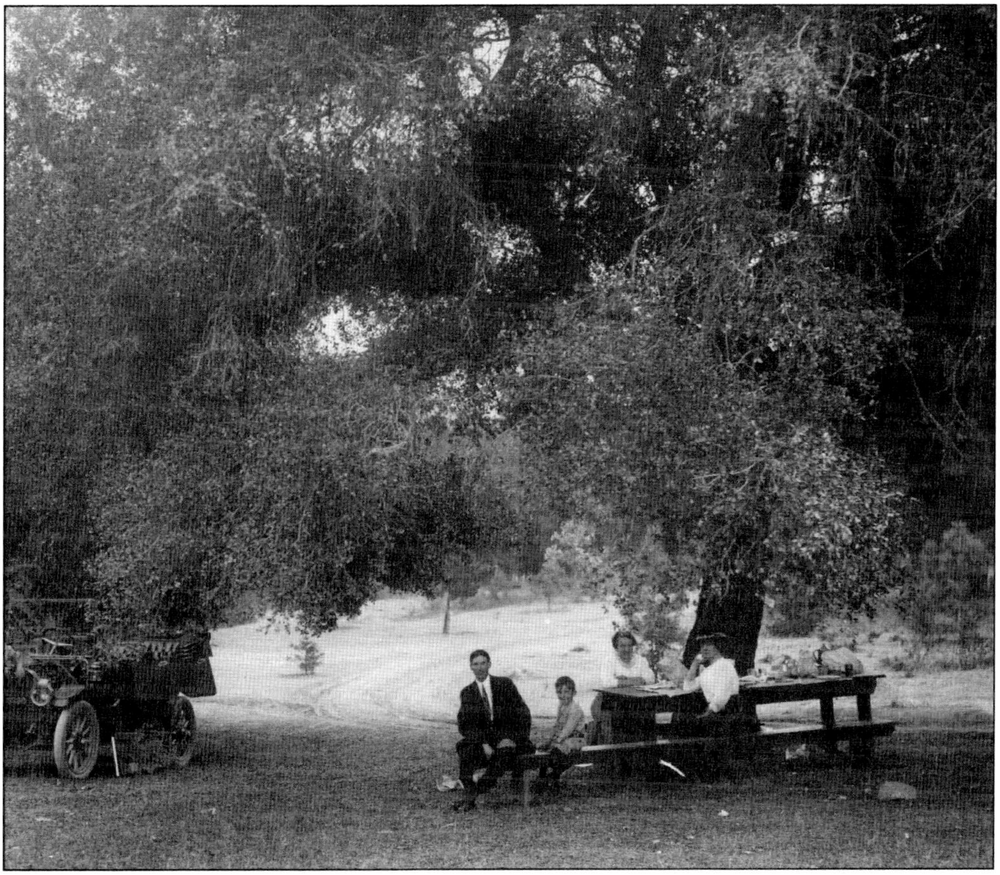

Waldo H. Dingman and family stop for some outdoor enjoyment and a photograph under this lofty oak tree at Foster Memorial Park. Dingman was an early Ventura County photographer and came to the area in 1915. He was also a pharmacist and one of the 35 members to sign the charter roll of the Ventura Rotary Club in 1919. (Courtesy of the Museum of Ventura County.)

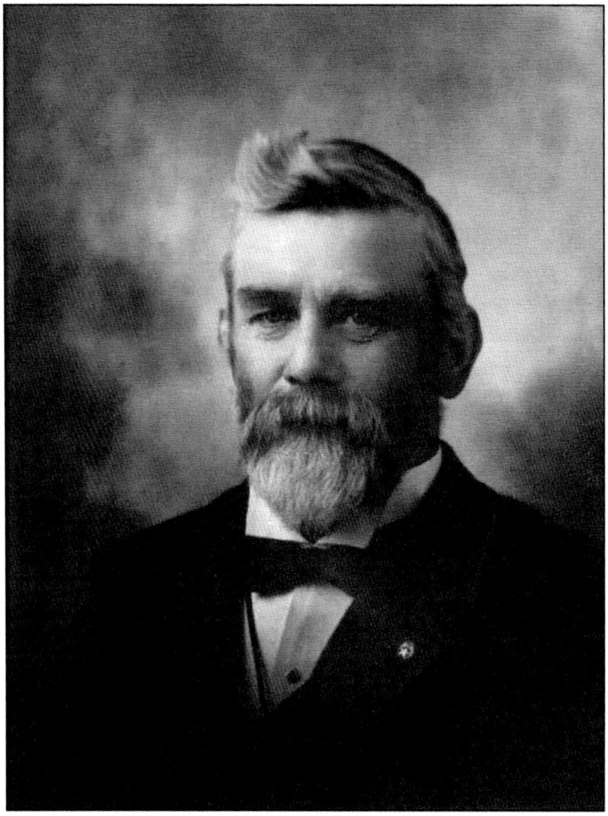

County pioneer Eugene Preston "E.P." Foster was an apricot grower, banker, philanthropist, and lover of trees. He lead the opening of travel between Santa Barbara and Ventura Counties and the planting of trees along county roads and highways. Around 1906, E.P. and his wife, Orpha, purchased 65 acres of wooded land along the banks of Ventura River and Coyote Creek at the gateway to Casitas Pass Road. The Fosters donated the land to the county as a memorial to their son, Eugene Cheney Foster (right), who died at age seven, establishing the second county park. The Fosters encouraged adjoining landowners, including Southern Pacific Railroad, to donate more land, increasing the size of the park to approximately 200 acres. Among his many titles, E.P. Foster is also known as the "Father of the Ventura County Parks Department." (Above, photograph by Brewster; both, courtesy of Phil Foster Ranger.)

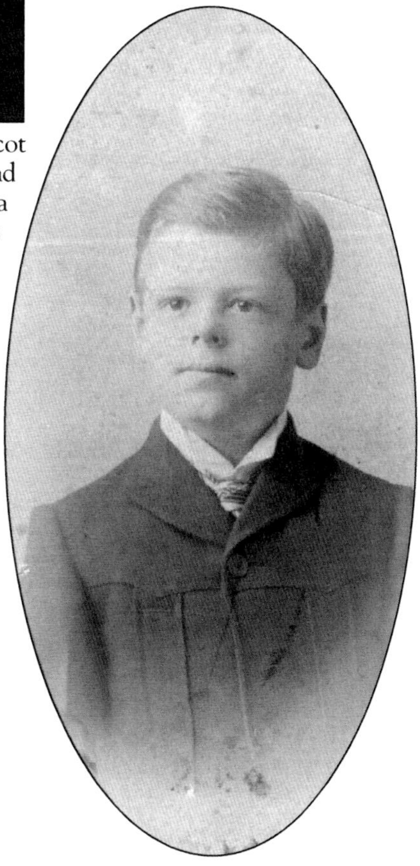

The lofty pines and wide oak trees of Foster Memorial Park picnic area furnished a lovely framework for any group portrait. This section of the park, located at Red Mountain, was designated for day use only. The long picnic tables provided plenty space to accommodate growing families, such as the one pictured at right. In this 1958 photograph, three generations of Pluim family members do their best to smile for the camera. (Courtesy of Robin Young.)

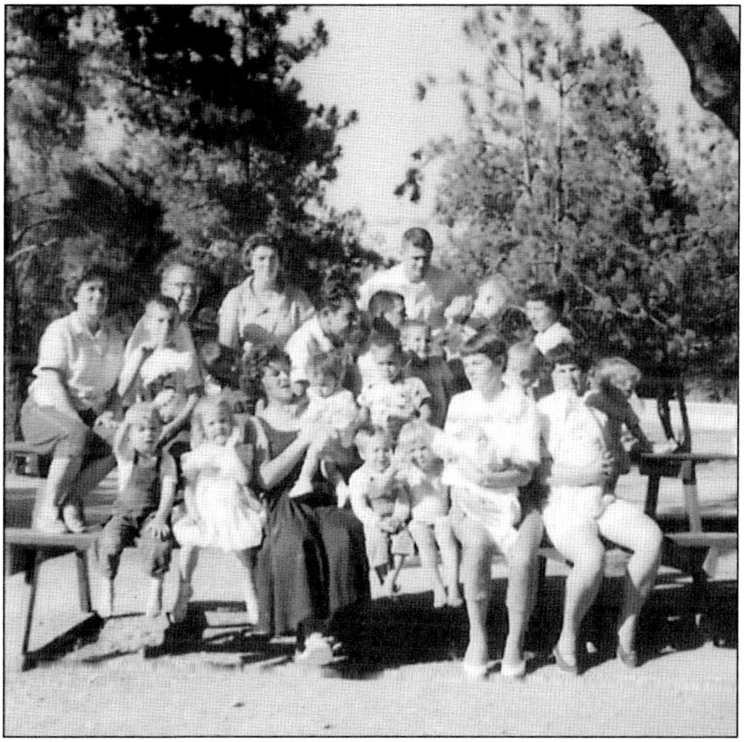

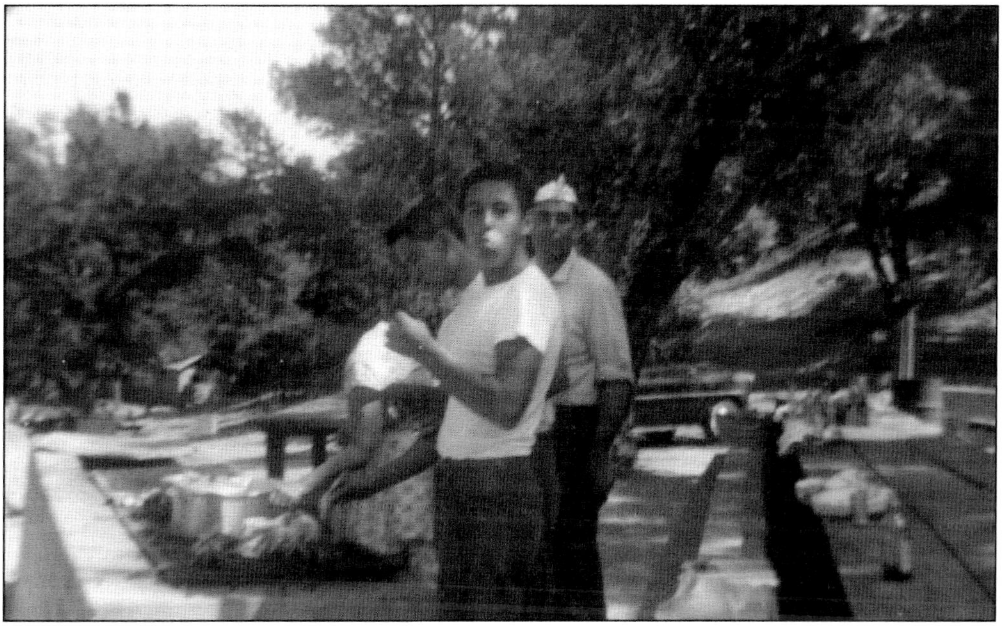

As residents of the Canet Ranch, the Pulido family had an abundance of acreage to hunt game on, but the ranch offered no barbecue facilities. On the slope of Red Mountain, the Pulidos found a spacious barbecue pit as well as a favorite outing spot. The park was also equipped with a merry-go-round, swing set, and badminton court. Pictured here in the late 1950s from left to right are Carmen Pulido, unidentified, Mike Pulido Jr. and Mike Pulido Sr. (Courtesy of Erma Lorenzana.)

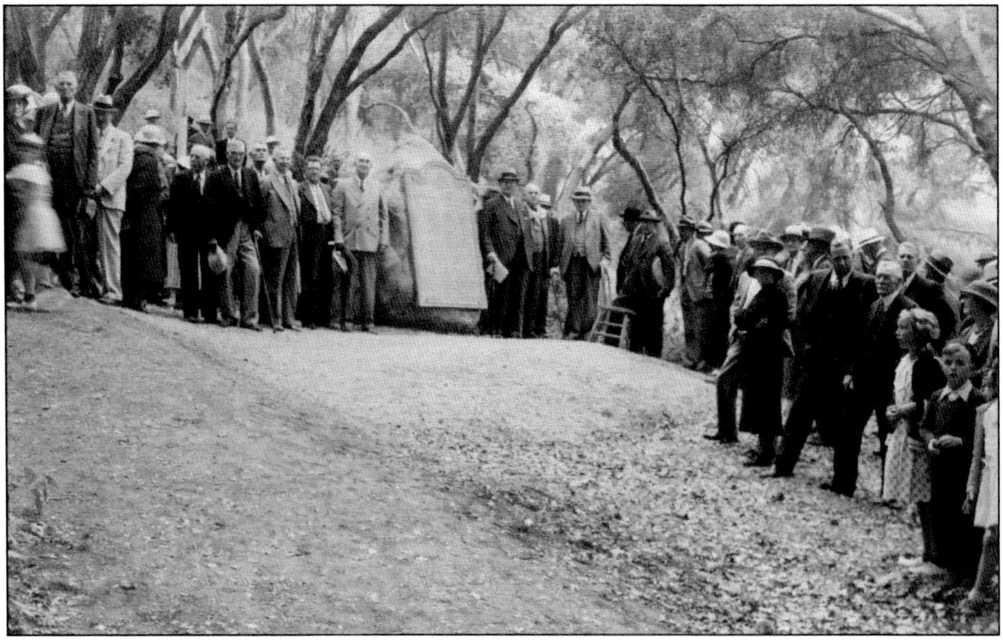

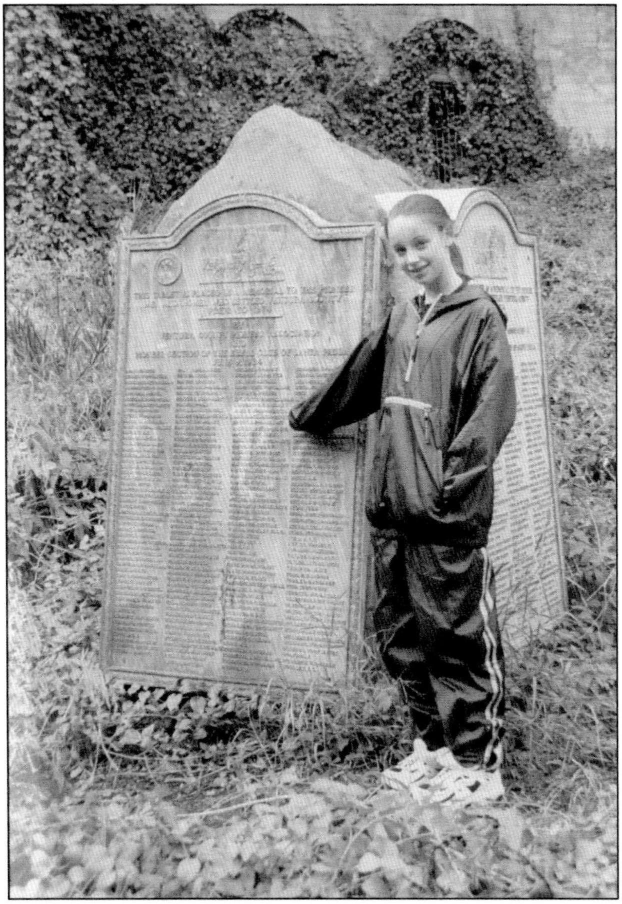

In June 1934, a boulder made of Sespe brownstone was dedicated to the memory of the pioneer men and women who settled in Ventura County prior to 1873 by the Ventura County Pioneer Association and the Pioneer Section of the Ebell Club of Santa Paula. The dedication was held in Foster Park. The boulder, bearing a large bronze tablet inscribed with the names of 201 pioneers, was erected directly below the amphitheater, facing Casitas Pass Road. In the 1996 photograph on the left, Alison Maulhardt points to the name of one of her great-great-grandfathers, Jacob Maulhardt. Another great-great-grandfather of Alison listed on the tablet is John Borchard. The memorial stone has since been relocated to the Museum of Ventura County. (Above, courtesy of the Museum of Ventura County; left, courtesy of Jeff Maulhardt.)

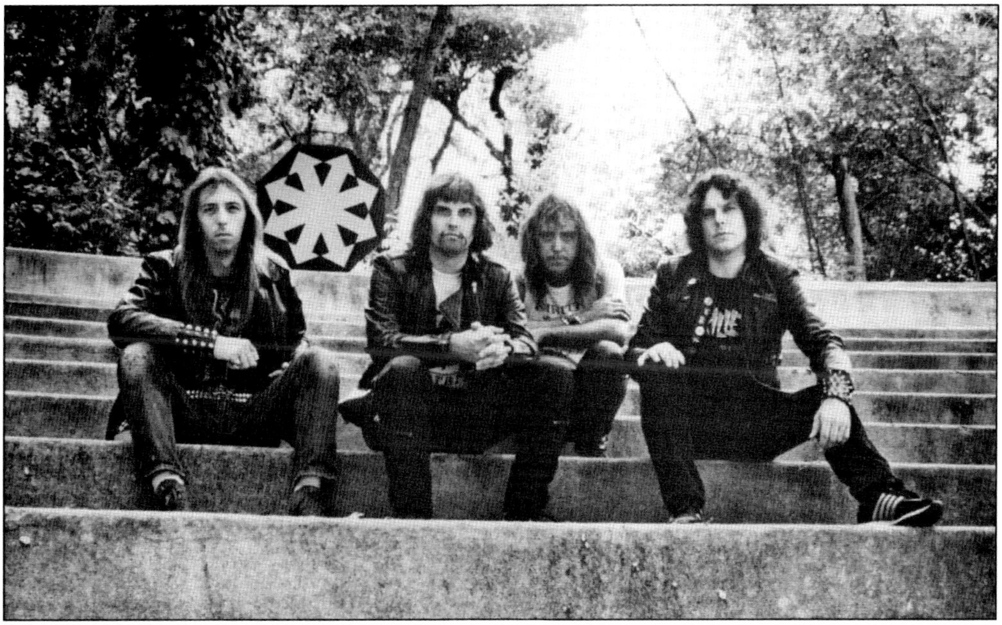

The Foster Park Bowl was built in 1928 up against the hillside of Red Mountain. In 1936, the venue hosted the first symphony concert held in Ventura County, performed by the Santa Barbara Symphony Orchestra. Pictured above are members of local heavy-metal rock group Cirith Ungol, which performed there during the late 1980s. From left to right are Tim Baker, Robert Garven, Jerry Fogle, and Mike Vujea. (Photograph by Greg Hazard, courtesy of Robert Garvin.)

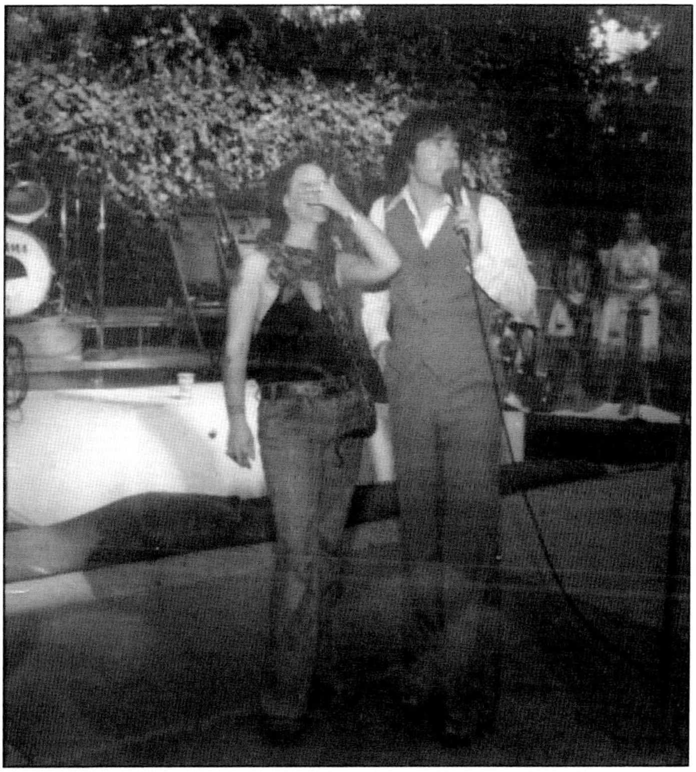

On stage at the Foster Park Bowl is former local disc jockey and comedian Les McDowell. McDowell was emcee for the Ventura County Arthritis Foundation's annual fundraisers during the late 1970s. Guests appearing on stage included celebrities such as local resident Sheb Wooly, who recorded "Purple People Eaters" in 1958. As part of his comedic repertoire, McDowell would pick out individuals from the audience such as this woman wearing her pet snake. (Courtesy of Les McDowell.)

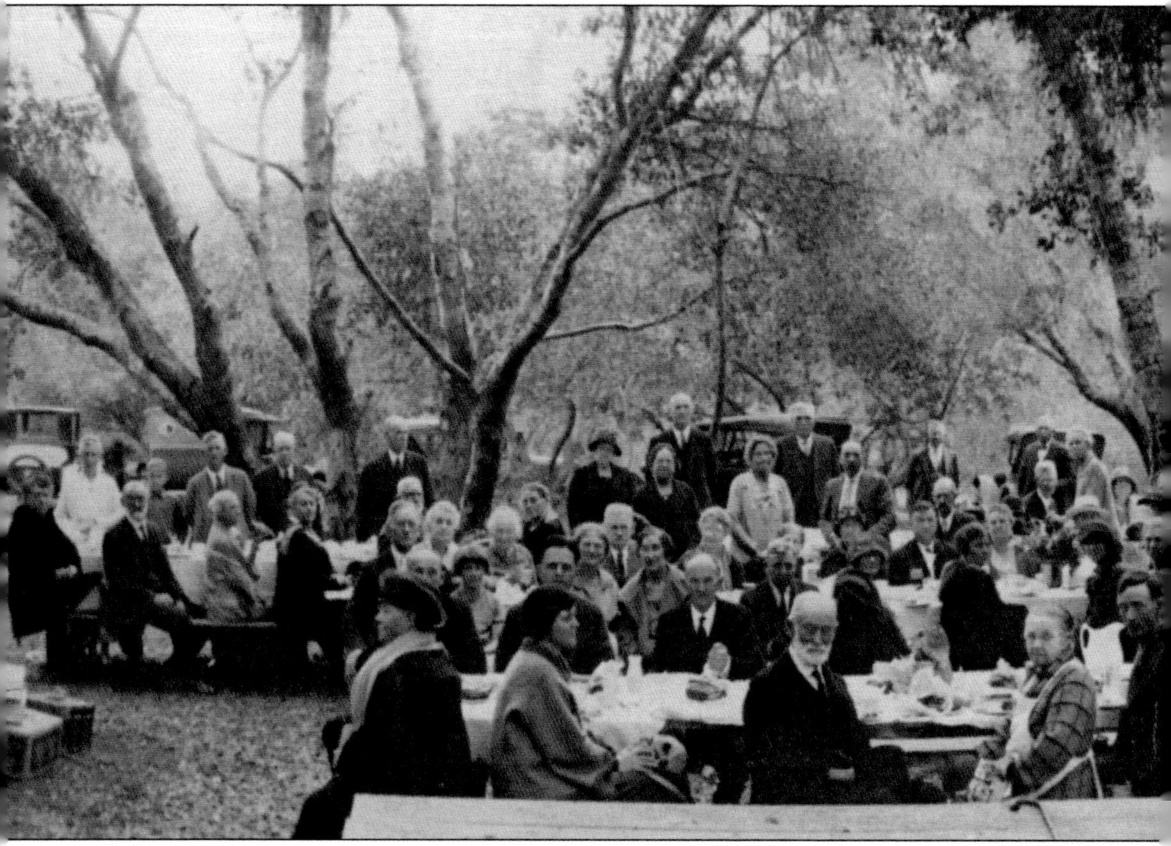

To keep the close bond and preserve their memories as new settlers, the Ventura County Pioneer Society was founded by Cephas L. Bard, MD, in 1891. Bard called the first meeting, held at the Ventura courthouse on September 19, where 62 men signed the charter roll. The society was originally made up of men who had settled in Ventura County before 1873. Bard was president until his death in 1901. Another general meeting was not called until May 1911, and it was held

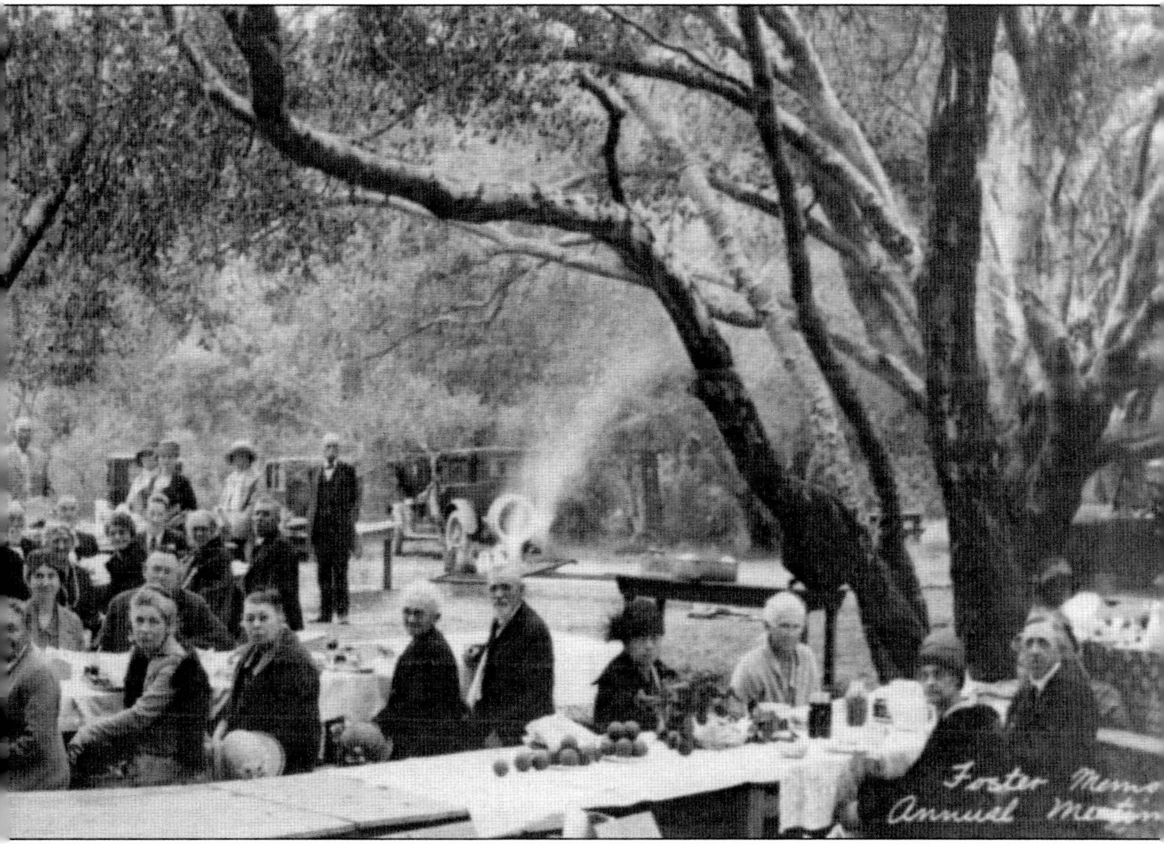

at Foster Memorial Park. It was the largest gathering of the pioneers since Bard's death. After that point, the pioneers held their annual meetings at the park, such as this meeting, which took place in 1925. Eventually, membership opened to women as the Pioneer Section of the Ebell Club of Santa Paula, which was responsible for the placement of the stone pioneer memorial. (Courtesy of the Museum of Ventura County.)

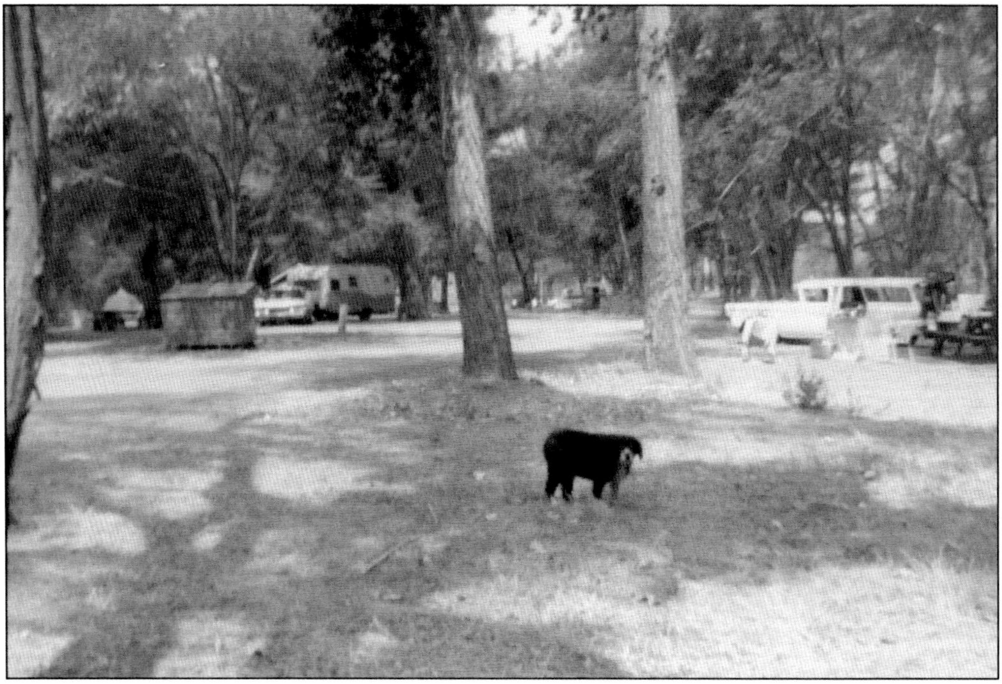

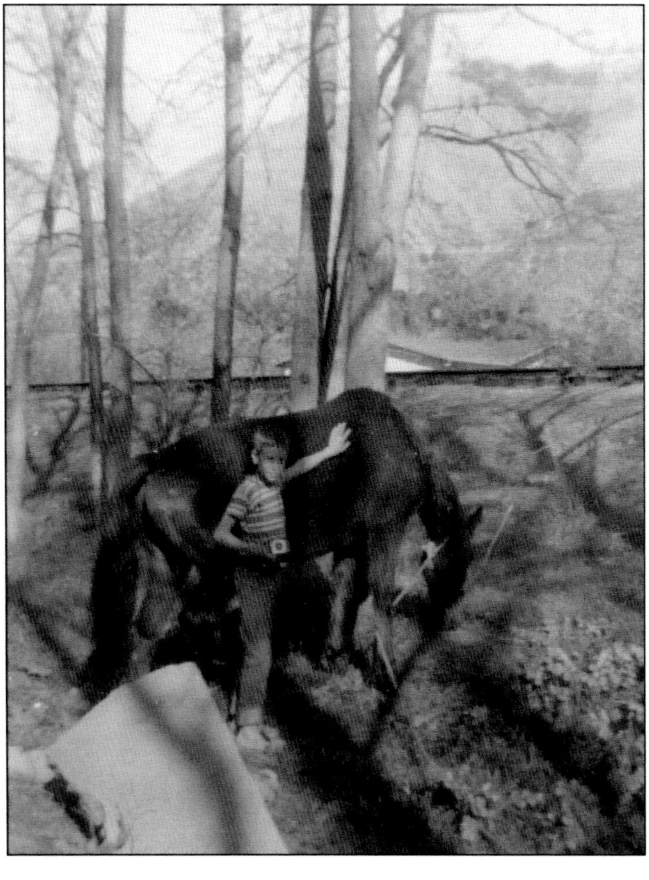

Before leash laws, the family pooch could roam as freely in the park as any camping human. In the background facing north, campers unhitch their trailers. This section of the park, located east of the river and west of the railroad, was the designated camping area. Occasionally, a free-roaming horse could be found grazing its way through the park. Pictured on the left, Joe Wayne Alferes poses with the unmanned horse while his cousin, Gene Hale, snaps a photograph. The boys loaded their Brownie cameras and took to capturing the days of their youth. Little did they know the historical significance of this 1965 image. Atop the embankment in this eastern view sits the railroad track, which separated the residential area from the park. Note the rooftop in the background. (Both, courtesy of Annie Cody.)

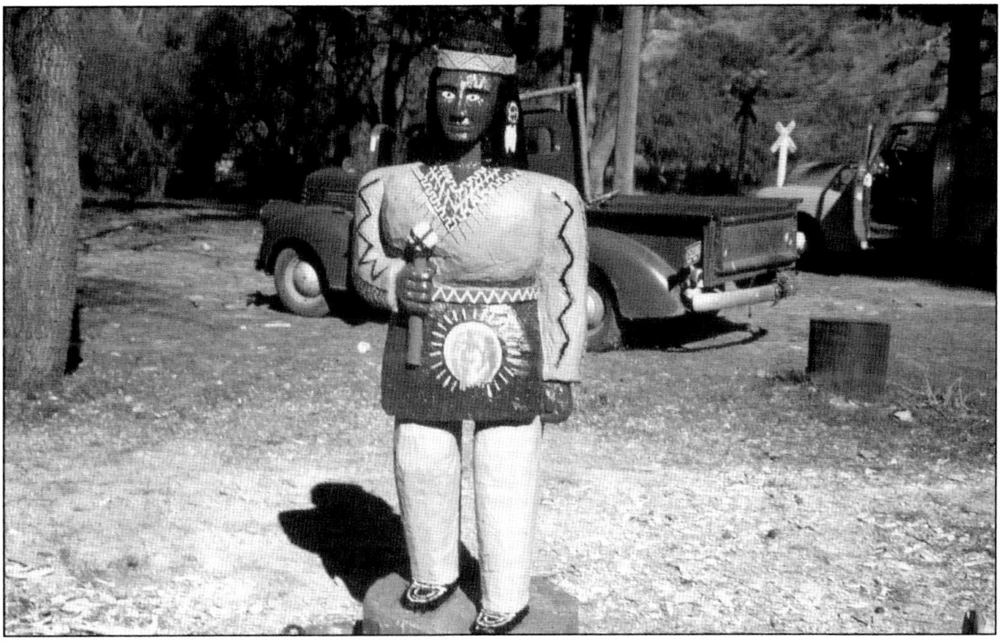

In the fall of 1960, anyone crossing over the Pacific Railroad from Ventura Avenue into the northern entrance of Foster Park Campgrounds would likely run into this bigger-than-life, freshly carved and painted native Indian statue (note the railroad crossing sign). Nomadic Cherokee Indian Ralph Gallagher, a third-generation wood sculptor, and his cousin, Gene Delaney, set up their workshop in the park for the winter. (Author's collection.)

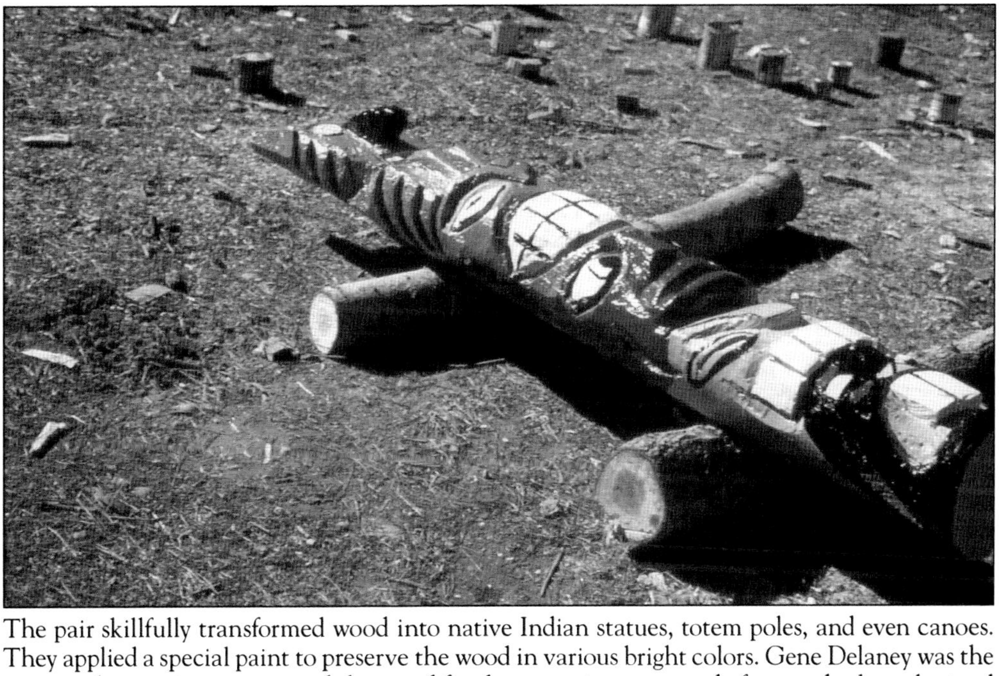

The pair skillfully transformed wood into native Indian statues, totem poles, and even canoes. They applied a special paint to preserve the wood in various bright colors. Gene Delaney was the totem pole–carving expert, and the wood for these carvings was made from cedar logs obtained in Placerville, California. The native Indian artwork was made to order and sold for $150 or more. (Author's collection.)

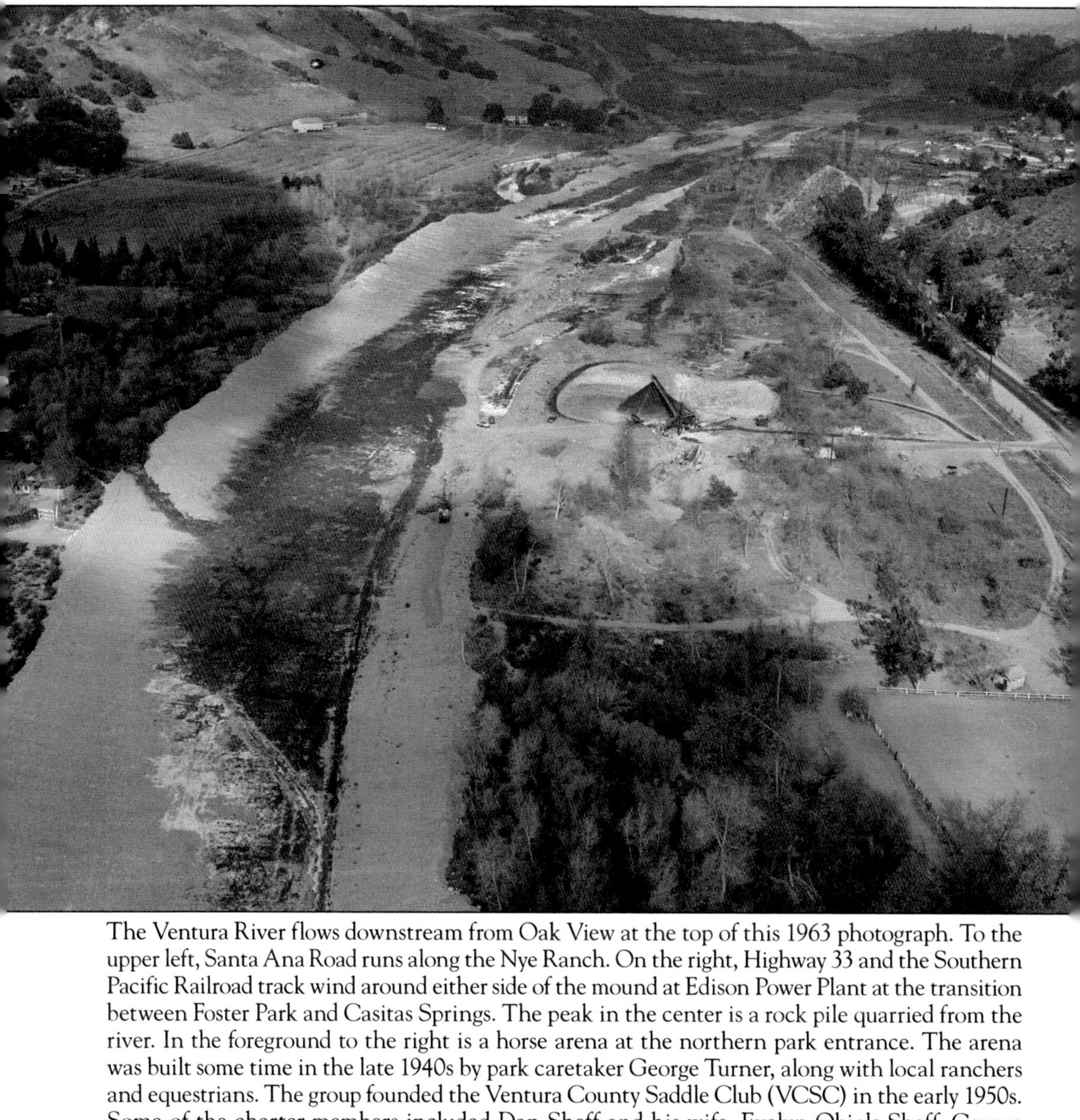

The Ventura River flows downstream from Oak View at the top of this 1963 photograph. To the upper left, Santa Ana Road runs along the Nye Ranch. On the right, Highway 33 and the Southern Pacific Railroad track wind around either side of the mound at Edison Power Plant at the transition between Foster Park and Casitas Springs. The peak in the center is a rock pile quarried from the river. In the foreground to the right is a horse arena at the northern park entrance. The arena was built some time in the late 1940s by park caretaker George Turner, along with local ranchers and equestrians. The group founded the Ventura County Saddle Club (VCSC) in the early 1950s. Some of the charter members included Dan Sheff and his wife, Evelyn Obiols Sheff, George Carpenter, George Payne, and sisters Babe and Kay Dent. Turner, too, had been one of the club's first presidents. The arena was used for classes and shows in Western horsemanship, trail riding, gymkhana, and barrel racing. (Photograph by Walt Dibblee©, courtesy of Steve Dibblee.)

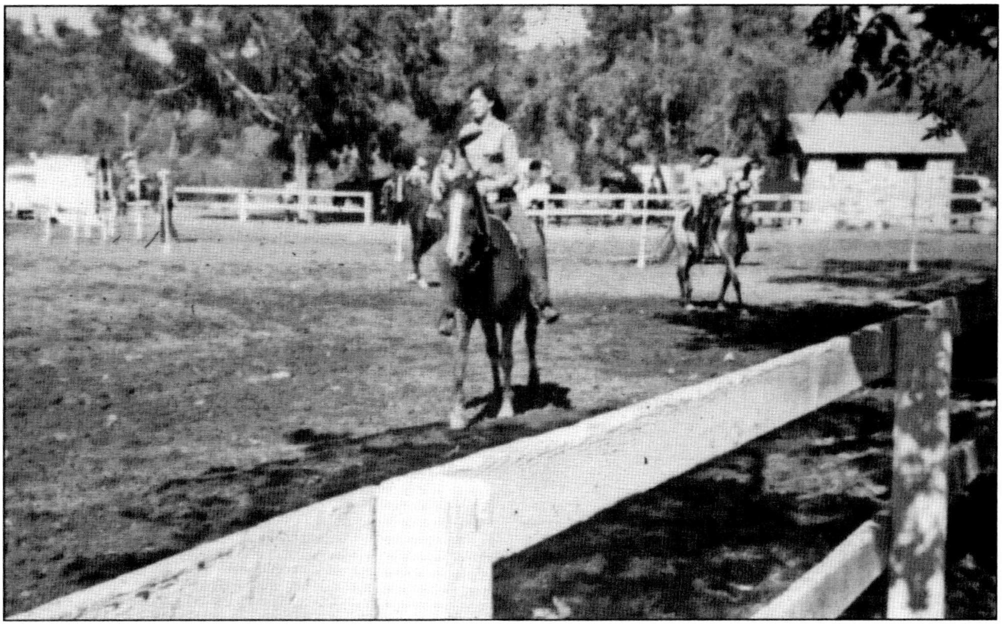

The notation on the back of the above 1965 photograph stated this was the first rodeo Burley Drew had ever watched. To Drew, a visitor from the East Coast, a rodeo is what it appeared to be. Other than barrel racing on a small scale, the arena did not host actual rodeo events. In this northern view, the stone building in the upper right background is a restroom, now used as a park storage shed. Looking west beyond the 1965 Ford Mustang parked along Highway 33 (below), riders line up inside the arena. At this point, contestants are either waiting for judges to award ribbons or to be picked out for a specific performance. (Both, courtesy of Drew Mashburn.)

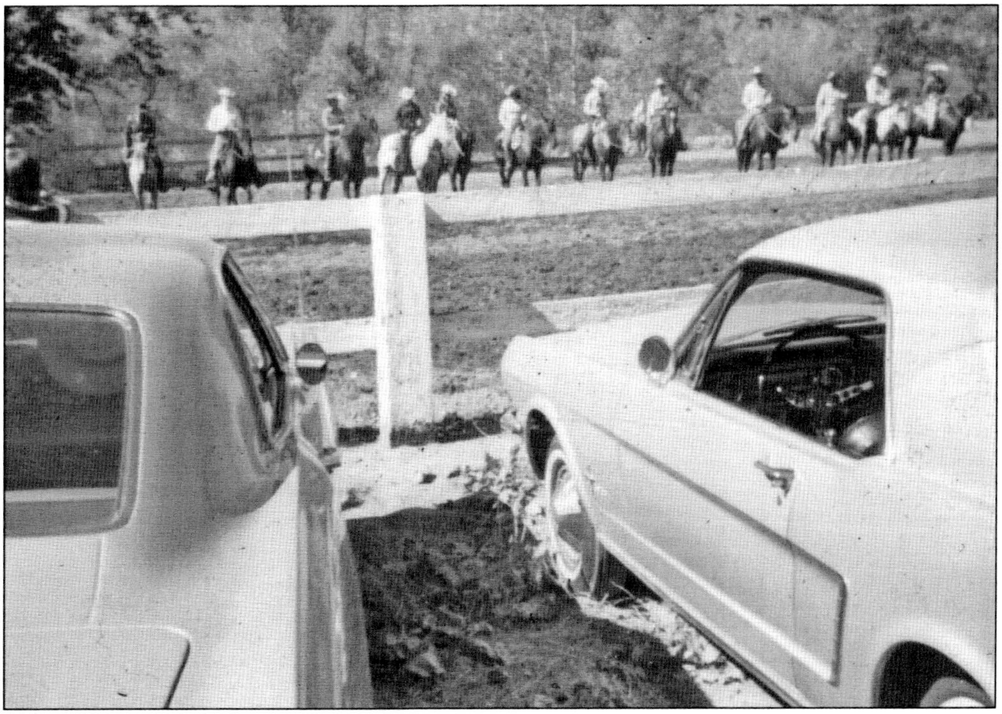

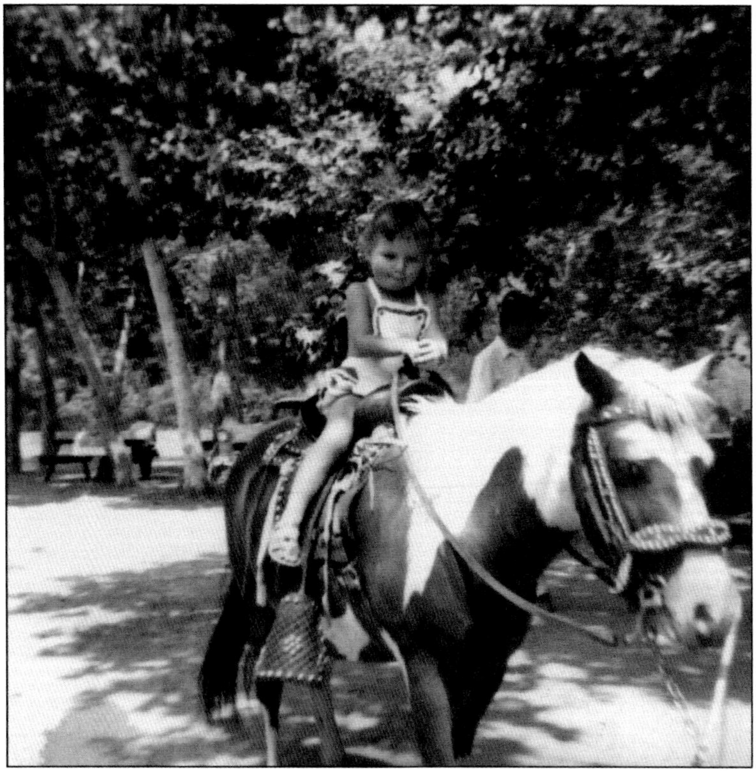

Folks sit under the familiar Foster Park sycamore trees while three-year-old Dianne Cook, the daughter of Casitas Springs residents Blaine and Joan Cook, gets a childhood thrill on a pony ride around the park's picnic area in the mid-1950s. In her teenage years, Dianne became a VCSC member. (Courtesy of Blaine E. Cook.)

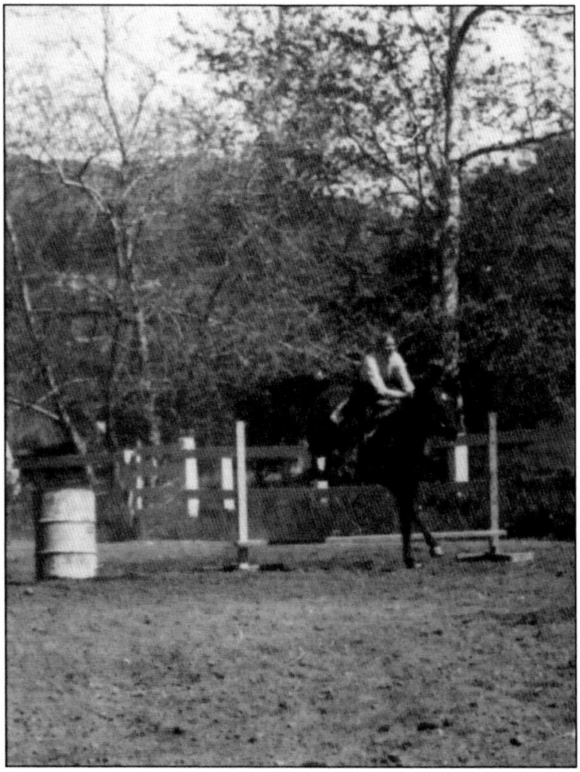

In this photograph from 1969, 16-year-old Dianne Cook makes a jump at the park arena. As a VCSC member, her favorite activity was barrel racing. She recalls that her fondest memories at the arena were the times her late father proudly watched as she was awarded trophies she won during such competitions. (Courtesy of Blaine E. Cook.)

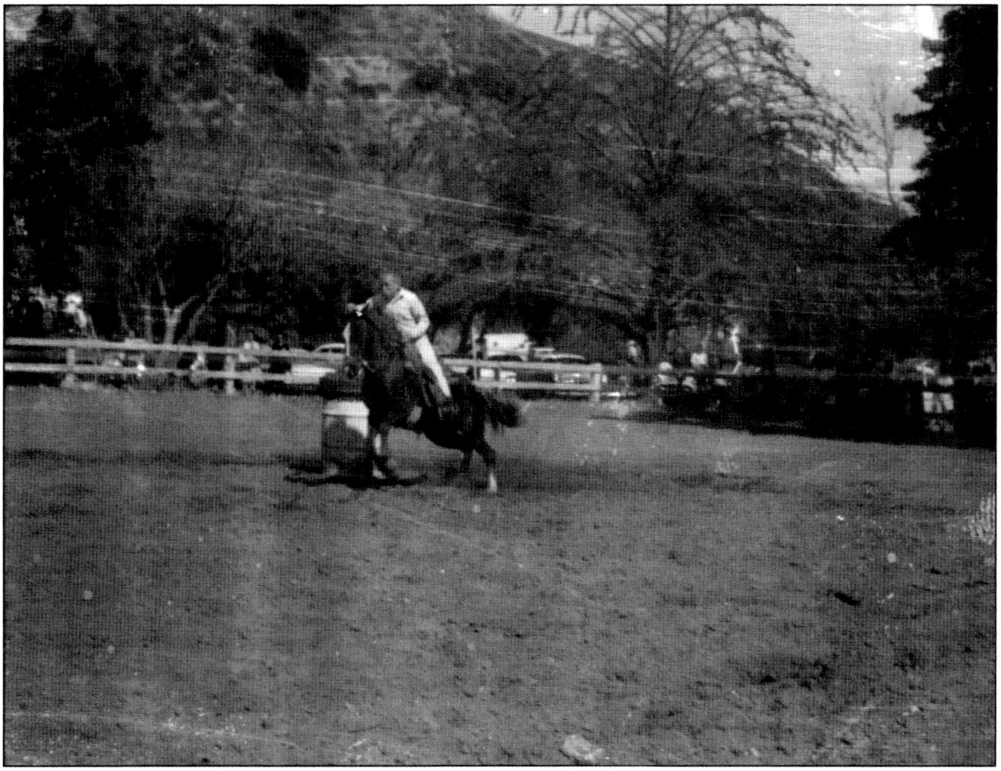

Great things can arise from humble beginnings, even in Foster Park; such is the story of this young VCSC member, Ted "Teddy" Robinson. Robinson, twice awarded the prestigious title of World's Greatest Horseman, started on a career path as a world champion cow horse trainer at age 10 when he began competing at the Foster Park arena. In the photograph above, spectators line around the arena fence as 11-year-old Robinson shows off his barrel-racing skill. His love of horses and dedication to the sport earned him many trophies in gymkhana and barrel racing competitions. At right, Robinson displays his trophies as he stands with prized pony Rex in a 1961 photograph taken at his Casitas Springs home on Park View Drive. (Both, courtesy of Ted Robinson.)

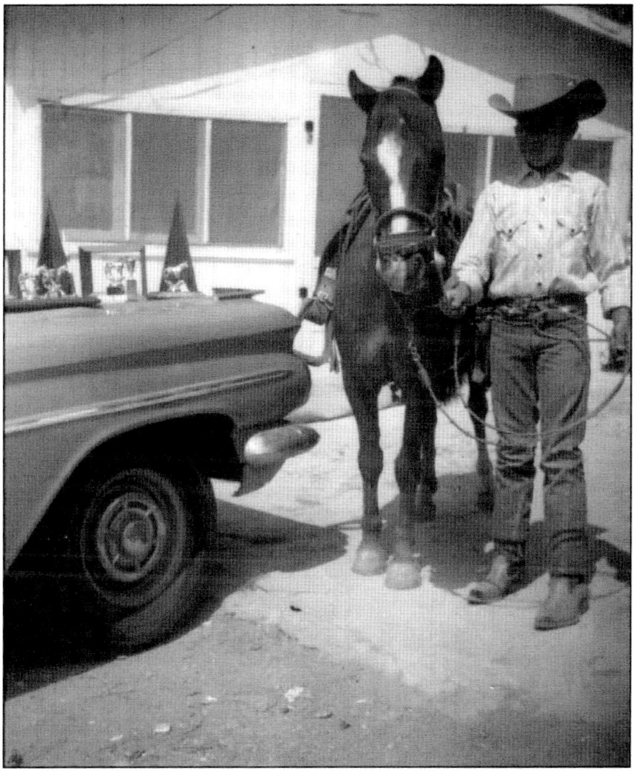

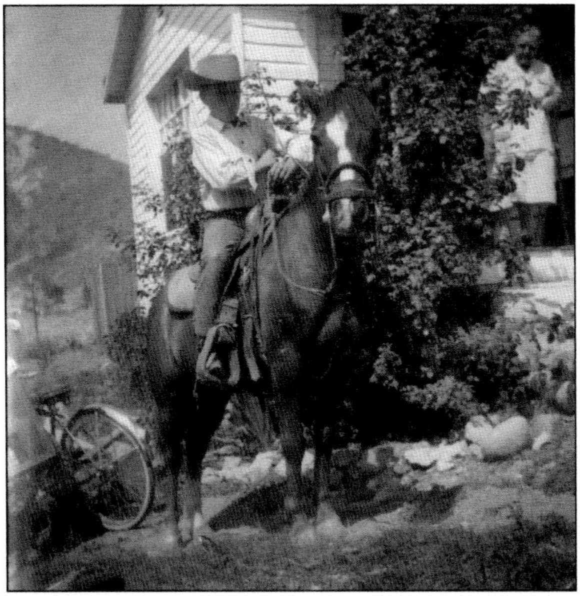

Ted Robinson's love for horses began as a toddler. To indulge his fascination, his parents purchased some ponies and set up a pony ring at their home in Oak View. He was a natural and later joined the VCSC. The Robinsons eventually moved to this Casitas Springs house. Robinson sits on his pony Rex while his grandmother Nora Goodall watches. (Courtesy of Ted Robinson.)

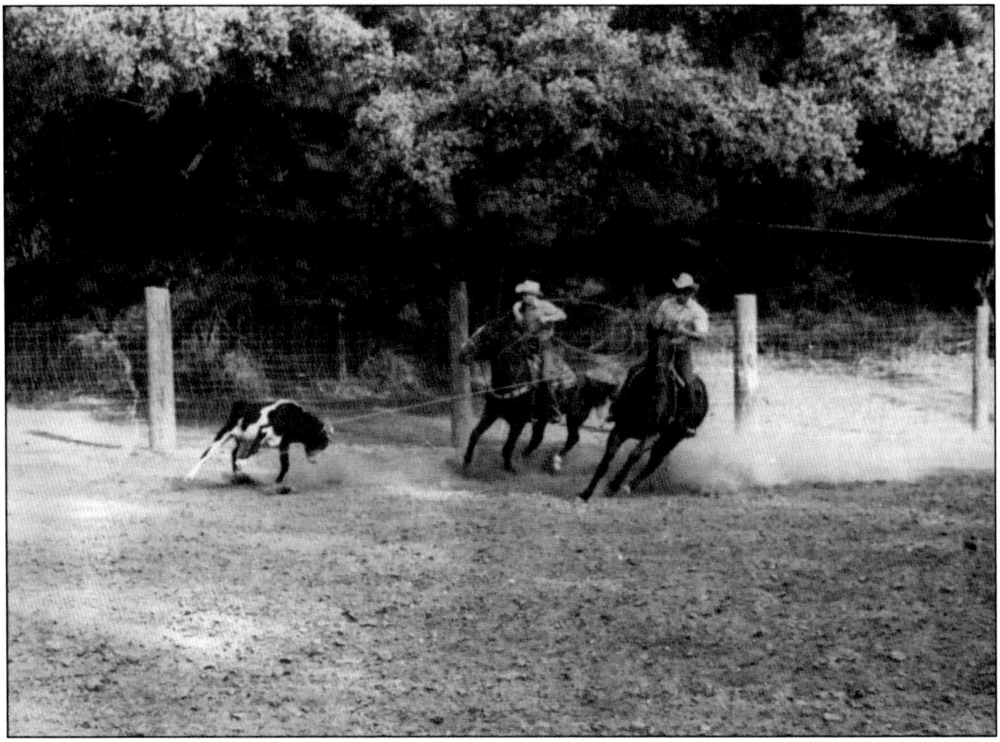

In the late 1970s, Robinson developed an interest in training reined cow horses. By the early 1980s, he purchased a ranch in Oak View, operating his own training stable. Robinson has since become a legend in the world of reined cow horse training, breaking records with seven NRCHA (National Reigned Cow Horse Association) Open Snaffle Bit Futurity World Championships and two World's Greatest Horseman titles. Robinson (right) and buddy Harvey Hooten are pictured here in 1969 roping at another Foster Park arena near the Casitas Dam. (Photograph by Sunny Northern, courtesy of Ted Robinson.)

Six

The Fun and Fury of the Ventura River

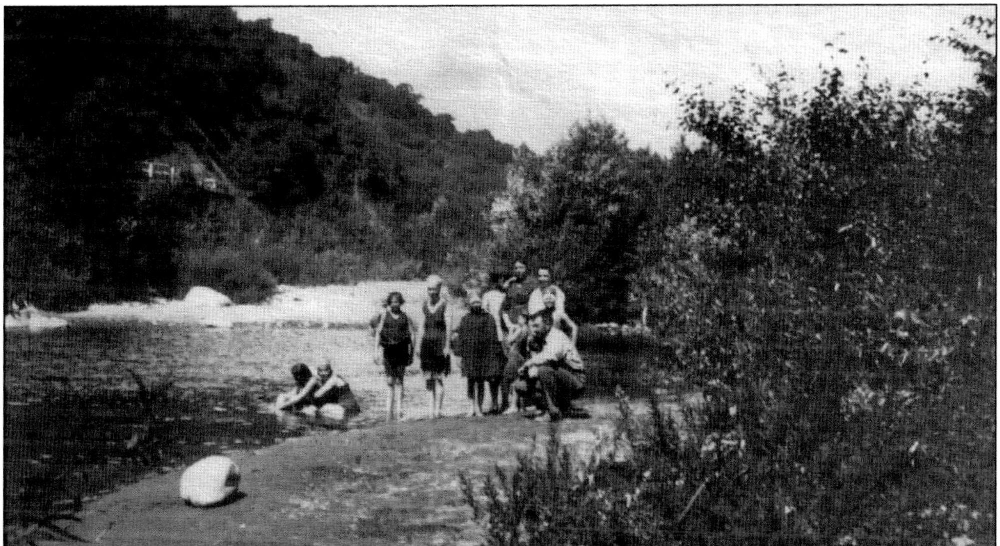

Before progress had made its mark in the Ventura River Valley, pools of water were wide and deep and provided more than just a picnic in the park. This pool was located on the banks of the river in Foster Memorial Park. In the right corner is a sandy area, something no longer seen along the river. A closer look reveals the face of a child in the bushes, pictured here around 1925. (Courtesy of Brian Aikens.)

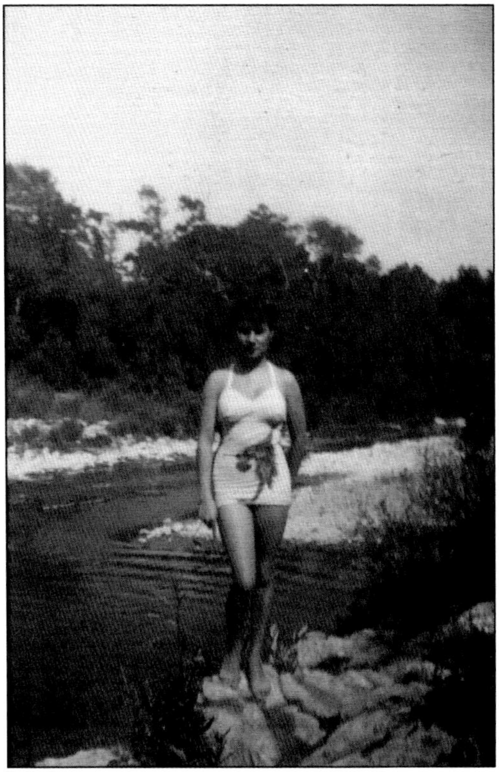

Pictured here around 1953 is Patricia "Pat" Turner, daughter of resident park caretaker George Turner. Pat stands at the bank of her favorite swimming hole, which was located south of the Foster Park Bridge. A narrow road on the west side of the bridge, running along Red Mountain, made this pool of refreshment easily accessible. (Courtesy of Barbara Turner Randall.)

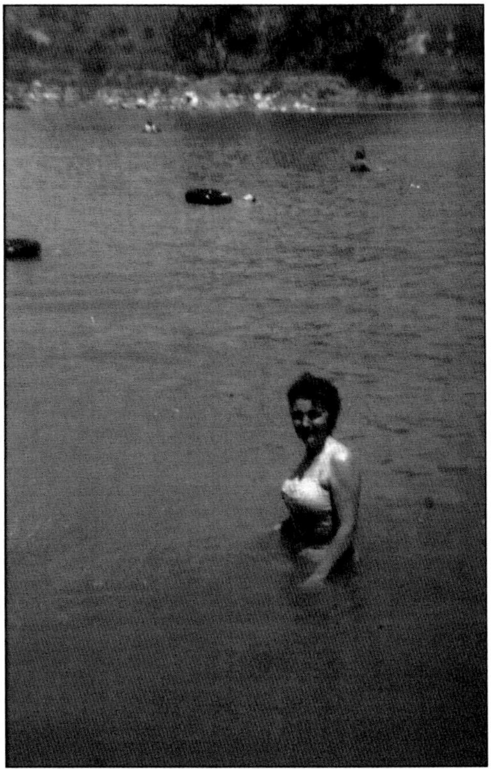

Bernice Cassidy stands waist deep in this Ventura River swimming hole north of Foster Park. In February 1962, the rain came pouring down. The five-day deluge brought 20 inches of rain, filling the nearly empty Casitas Lake bed with 53,000 acre-feet of water and overflowing the banks of the river. (Courtesy of Vicky Beria-Jefferson.)

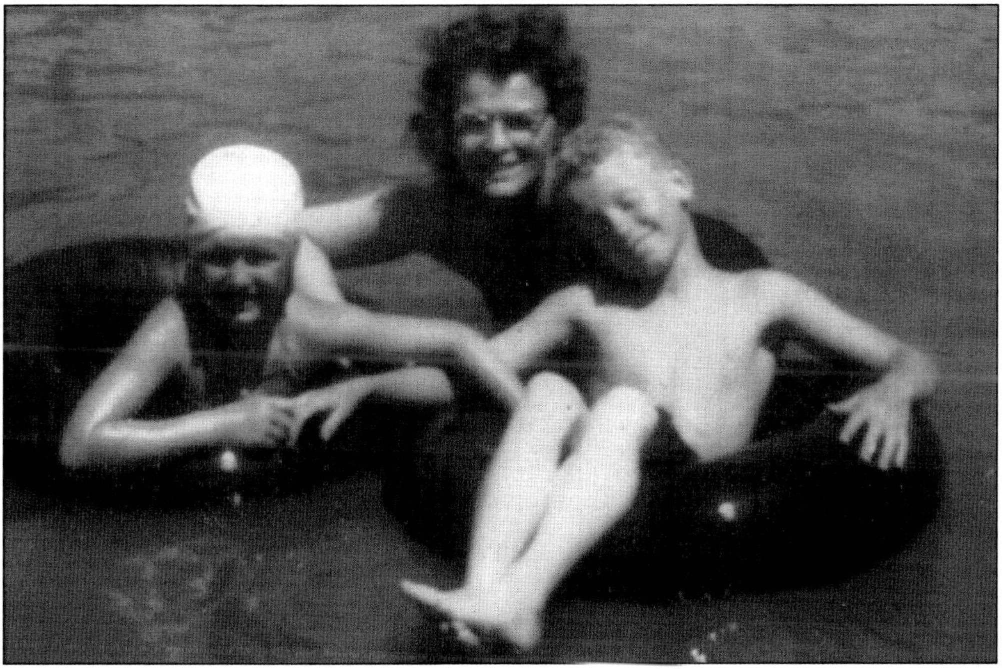

The rainfall of February brings an expression of summer bliss to young Bobby Flowers as he savors the moment. Bobby and his sister Vicky take a break from tubing the river for a memorable family photograph with their mother, Arlene Flowers. Vicky is wearing a swimming cap, something not seen too often anymore. (Courtesy of Vicky Beria-Jefferson.)

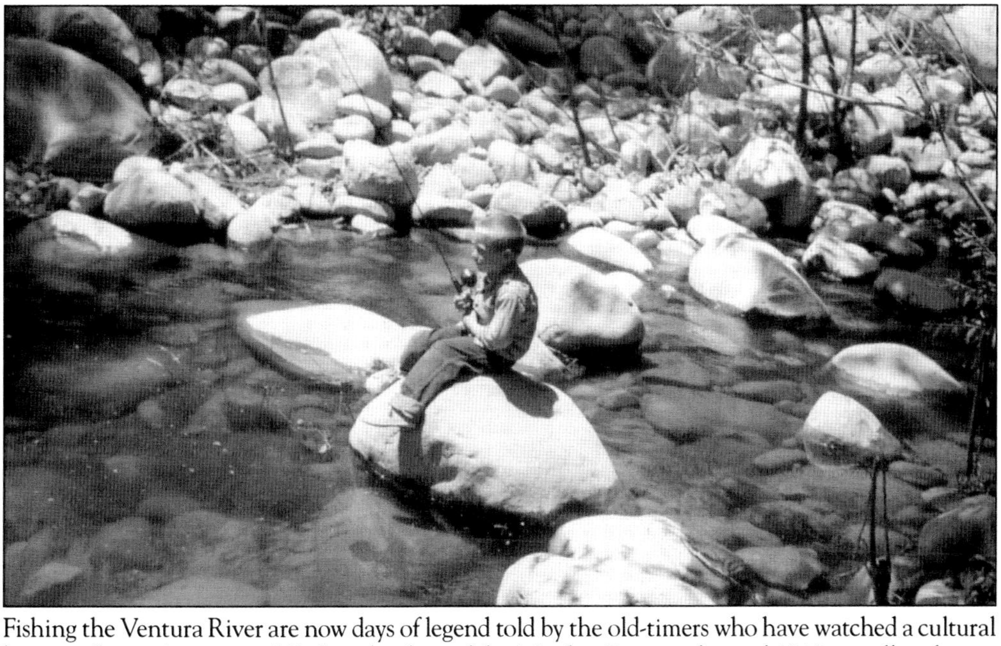

Fishing the Ventura River are now days of legend told by the old-timers who have watched a cultural heritage "gone down river." Before the days of the Matilija Dam in the mid-1940s, steelhead trout made their way upstream from the ocean to spawn. The Matilija Creek (above), a tributary of the Ventura River, saw its share of steelhead. Unfortunately, the young angler in this 1963 photograph, Jeff Pluim, never did. (Photograph by Joseph P. Pluim, author's collection.)

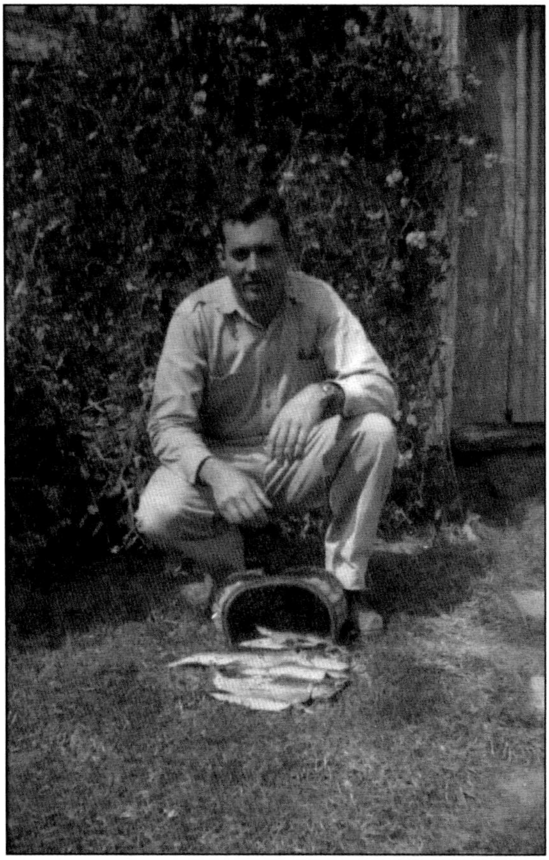

Born in 1918, lifelong Ventura resident John Colla spent many hours fishing in the Ventura River. His rookie angler days began as a young lad on the Ventura pier. As he sharpened his skills, he fished his way up the Ventura River. In the early years, Colla recalls, fishing was only allowed up the river to the railroad bridge at the end of Main Street. A popular spot in that area was called the Dump Hole, named for its proximity to the city dump. In the 1930s, legal fishing was opened up to the Foster Park Bridge. It was there that Colla found his favorite fishing spot below the bridge. Colla displays his catch of young trout in the 1946 photograph on the left. Pictured below, overlooking the Foster Park bridge is a downstream view of the river during a rainy season in 1962. (Left, courtesy of John Colla; below, author's collection.)

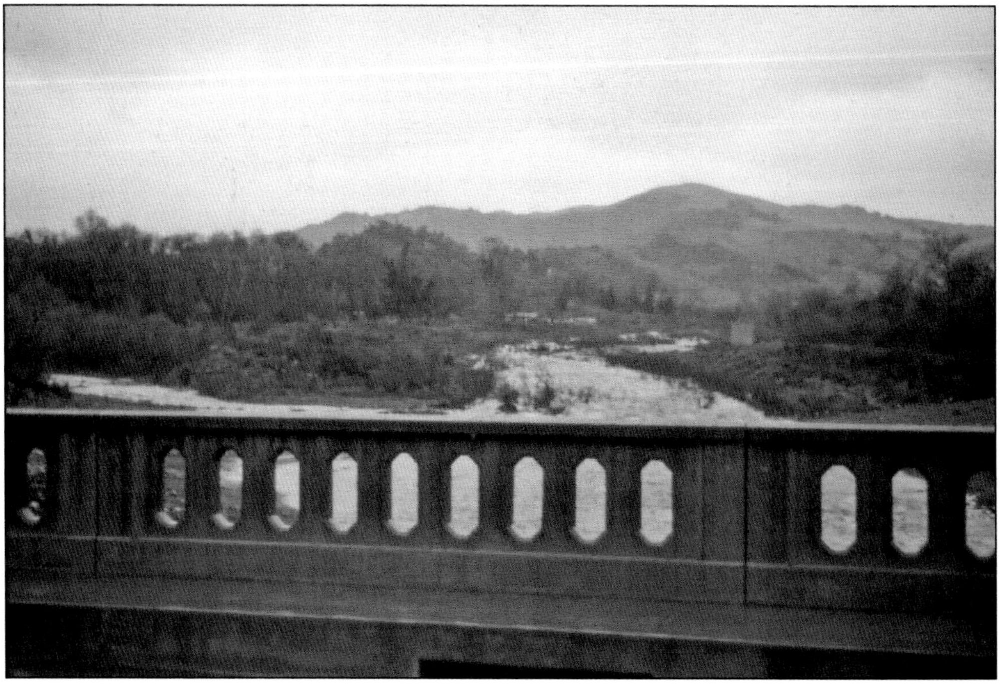

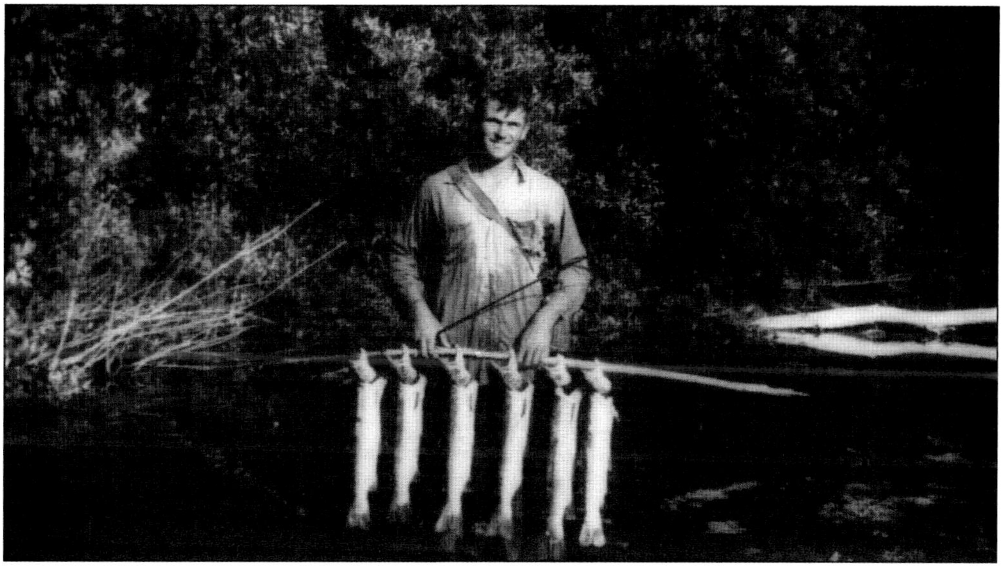

Edgar Henke, standing in the Ventura River near the Foster Park Bridge, displays his catch of six steelhead trout. Henke, a former San Francisco 49er and former Ventura resident, recalls his early years fishing the river. On the first of May, when rainbow trout season opened, all a child needed was a note from a parent to be excused from school to fish on opening day. (Courtesy of Edgar Henke.)

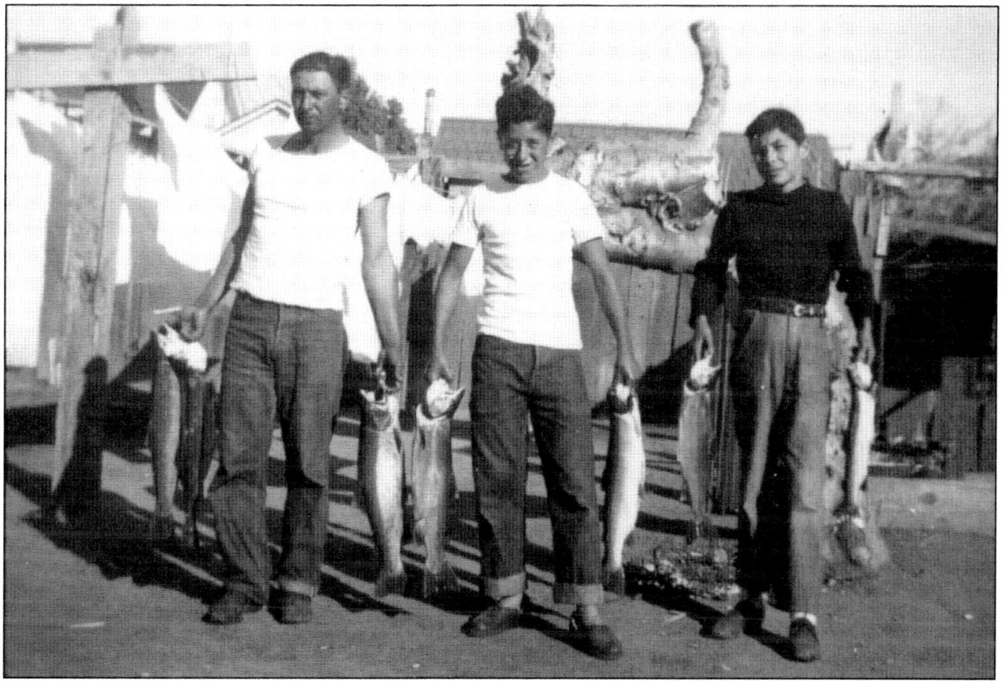

John Lorenzana (far right) remembers those free May 1 get-out-of-school days. If a student was absent on that day, the school truant officer, Red Connel, would show up at the fishing site to make sure an absent student was fishing and not ditching. Connel, an angler himself, taught fly-tying lessons after school. Pictured in this 1946 photograph with Lorenzana are his father, Victor Lorenzana (left), and cousin Ed Romero. (Courtesy of John Lorenzana.)

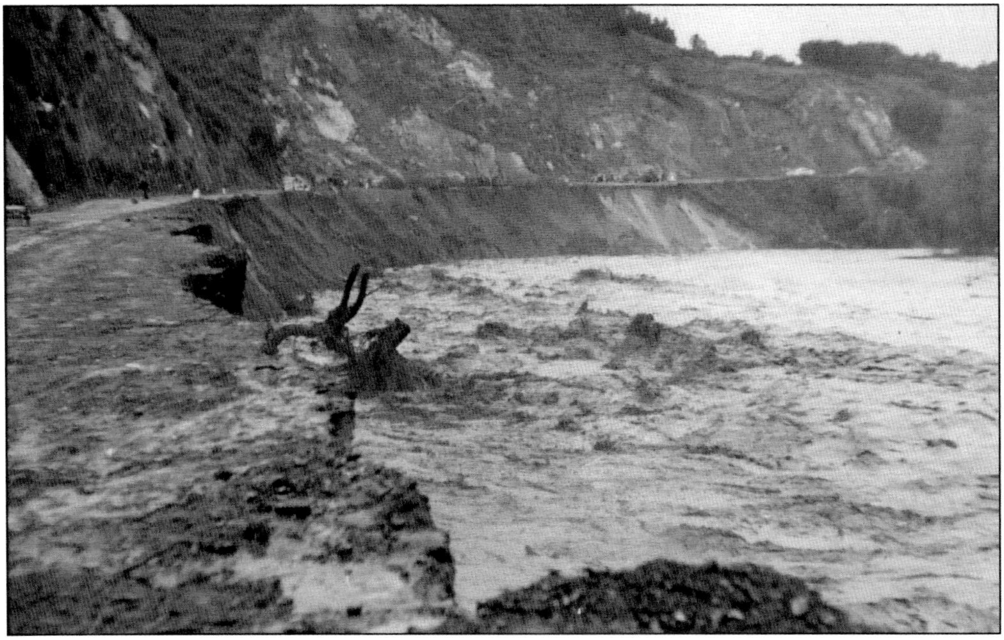

This body of water bears more resemblance to an ocean than a creek. In March 1938, a series of storms bombarded Southern California, causing major damage to Ventura County. In the photograph above, onlookers line the Arnaz Grade on Highway 33 in awe as they watch the swollen San Antonio Creek violently churn its way downstream. San Antonio Creek originates on the southerly slopes of the Topa Topa Mountains and joins the Ventura River and Coyote Creek west of Highway 33, about two miles north of Foster Park. With the convergence of three streams near Foster Park, the flooded residence pictured below is fortunate to have a low watermark around its exterior. It is to be hoped the residents had a rowboat as well. (Both, courtesy of the Leslie Ray Moore family.)

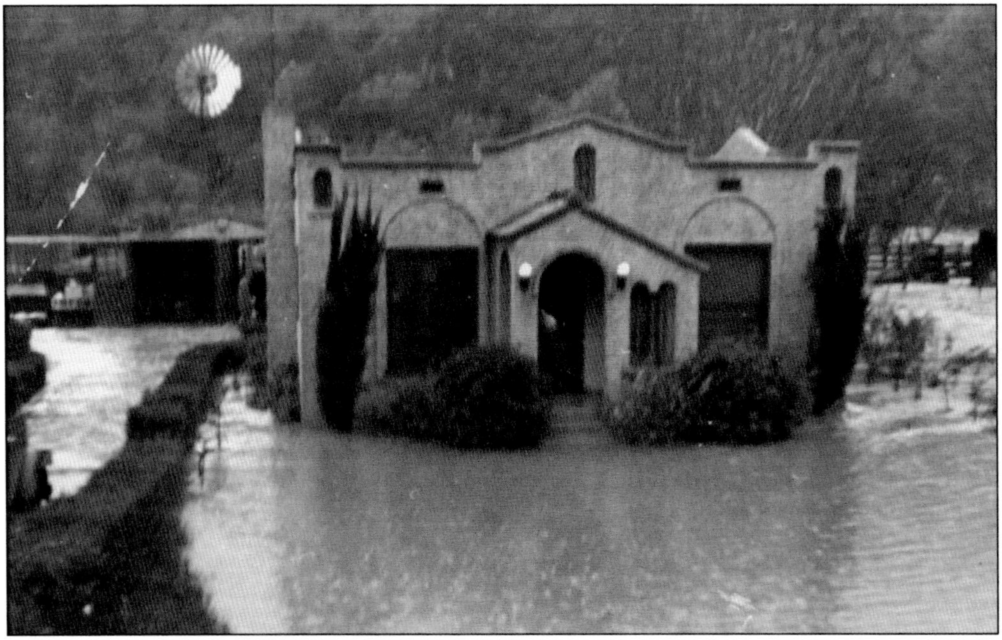

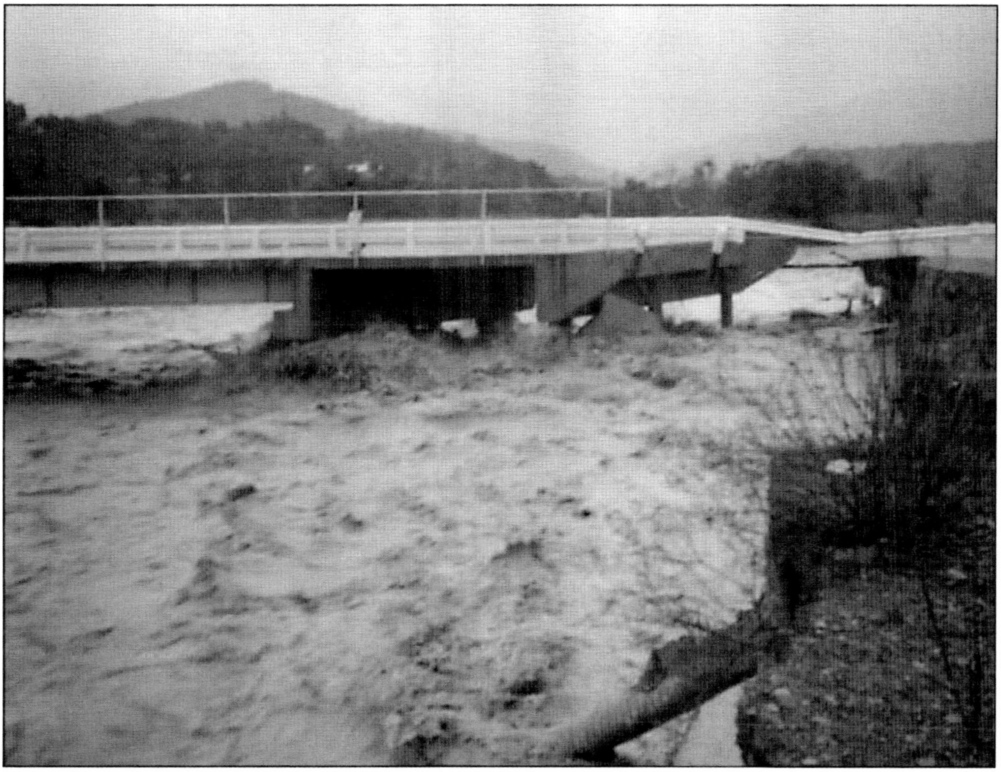

In 1969, once again, the heavens opened and poured down a rain of monstrous proportions, causing one of the biggest disasters in the county's history as tropic storms pounded the area. Creeks and streams burst, and the Ventura River went wild, taking out anything standing in its way, including the two bridges in these photographs. The bridge above is located on Highway 150, northeast of Lake Casitas. Pictured at right, the Santa Ana Bridge, located in Oak View, was reduced to an island. It was reported that sightseers walked out on the bridge while one side was still intact. Floodwaters surrounded the bridge and took off that end, leaving them stranded. They were later rescued by helicopter. (Both, courtesy of Kathy Hartman.)

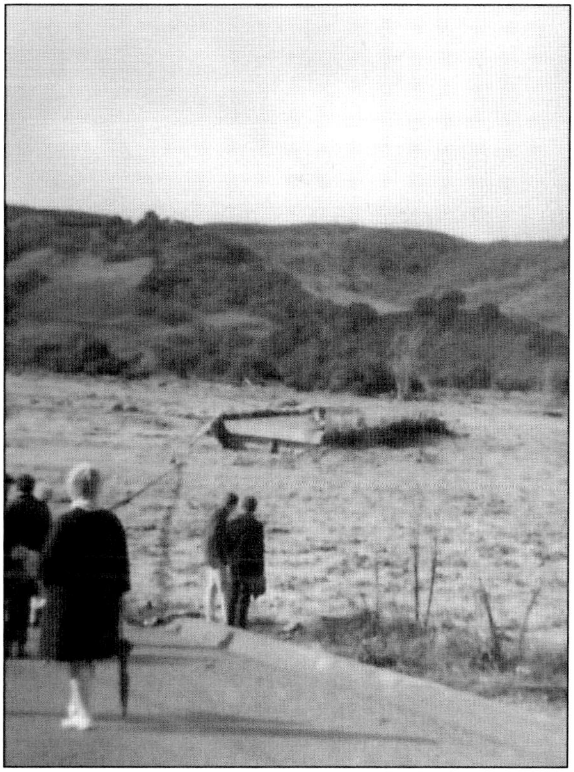

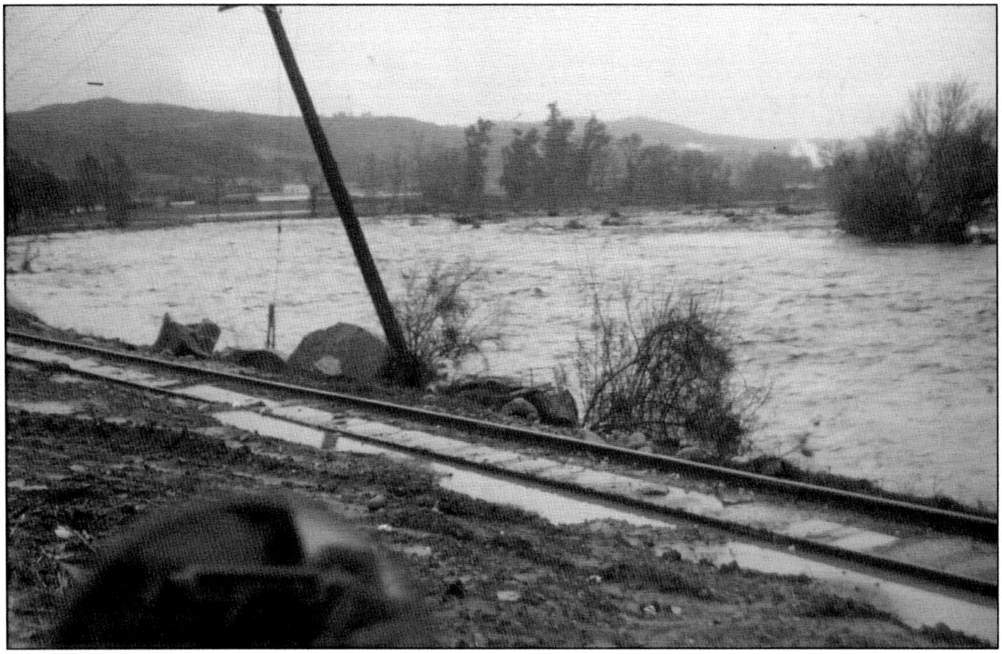

Downstream in Foster Park, it does not look like the train will be making its daily run to Ojai—it never did again after it was undermined in areas by ravaging flood waters. In the left foreground, an image of Mike Pulido Jr. appears in the side-view mirror of a car as he snaps a shot of the devastation. (Courtesy of the Mike Pulido Sr. family.)

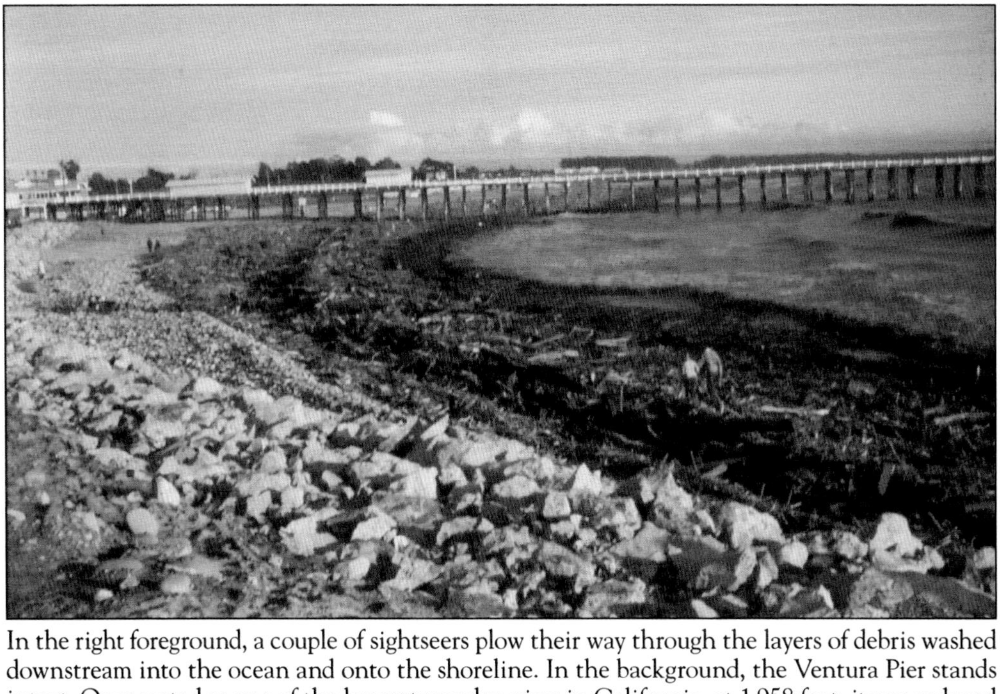

In the right foreground, a couple of sightseers plow their way through the layers of debris washed downstream into the ocean and onto the shoreline. In the background, the Ventura Pier stands intact. Once noted as one of the longest wooden piers in California, at 1,958 feet, it was reduced over the years from storm damage and a lack of funding to restore its length. (Courtesy of the Mike Pulido Sr. family.)

Seven

The Casitas Dam Undertaking

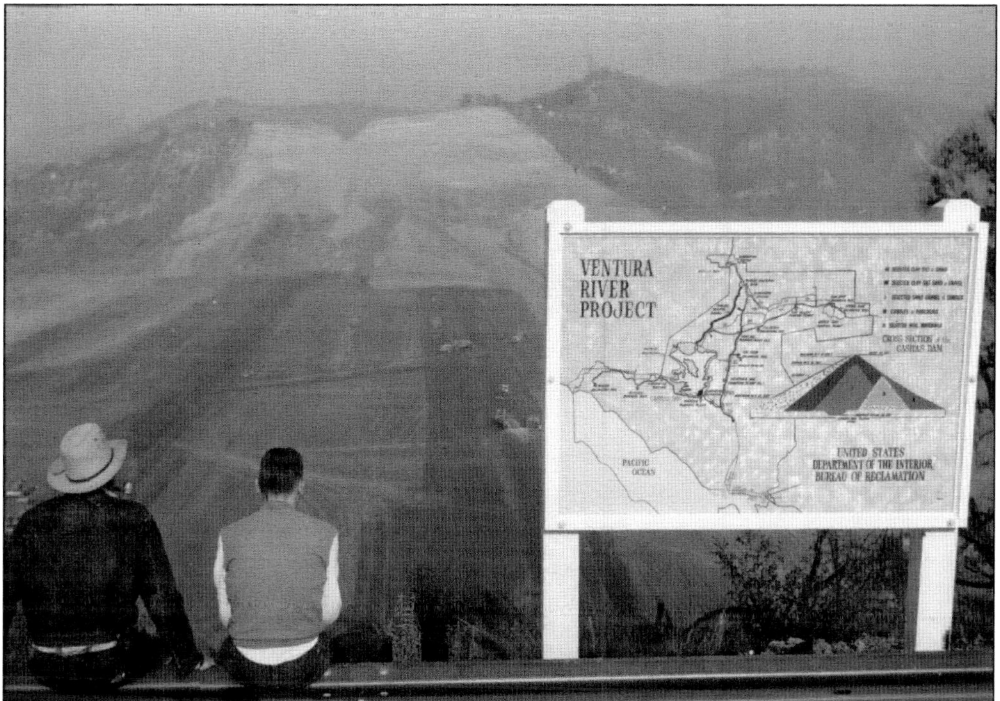

To provide water for agriculture and personal use, the Ventura River Water Project was formed by the US Department of the Interior Bureau of Reclamation in 1956. Heavy equipment moved 9,500,000 cubic yards of dirt, gravel, and sand to create one of the world's largest earth-filled dams with a 254,000-acre-foot capacity. Spectators are perched at the observation point provided along with a cross-section sign for public viewing. (Courtesy of the Casitas Municipal Water District [CMWD].)

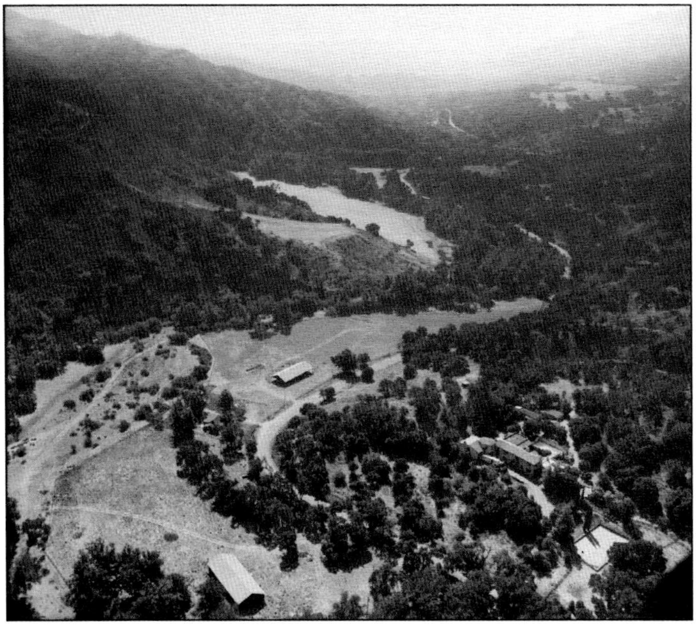

Casitas Pass Road winds its way through the Santa Ana Valley in this 1956 aerial photograph facing northwest. To the right is the historical Rancho Casitas Hacienda, owned by Walter and Edith Hoffman, and the site for the new Lake Casitas Dam. The ranch bred workhorses and racehorses and once provided a stagecoach roadhouse that supplied fresh team horses for coaches traveling along Casitas Pass Road. (Photograph by Walt Dibblee©, courtesy of Steve Dibblee.)

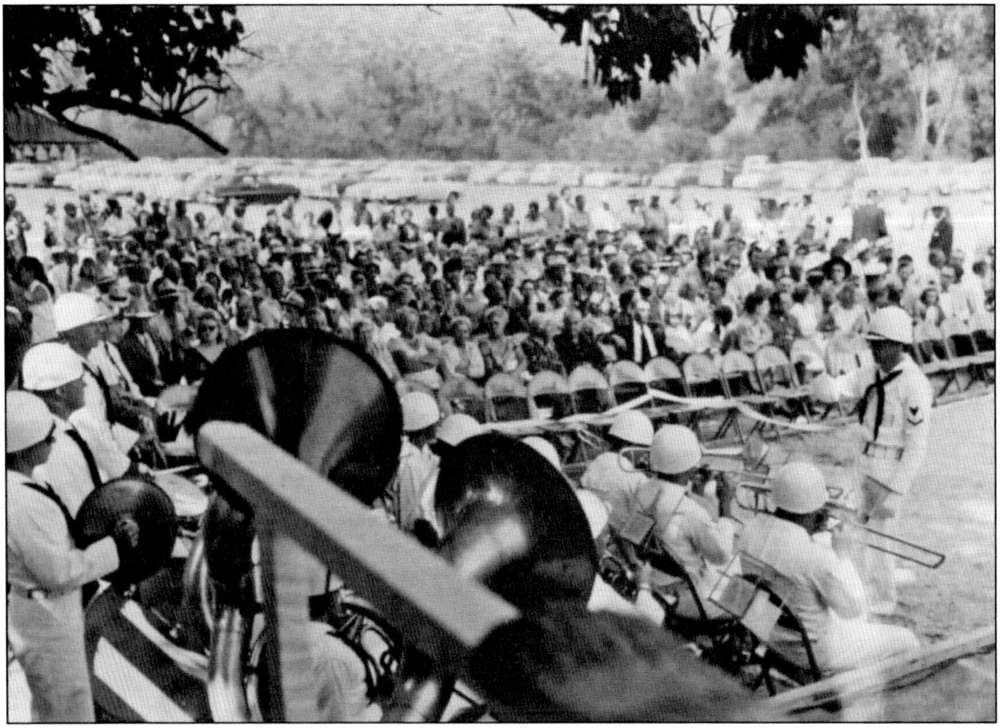

The sound of horns, cymbals, and drums of the naval band in the foreground provides the pomp to set off the Ventura River Water Project ground-breaking ceremony held on August 27, 1956. In the background, parked cars and an audience fill the space once occupied by the stately Rancho Casitas. (Courtesy of CMWD.)

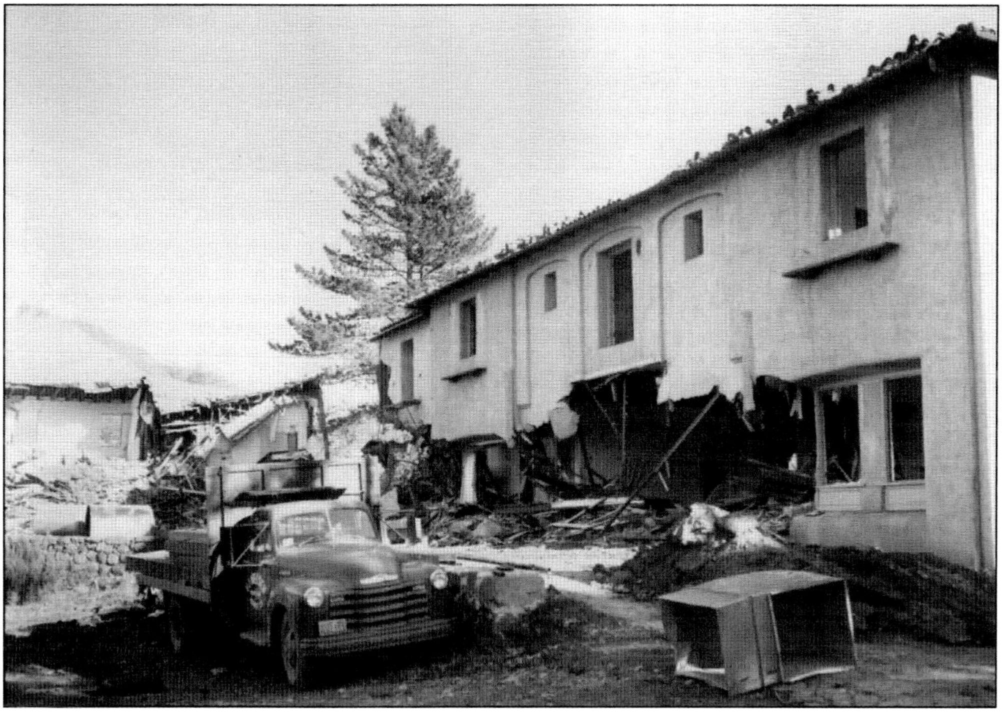

The Hoffman Ranch house was used as an office during construction of the dam. Since it was in the lake bed, it had to be removed upon completion. Before the house was dismantled, anything of historical or architectural value was removed. Historical items such as brick tiles were given back to the Ventura Mission, from which they originated. Architectural items became property of the contractor to be sold. To keep the lake bed clear of debris, homes such as the Hoffmans' hacienda were burned after dismantling. (Both, courtesy of CMWD.)

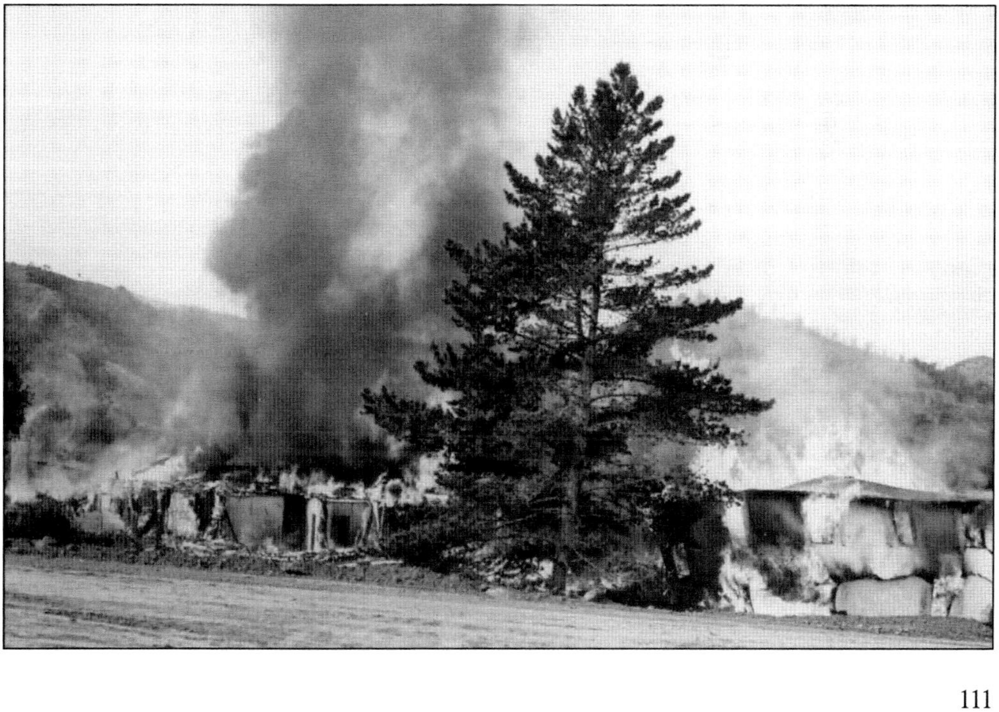

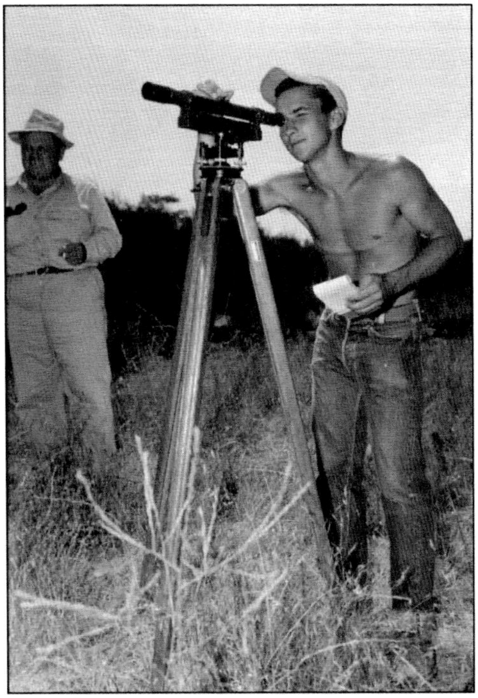

The Ventura River Project was ideal for the summer training of budding engineers. In this August 1957 photograph, Joseph Hill soaks in the warmth and sun of the Santa Ana Valley while assisting engineers. Hill was a second-time summer student engineer trainee of the US Bureau of Reclamation and a civil engineering major at the University of Michigan. (Courtesy of CMWD.)

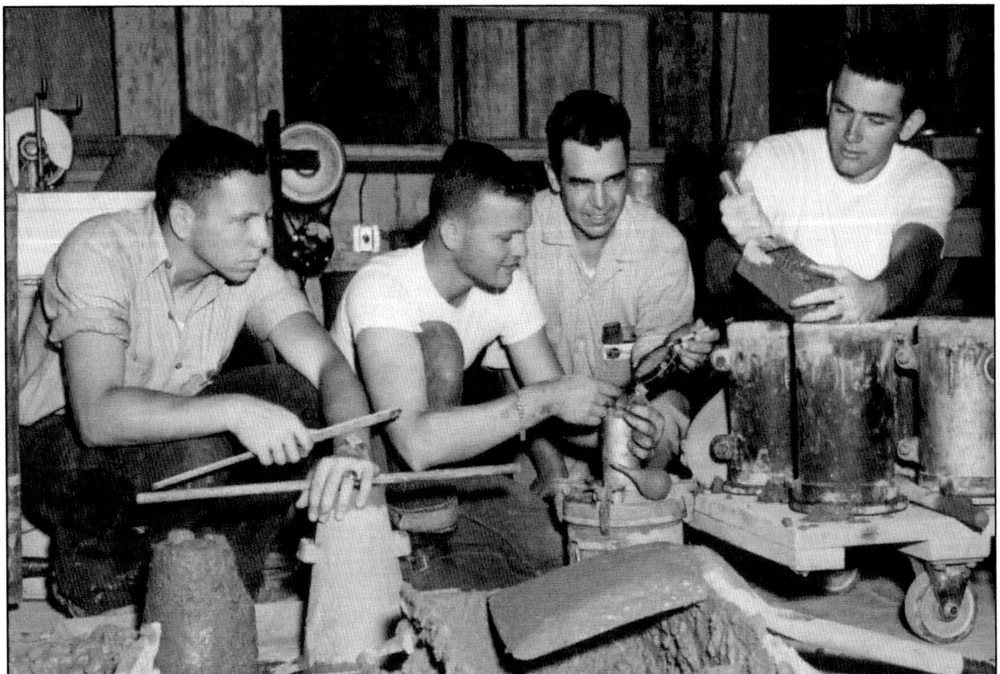

Spending the summer months working in the Ventura River Project Earth and Concrete Laboratory, student trainees receive instruction from concrete specialist Roderick Bliss (third from left). Students pictured in this July 1957 photograph are, from left to right, Robert Keck (Stevens Institute of Technology, New York), Currie Lockett (Stanford, California), and Larry Vinsonhaler (College of the Pacific, California). (Courtesy of CMWD.)

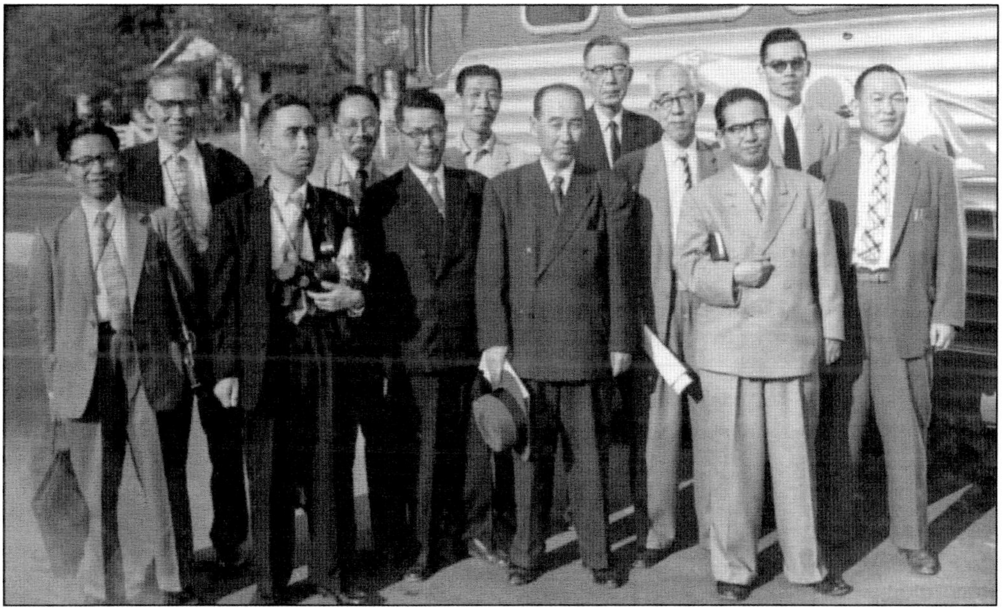

The Ventura River Project created international interest, bringing visitors from all over the globe for training and observation purposes. This group of men who visited the project in 1958 are composed of engineers, industrialists, and businessmen from Japan, known as the Land Development for Irrigation Team: Agriculture, Forestry, and Fisheries Productivity Conference of Japan. (Courtesy of CMWD.)

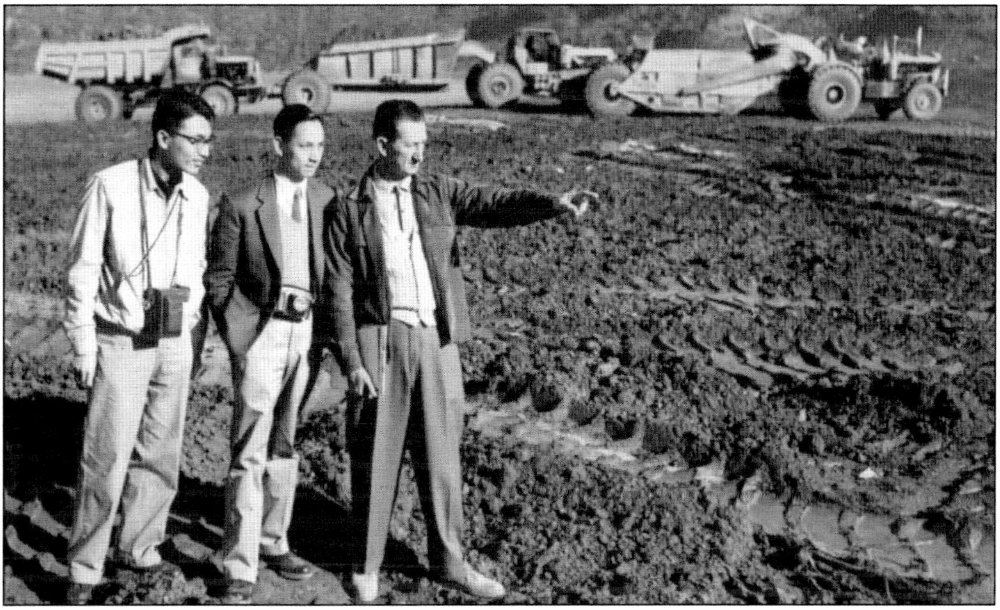

Earth movers line the background of this January 1958 photograph of the dam construction site. To the right is US Bureau of Reclamation engineer for the Ventura River Project John Corwin. Engineers Ru-Huo Hsu (left) and Ta-Ying Fan (center) from the Shimen Dam Project of Taipei, Taiwan, stand cameras ready as Corwin gives a tour around the construction area. Other visitors to the project site came from Turkey, Ethiopia, India, Iraq, Australia, and Venezuela. (Courtesy of CMWD.)

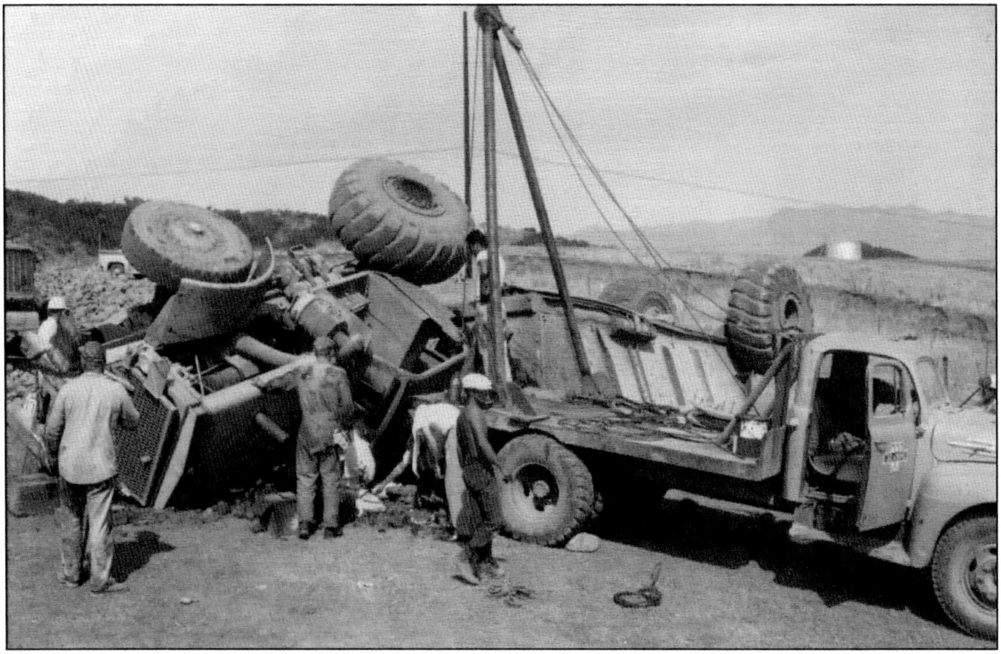

Large undertakings are not always executed without misfortune. In this photograph, a rescue operation is in progress to free the pinned driver of this overturned dump truck. Pictured is a winch truck attempting to lift the truck cab enough to free the driver's leg, which was pinned under the top of the truck's cab. (Courtesy of CMWD.)

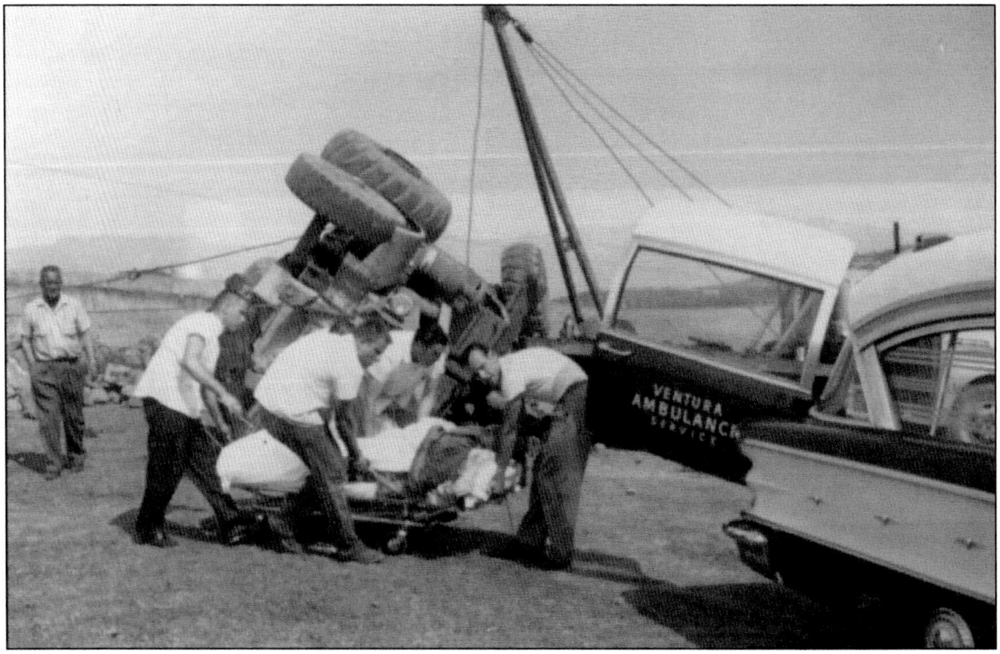

The victim, Oscar Kauffman, was pinned under the overturned 17-cubic-yard bottom-dump truck for more than an hour. After being freed from under the cab, he was moved to the waiting ambulance. Though he survived the accident, unfortunately, Kauffman's left leg was amputated up to the hip. (Courtesy of CMWD.)

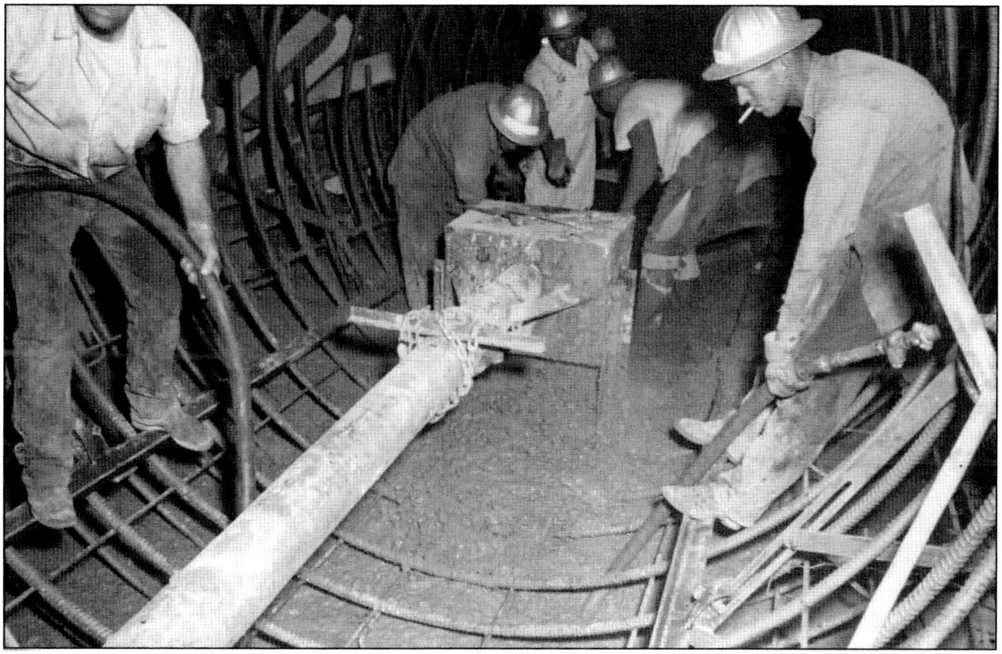

In this photograph, workers set forms for the first concrete pouring stage in the outlet works gate chamber. This outlet structure was built under the dam and is part of the waterworks system. As valves are opened at different levels, water from the lake enters into the pipeline system that leads to the kitchen sink. (Courtesy of CMWD.)

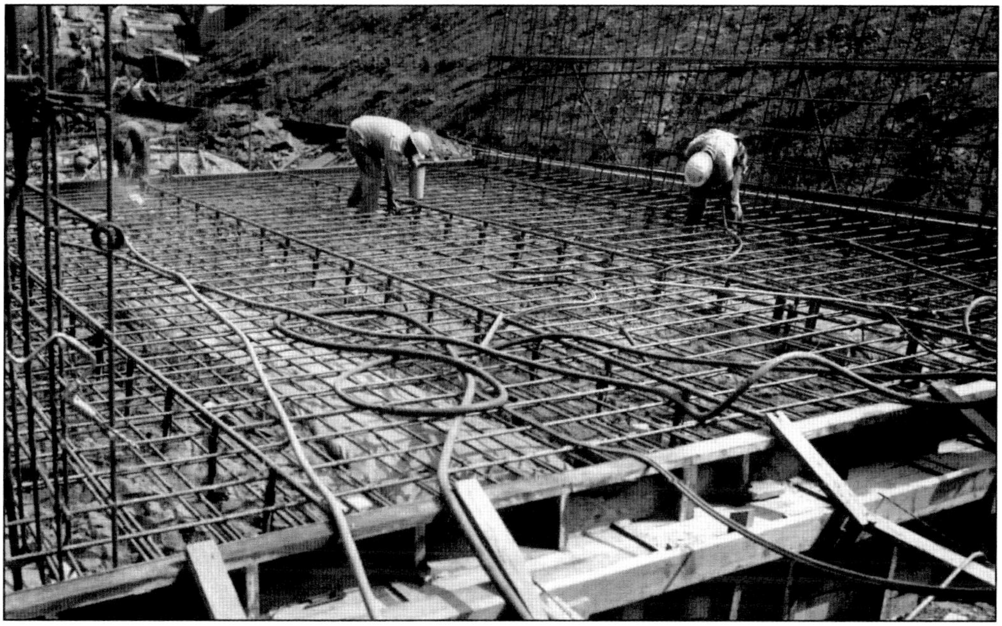

Workers lay rebar before pouring the cement slab for this chlorination facility, used for disinfecting water. As water is released into the pipeline system, it travels along chlorination facilities, which are located at crucial points of the pipeline. The facilities are equipped with valves and tubes that contain chlorine injected into the water at a controlled rate based upon water usage. (Courtesy of CMWD.)

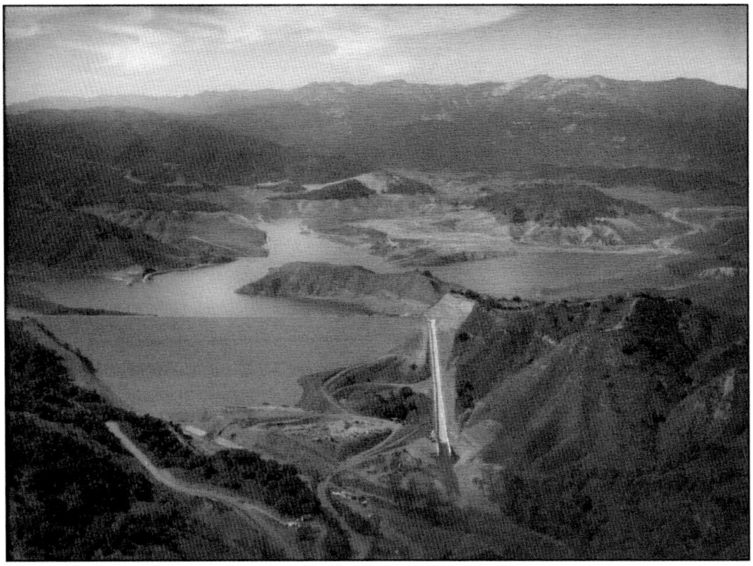

The dam was completed in 1958 but remained virtually empty for nearly four years. Fortunately, in February 1962, storms dumped 20 inches of rain within a five-day period, filling the lake with 53,000 acre-feet of water. In the center of this image, vehicles travel along the axis of the dam. (Photograph by Walt Dibblee©, courtesy of Steve Dibblee.)

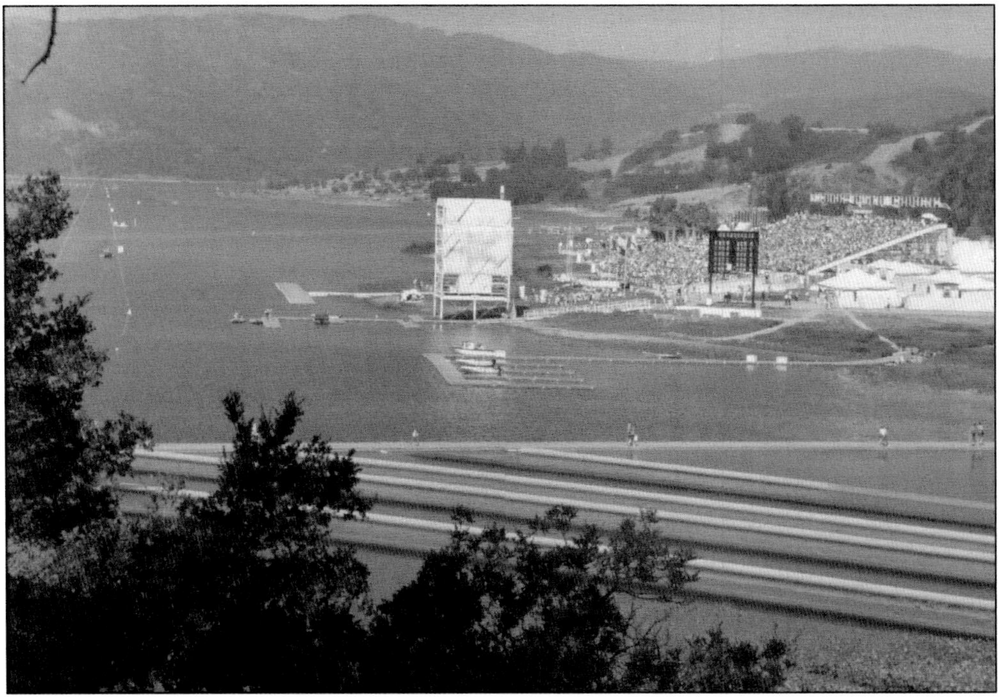

In 1984, Los Angeles hosted the Summer Olympics. The Casitas Water Board was approached by the Olympic committee to host the canoeing and rowing events. After careful negotiations, the board agreed. In the center of this image stands an Olympic sign before a full grandstand to the right. A jet-float bridge was also installed. The lake hosted a total of 14 events, and everything was removed afterward. (Courtesy of CMWD.)

Eight

State Division of Highways, an Archeological Dig, and Signs of the Time

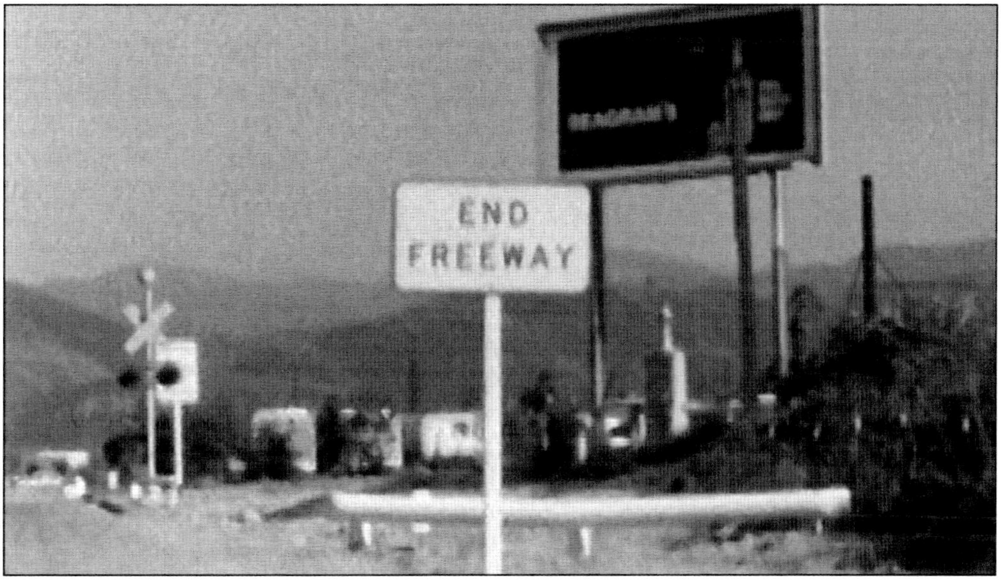

As the population growth after the Ventura Avenue oil boom continued to expand northward into the Ojai Valley, so did the need for highway improvement. The Ojai Freeway reached this point, just north of Sell Road, in 1956. Plans by the California Division of Highways had been made to extend the freeway to Ojai through the eastern hillsides along Highway 33. (Courtesy of KCBS-TV©.)

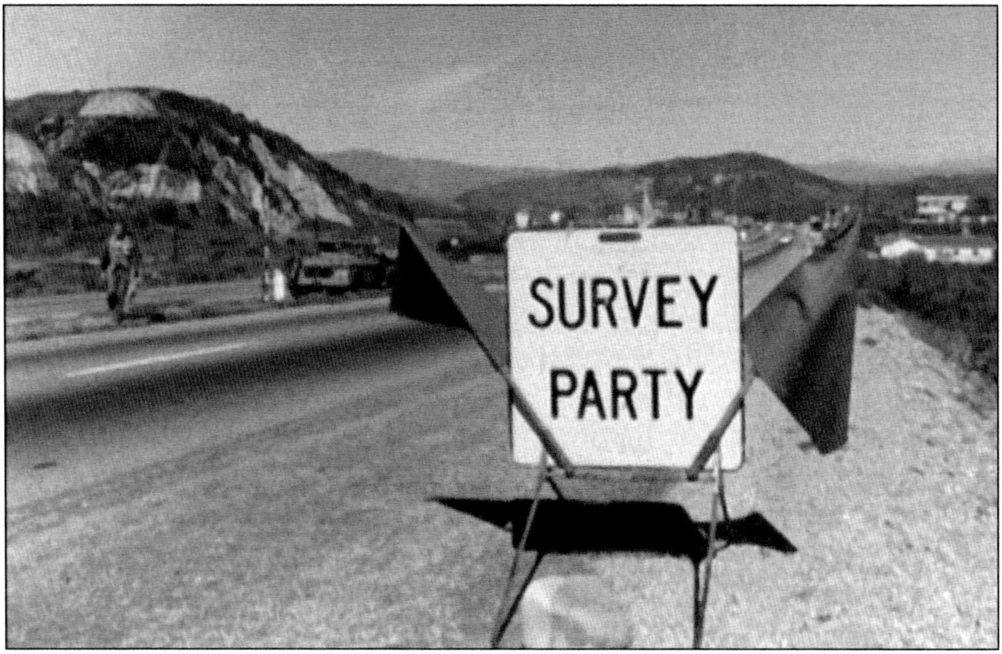

A later decision to save taxpayers money changed the course of the planned route of the freeway. The new route would not go through the hillside but run along Ventura Avenue, straight through the tiny community of Foster Park. A survey party scopes out the new route prior to commencing construction in May 1966. (Courtesy of KCBS-TV©.)

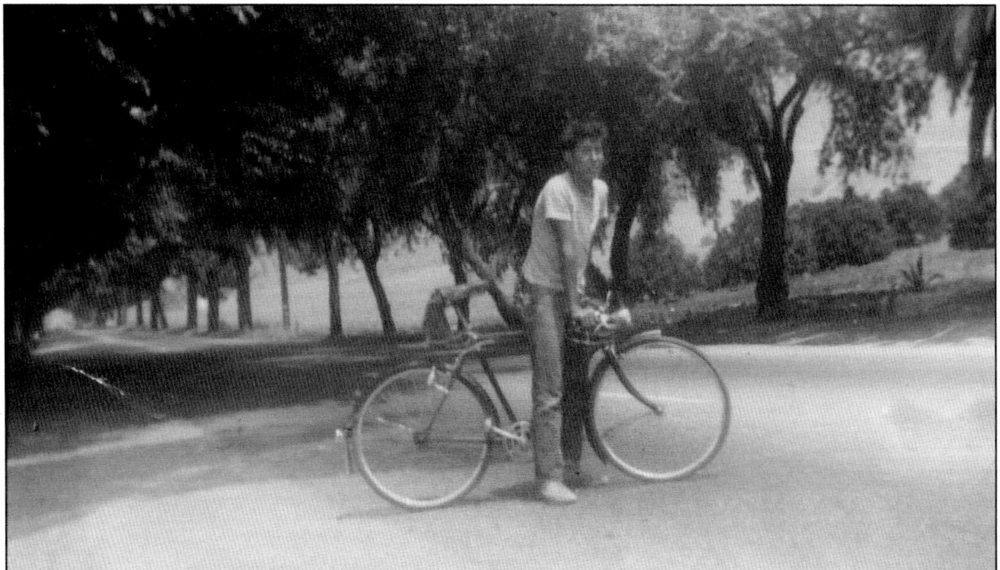

Lush pine trees create a lovely canopy along Highway 33 just south of Foster Park. Billy Duran, a resident of the Canet Ranch, stops on the desolate highway to pose with his new three-speed bicycle. This mid-1950s photograph was taken just north of the Ventura water treatment plant. The Canets' bean field is in the background—a bean field about to make history. (Courtesy of Gracie Duran Varela.)

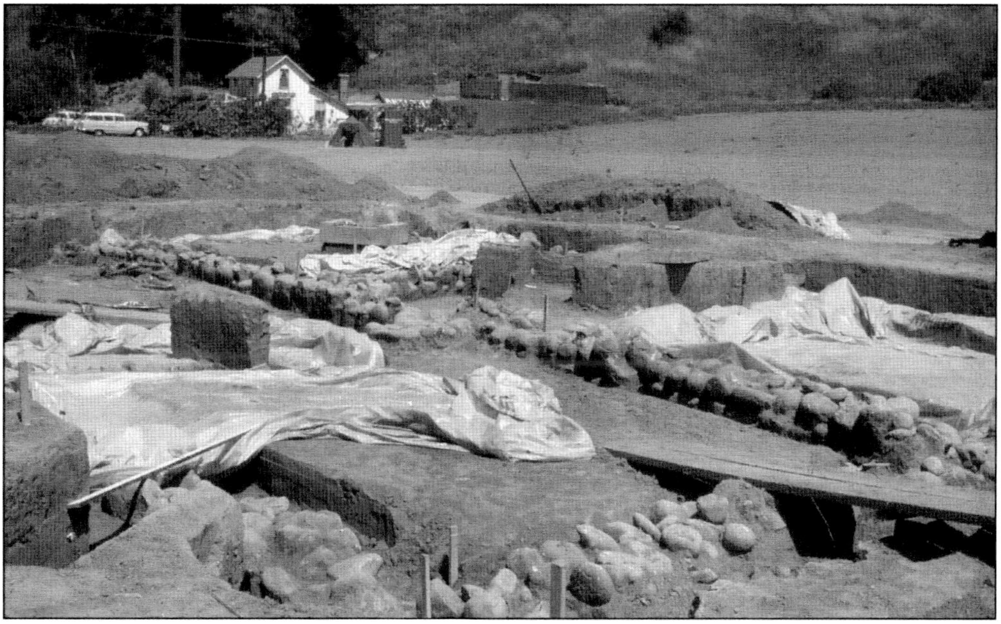

It was a race against the clock to uncover the ruins of a mission chapel in the bean field of the Canet Ranch. After reading different history books that referred to a chapel in the vicinity of the southern edge of Foster Park, a group of archeologists acquired the funding to excavate. The excavation began in March 1966, only months before bulldozers cleared a path through the field. (Courtesy of the Mike Pulido Sr. family.)

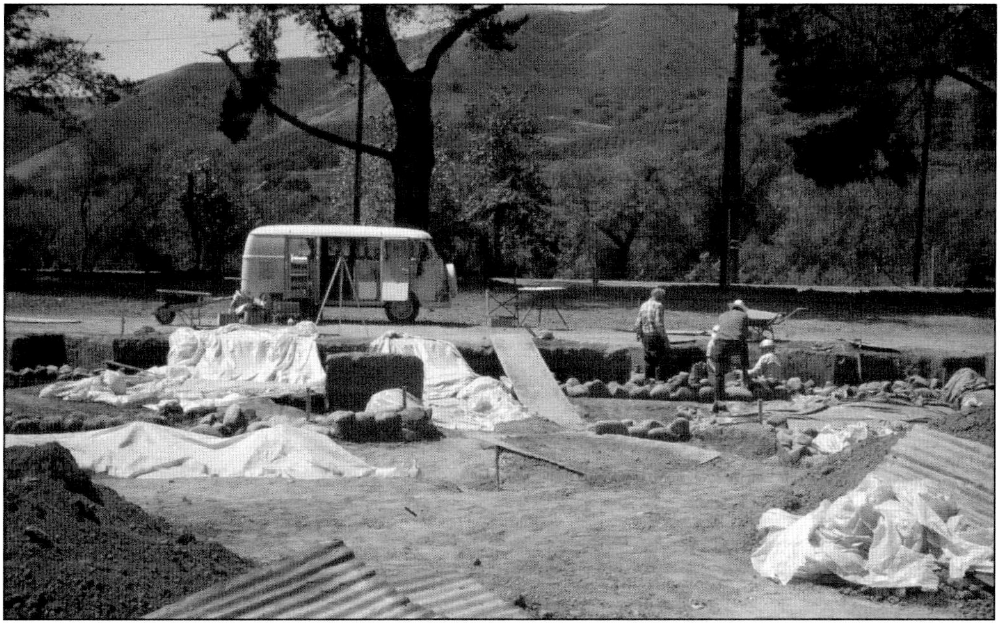

With the help of Canet Ranch foreman Mike Pulido, archaeologist Roberta Greenwood and her team unearthed the ruins just in time. Pulido, who plowed the field, had discovered Spanish coins, broken pottery, and adobe tile fragments in the same area his plow hit rocks over the years. Pointing out the area, the foundation of the lost San Gertutis Chapel was found. Pictured here is Pulido talking with the archeological team. (Courtesy of the Mike Pulido Sr. family.)

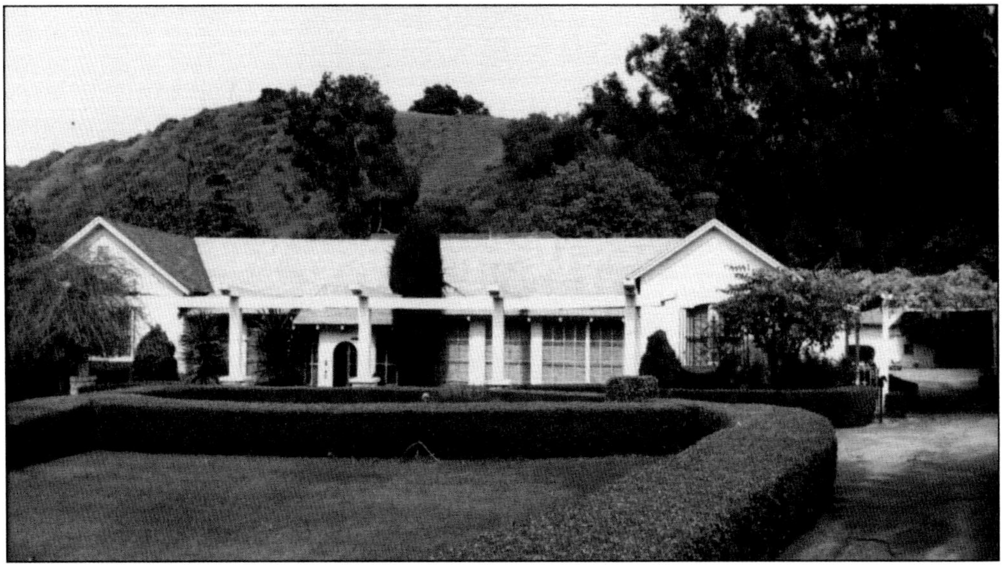

Facing east is a front view of the lovely Canet Ranch house. A single gas pump once stood to the right of the hedge-lined driveway, and inside the hedge near the front of the house was a fountain and a small fishpond. The driveway to the house started at Highway 33 and led straight along the bean field. (Photograph by C. Robert Lee©; courtesy of C. Robert Lee.)

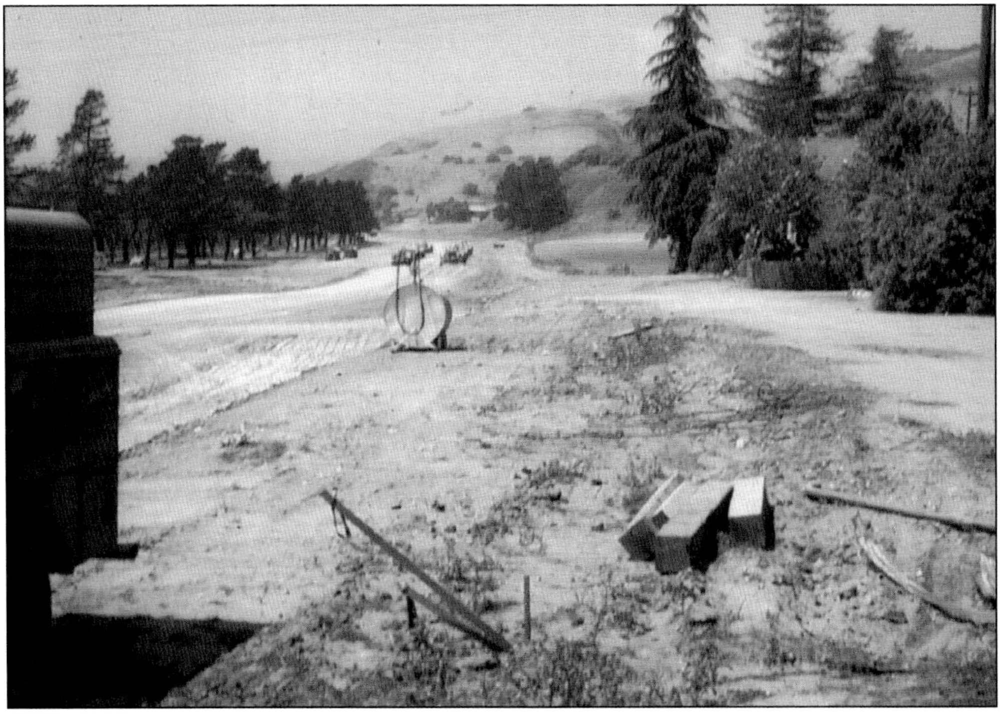

In this picture facing north, heaving equipment vehicles approach the scene, evoking images of military tanks out to conquer. To the right is what is left of the box hedge that once graced the long driveway to the ranch house, which had also been taken out, along with a large portion of the bean field. When the construction of the freeway was completed, vehicles were now 15 feet from the front door. (Courtesy of the Mike Pulido Sr. family.)

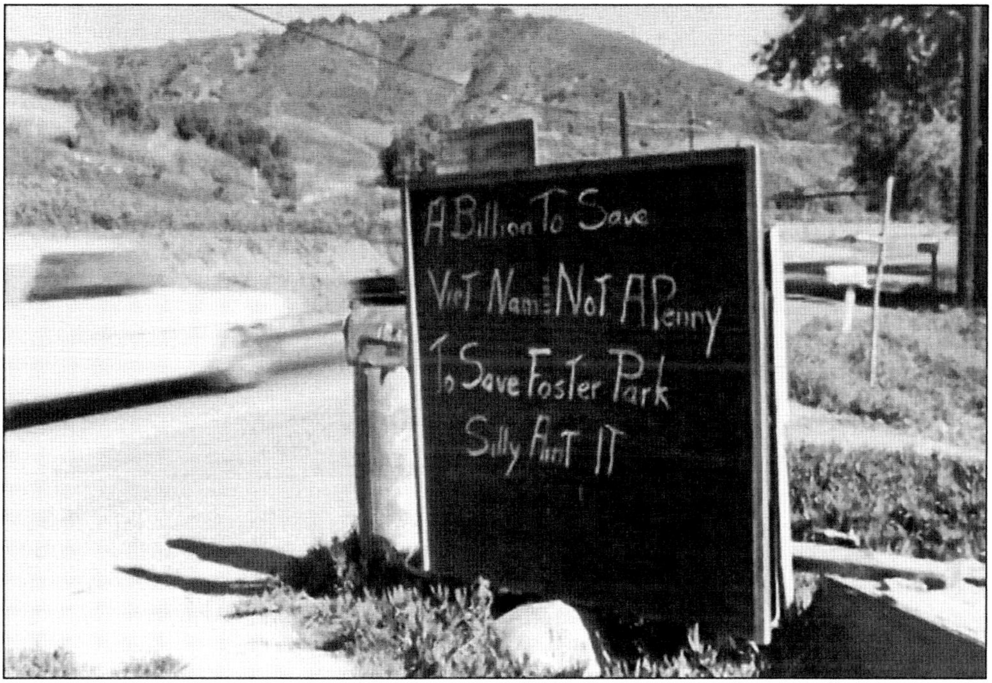

When Foster Park residents received notice of the town's impending doom, some folks did not take it well—especially the elderly, like Charlie Hoffman, who had much invested in the area and wanted to live out his years there. The blackboard messages of humor and wisdom turned to anger and sarcasm, such as the message above, "A Billion To Save Viet Nam Not A Penny To Save Foster Park. Silly Aint It." The sign below was in response to a comment President Johnson had made: "Don't You Get Tired Of Hearing Johnson Telling Us How Well Off We Are?" In a television interview, he stated that "The Division of Highways has more power than the Czar of Russia." Hoffman was eventually compensated by the state and found a new home and shop in Casitas Springs. (Quote and images courtesy of KCBS-TV©.)

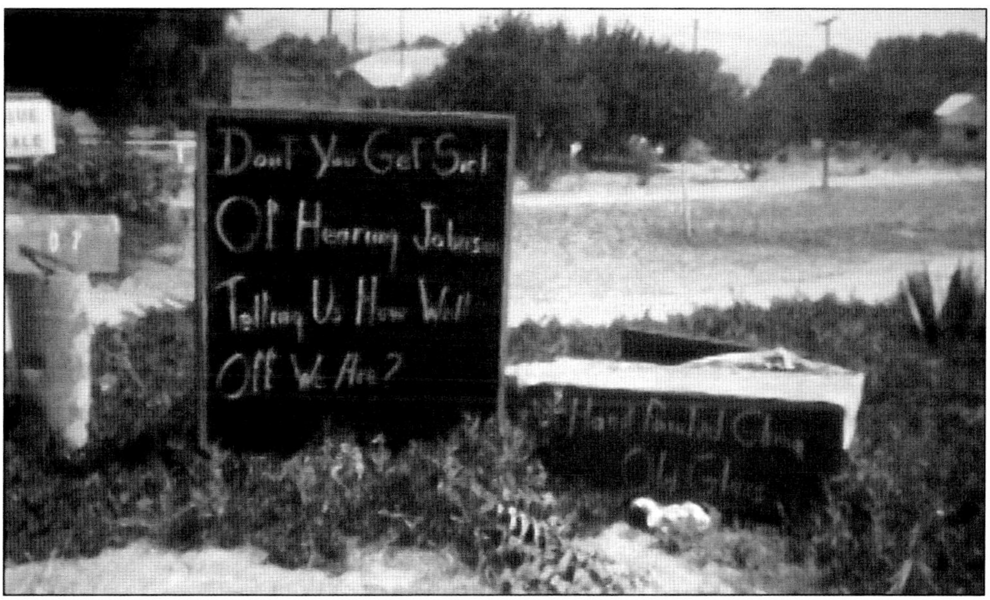

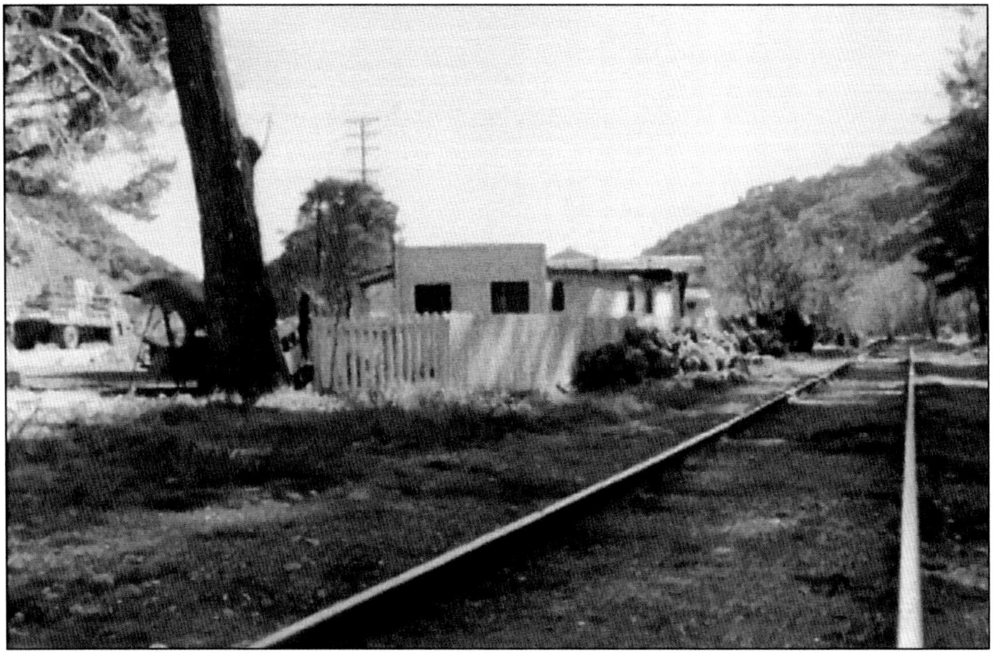

From the north end of town looking south, the railroad track ran between the park and the residential area. The house with the picket fence is the home of Ruby Combs, another elderly citizen who did not want to leave. Like Charlie Hoffman, Combs felt that the state could not compensate her enough to find a comparable home. (Courtesy of KCBS-TV©.)

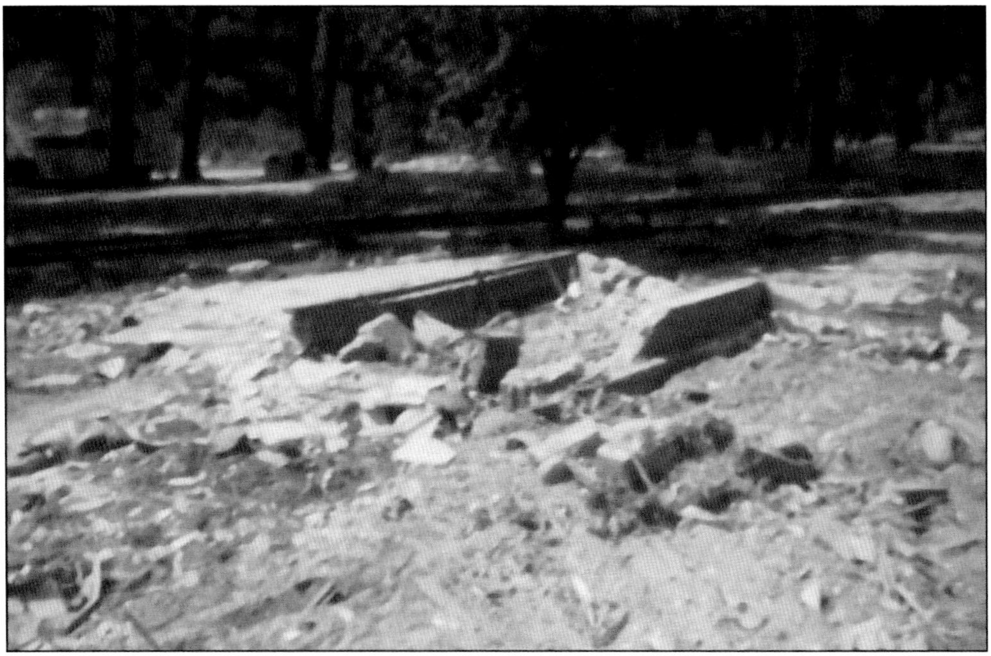

A partial foundation is all that is left of Ruby Combs's house in this 1966 image. Combs, too, was eventually compensated and moved to Casitas Springs. The Foster Memorial Park is now quite visible from Highway 33. In the background stands a trailer in the park. Perhaps it belonged to a former resident with nowhere else to go. (Courtesy of KCBS-TV©.)

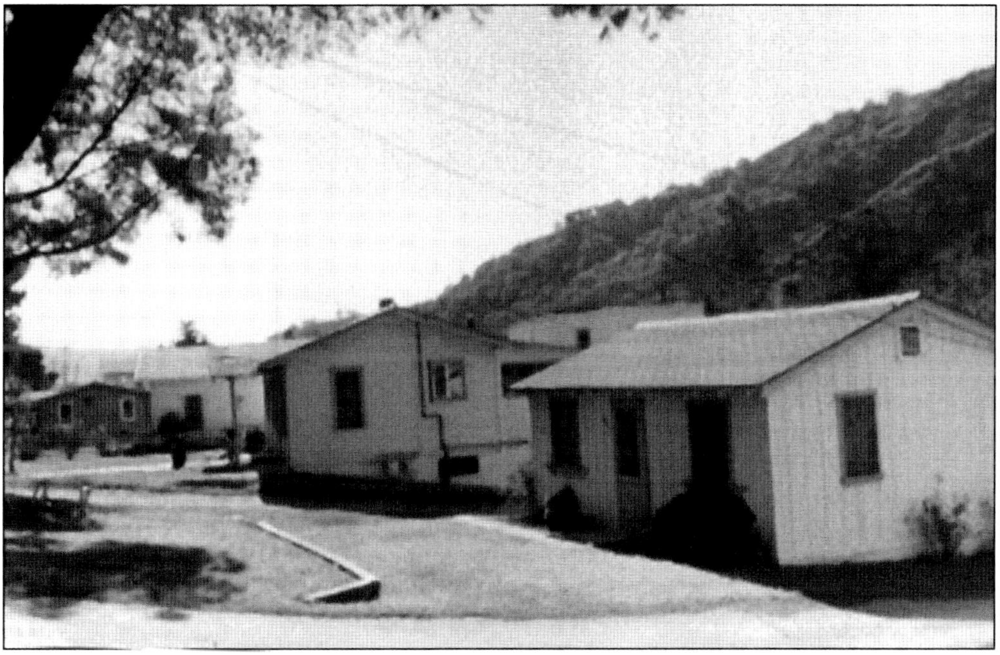

In this 1965 photograph, facing southwest are a row of houses along Highway 33. At the end is the house owned by Glen Kieborz, which had been rented to the Alferes family for many years. The house next door was the home of Joe and India Pluim, who had lived in Foster Park since 1939. The homes in the foreground, too, belonged to longtime residents. (Courtesy of KCBS-TV©.)

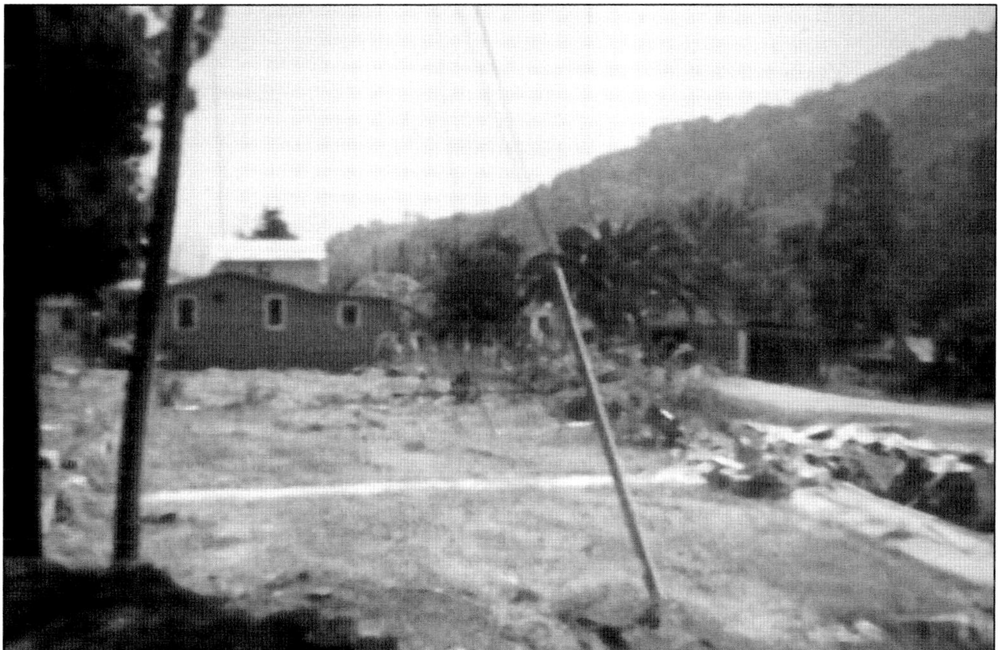

This image of the same row of homes, all removed except one, was captured in October 1966 after the bulldozers began construction of the Ojai Freeway extension. Demolition was completed as residents moved out, but some folks stayed until the bitter end. (Courtesy of KCBS-TV©.)

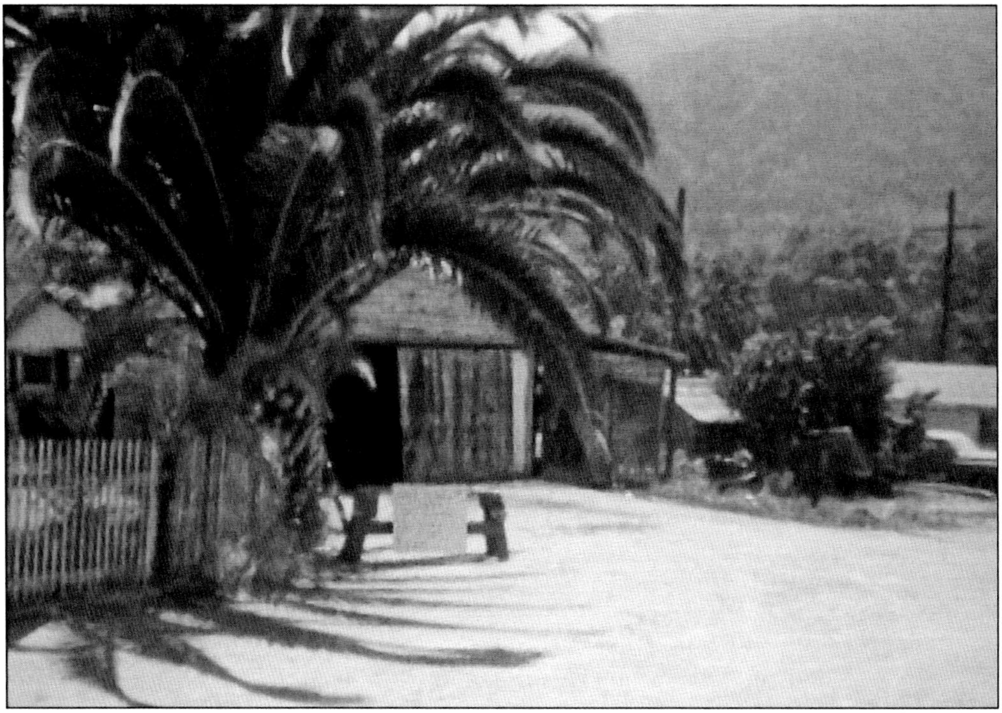

After the Alferes family moved out of the house in 1965, the landlord continued to rent out the dwelling. With the town under destruction, it was hard to know which homes were still occupied. Also, looting and trespassing could be issues. To protect their privacy, the latest occupants erected this sign on a sawhorse, which reads, "Not sold, owner still living here, Keep Out." Though the house and the town have disappeared, the palm tree is still very visible at the end of the freeway and stands as a marker and a memorial for those who once lived there. (Above, courtesy of KCBS-TV©; below, author's collection.)

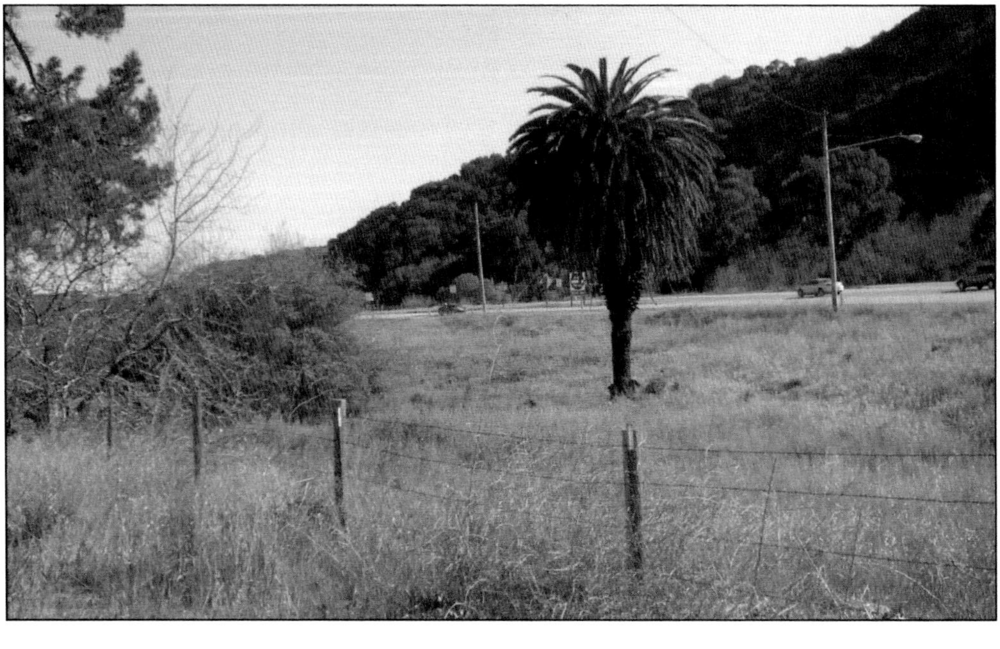

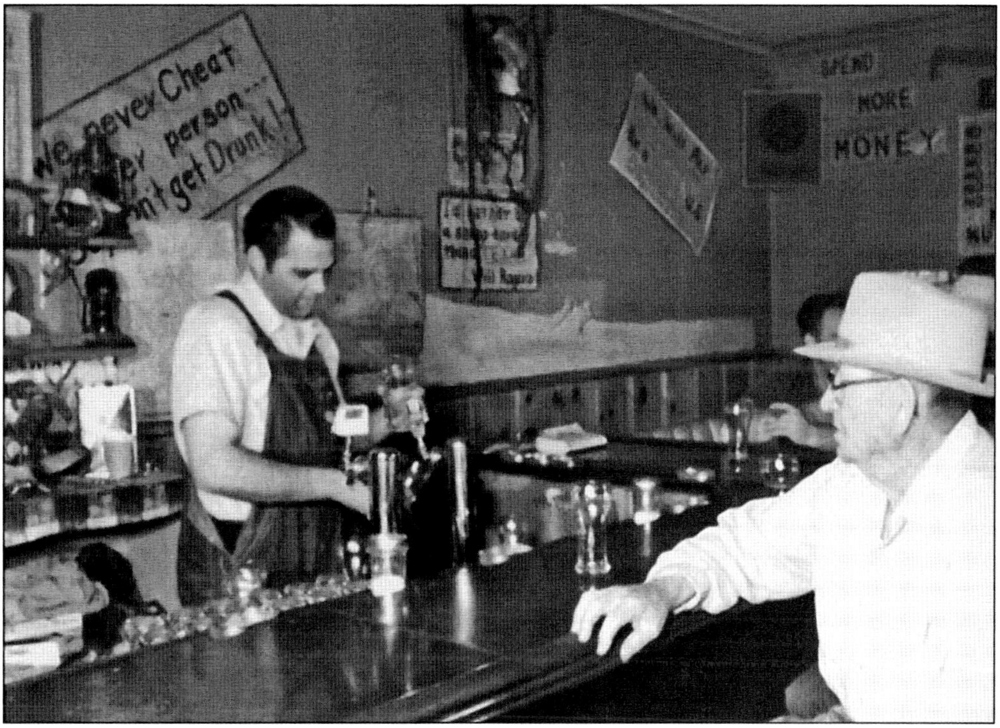

The news of the state's new freeway route did not get Fred "Okie" Leaf too worked up. In a 1968 *Star-Free-Press* interview, Leaf stated that Foster Park was "a slum area where septic tanks overflowed and the cockroaches crawled. I was glad to get out of there." Leaf found a new Okie's location in Santa Paula. (Courtesy of KCBS-TV©.)

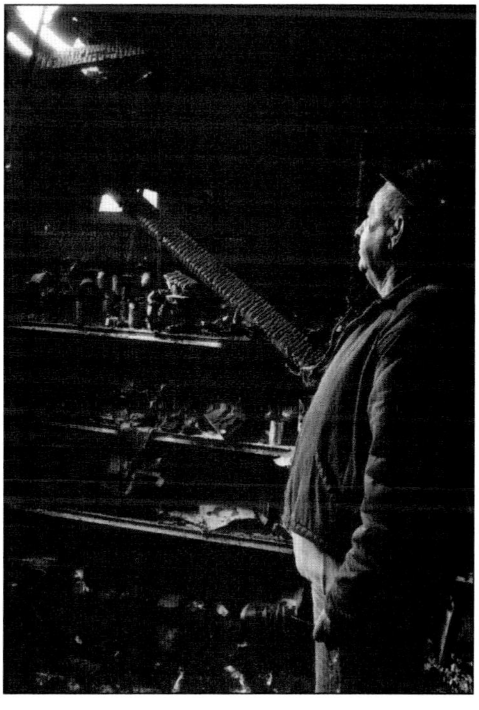

Gene Boles, owner of Foster Park Market, was not too thrilled about the state takeover of the town. When a tin barn that had been brought in by the state disappeared, Boles was arrested for suspicion of its disappearance. Charges were dismissed, and he was released. The tin barn later reappeared. He found a site to build a new store, but in the meantime, the market was destroyed by fire. Pictured at right, Boles assesses fire damage to the market. (Courtesy of the Museum of Ventura County.)

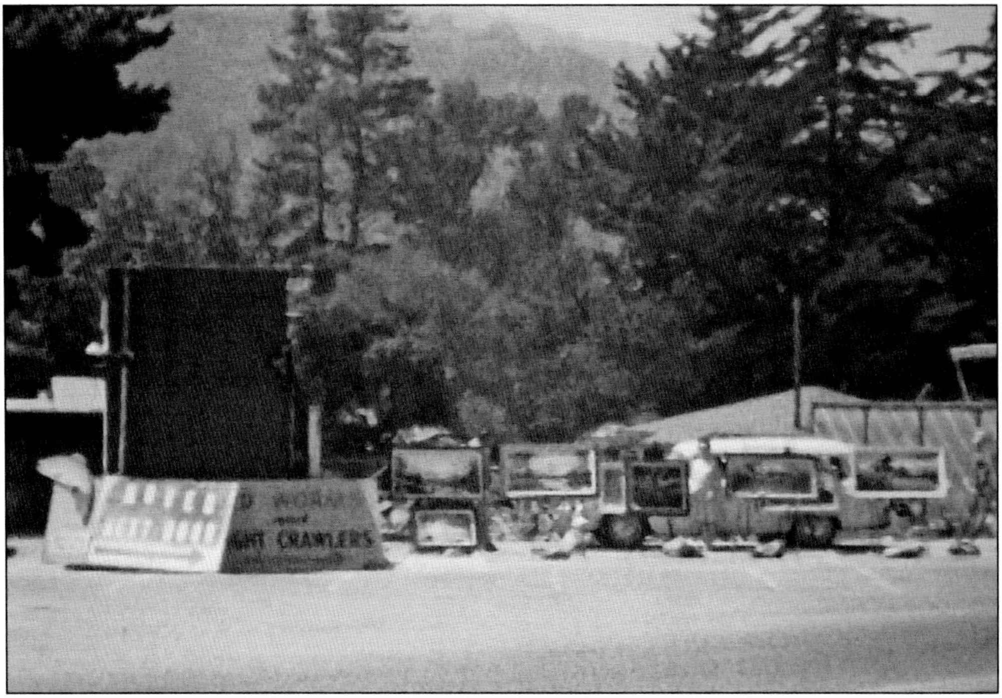

While waiting for the opening of the new market, the state allowed Boles to use the vacant liquor store. In the foreground to the left, Boles erected signs to alert folks to his temporary location. To the right on the former site of the market, an art dealer takes advantage of the space along the highway. (Courtesy of KCBS-TV©.)

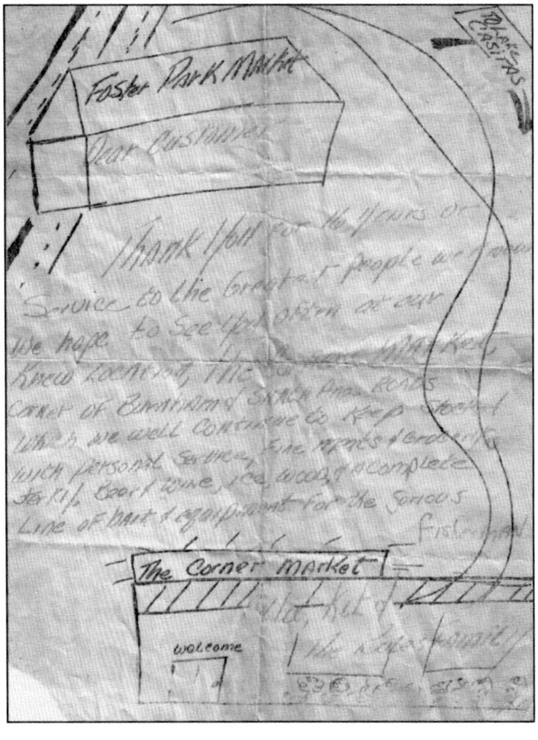

After moving into his new permanent location, Boles had a map made up with a letter he wrote for his loyal customers, which read, "Dear Customer, Thank you for 16 years of service to the greatest people we know. We hope to see you often at our new location, the Corner Market, corner of Burnham and Santa Ana Roads, which we will continue to keep stocked with personal service, fine meats and groceries, jerky, beer and wine, ice, wood, and a complete line of bait and equipment for the serious fisherman. Ollie, Kit and the Boles family." (Courtesy of Kit Mungo Jr.)

Bibliography

"The Casitas Chronicles." Casitas Municipal Water District public service pamphlet.

Emmons, Steve. "They're Digging Against Time in a Beanfield South of Foster Park." *Star-Free-Press*, March 16, 1966.

"Fight Against Highway Brings New Interest to Foster Park: Business Improving For Charlie Hoffman." *Star-Free-Press*, March 5, 1965.

Hillenger, Charles. "Archeologist Beat Freeway Bulldozers." *Los Angeles Times*, May 2, 1966.

Holt, Bob. "Ventura Holdup Ring Smashed." *Star-Free-Press*, March 15, 1962.

Leppard, Stan. "L.A. 'Lavender Hill' Mob Napped." *Herald-Examiner*, March 15, 1962.

"Sage of Foster Park Thriving in Casitas Springs." *Oak View Journal*, February 10, 1977.

Smith, Leo. "Foster Park, R.I.P." *Los Angeles Times*, September 10, 1992.

Story, Ralph. "California Division of Highways and Foster Park." *Ralph Story's Los Angeles*. Aired March 2, 1965 (Los Angeles: KCBS-TV).

———. "Foster Park Revisited." *Ralph Story's Los Angeles*. Aired October 9, 1966 (Los Angeles: KCBS-TV).

Weinstock, Carol. "Landmarks: County Historical Sites." *Los Angeles Times*, September 11, 1990.

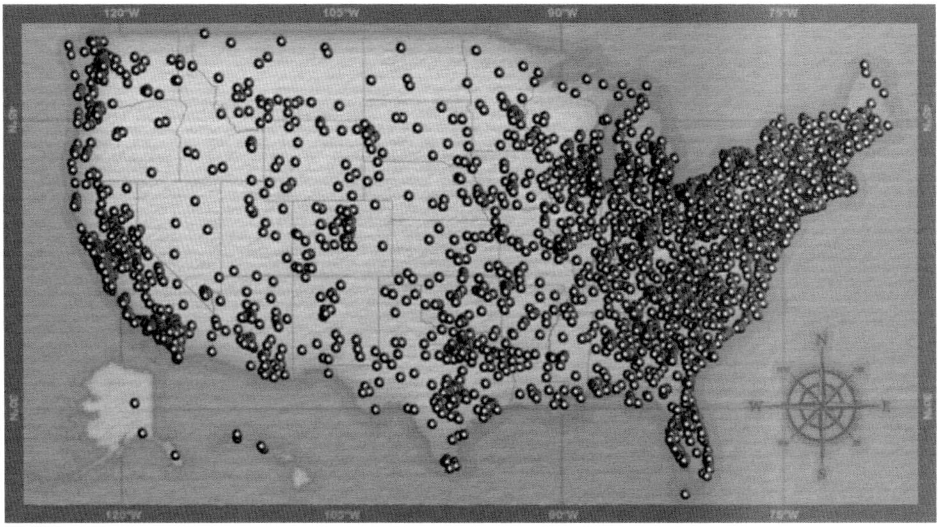